Jelena Obradović-Wochnik is Lecturer in Politics and International Relations at Aston University, Birmingham.

ETHNIC CONFLICT AND WAR CRIMES IN THE BALKANS

The Narratives of Denial in
Post-Conflict Serbia

JELENA OBRADOVIĆ-WOCHNIK

I.B. TAURIS

LONDON · NEW YORK

Published in 2013 by I.B.Tauris & Co Ltd
6 Salem Road, London W2 4BU
175 Fifth Avenue, New York NY 10010
www.ibtauris.com

Distributed in the United States and Canada
Exclusively by Palgrave Macmillan
175 Fifth Avenue, New York NY 10010

Library of Balkan Studies, vol. 1

ISBN 978 1 84885 003 3

A full CIP record for this book is available from the British Library
A full CIP record for this book is available from the Library of Congress

Library of Congress catalog card: available

Typeset by Newgen Publishers, Chennai
Printed and bound by CPI Group (UK) Ltd, Croydon, CR0 4YY

CONTENTS

ACKNOWLEDGEMENTS

I have been fortunate to have the advice and support of a great number of friends and colleagues over the years that this book has been in development. I am grateful to Elizabeth Edginton and Katarzyna Wolczuk for the supervision of my PhD thesis, which eventually became this book. My thanks also go to the Economic and Social Research Council and the Postgraduate Incentive Fund from the Centre for Russian and East European Studies at the University of Birmingham, for providing funding for my postgraduate research work. Parts of this manuscript were completed whilst on a Visiting Research Fellowship at the Aleksanteri Institute, University of Helsinki, and I am grateful for the support and enthusiasm this research received during the fellowship. Since then, the School of Languages and Social Sciences at Aston University has provided a fantastic working and intellectual environment for the completion of this book.

My deepest thanks also go to family, friends and colleagues who have commented and offered insights, interest and encouragement for this book during its many phases of development. In particular, I would like to thank Alexander Wochnik, Dragana Obradović, Dragan and Ljuba Obradović, Catherine Baker, Deema Kaneff, Lara J. Nettelfield, Ger Duijzings, Judy Batt, Hilary Pilkington, Tim Haughton, Ivana Bajić, Ljubica Spaskovska, Gesche Ipsen, David Gowan, Cai Wilkinson, Sean Cowland, Maayken van den Berg, Maria

Chli, George Vogiatzis, Sean Laphen, Dympna O'Sullivan, Matt White, Odeta Barbullushi, Lara Scarpitta, Alexandra Prodromidou, Aglaya Snetkov, Nicola Corkin, Amanda Russell Beattie, Anneliese Dodds, Ed Turner, and Eva Batista. Needless to say, this book would not have been possible without the generosity and help of all of my respondents in Belgrade, whom I cannot mention by name.

LIST OF ABBREVIATIONS

DS	Democratic Party
DSS	Democratic Party of Serbia
HDZ	Croatian Democratic Union
HLC	Humanitarian Law Centre
ICMP	International Commission for Missing Persons
ICTY	International Criminal Tribunal for the Former Yugoslavia
JNA	Yugoslav National Army
KFOR	Kosovo Protection Force
KLA	Kosovo Liberation Army
LDP	Liberal Democratic Party
NATO	Northern Atlantic Treaty Organisation
NGO	Non-governmental organisation
RECOM	Regional Commission Tasked with Establishing the Facts about All Victims of War Crimes and Other Serious Human Rights Violations Committed on the Territory of the Former Yugoslavia in the Period from 1991–2001
RSK	Republika Srpska Krajina
RTS	Radio Television Serbia
SAA	Stabilisation and Association Agreement
SDA	Party of Democratic Action
SDS	Serbian Democratic Party
SPO	Serbian Renewal Movement

SPS	Serbian Socialist Party
SRS	Serbian Radical Party
TRC	Truth and Reconciliation Commission
VRS	Army of Republika Srpska
UNMIK	United Nations Mission in Kosovo
UNPROFOR	United Nations Protection Force
YIHR	Youth Initiative for Human Rights

CHAPTER 1

INTRODUCTION

This book considers the experience of knowing, witnessing and speaking about atrocities.[1] As such, it presents a case study into what the often-used notion of 'confronting the past' might mean, and entail. Specifically, it considers how individuals of the 'ordinary' public in Serbia reflect upon, understand, talk and keep secrets about the 1991–1999 conflicts in Croatia, Bosnia and Herzegovina[2] and Kosovo and the atrocities, human rights abuses and war crimes which took place during this time, particularly those committed by Bosnian Serb and Serbian soldiers and the paramilitary. It presents the often 'untold stories' (Simpson 2008) of individuals whose voices and experiences are generally excluded from the broader debate about the past and considers how these narratives diverge from, resist and are invisible to the formal and civil society initiatives aimed at 'confronting the past' in Serbia. In doing so, the book also explores silence about and denial of the violent past, and considers how and where these dynamics manifest and what they might mean.

The conflicts in Croatia, Bosnia and Kosovo, 1991–1999, were marked by a high degree of violence against civilians. There is no description of those events that can do justice to the scale of atrocities, nor to the suffering endured by those caught up in the conflicts. According to the International Criminal Tribunal for the Former Yugoslavia (ICTY), set up in 1993 to prosecute those responsible for such atrocities, over 100,000 persons were killed in Bosnia alone, and approximately 2 million fled or were displaced (ICTY, n.d., a). In addition, the International Commission for Missing Persons (ICMP) estimates that at the end of the Bosnian conflict, of a population out of 3.4 million, 30,000 people were unaccounted for, whilst at present the fates of 10,000 still remain unknown (ICMP, n.d.). In Croatia, the ICMP states that some 5,500 individuals went missing, mainly between 1991 and 1992 and in 1995 (ICMP, n.d.). The ICMP highlights that the authorities of the Republic of Croatia have conducted excavations of approximately 143 mass grave sites and 2,000 individual grave sites, and have identified more than 3,380 missing individuals, whilst 2,020 are still registered as missing (ICMP, n.d.). In Kosovo, more than 4,000 individuals disappeared, and more than 2,000 are still unaccounted for (ICMP, n.d.).

These tragic legacies of the conflicts require justice and redress for victims. The field of transitional justice is concerned with victims' needs following such atrocities; making sure that states and individuals, complicit in such human rights abuses, are held accountable for them, and that populations of those states do not remain indifferent to past injustices (see e.g. Teitel 2003). These needs are usually met through the implementation of mechanisms such as war crimes tribunals or truth commissions, as well as domestic initiatives organised by civil society groups (Lambourne 2008). In general, transitional justice is seen as a preferred policy choice for post-conflict societies and as a package of necessary transformations required for a country or society to account for a violent or repressive past and proceed towards democracy (Sriram 2007). Although such mechanisms have been applied in Latin America, Africa and Asia the transitional justice process in the former Yugoslav countries has, according to Dragović-Soso and Gordy (2010:193), 'no close parallel in history'. The countries of Croatia, Bosnia, Kosovo and especially Serbia, are requested to participate in a range of criminal proceedings as well as 'to produce gestures of penance which embody genuine transformation in popular consciousness' (Dragović-Soso and Gordy 2010:193).

In this context, there has been much debate about Serbia's need to confront the past and to acknowledge publicly and legally its various levels of involvement in the atrocities committed during the 1991–1999 conflicts. In general, these expectations have been led by the international community as well as domestic civil society, but hardly at all by the government of Slobodan Milošević, as well as the leaders in charge since his fall on 5 October 2000.

Futhermore, post-Milošević Serbia's official responses towards its responsibility for the conflicts and atrocities has been half-hearted at best, and as a result, the process, which has in popular usage become known as confronting, facing or coming to terms the past,[3] has been led by a number of prominent Belgrade-based non-governmental organisations (NGOs). These NGOs, which include the Humanitarian Law Centre, led by Nataša Kandić, the Helsinki Committee for Human Rights, the Belgrade Centre for Human Rights, Women in Black, the Centre for Nonviolent Action, the Centre for Cultural Decontamination and the Youth Initiative for Human Rights (YIHR), have campaigned for a more open and transparent debate about the past in Serbia (see e.g. Kostovicova 2006; Fridman 2011). In addition to their work on issues such as domestic violence, conditions in Serbian prisons and human rights, they continue to carry out serious and important work related to the violent past, such as collecting information for future war crimes prosecutions, highlighting the cases of the missing as well as campaigning for a public debate on atrocities and war crimes committed by Serbs, against Croats, Bosniaks and Albanians.

Over the years, both the debate on confronting the past and the practice of transitional justice in Serbia have been complicated by several developments. First, Serbia's cooperation with the ICTY has always been inefficient, slow and at times non-existent (see e.g. Peskin 2008; Subotić 2009). The second complication arose out of the first: in order to speed up cooperation, for which there was great need given that the most wanted indictees, Radovan Karadžić and Ratko Mladić, were fugitives until 2008 and 2011 respectively, Serbia's cooperation with the ICTY was made a crucial condition for European Union membership. This, according to some observers, allowed the debate about the violent past to be subsumed into a debate about 'Europeanisation' (see Subotić 2009), thereby allowing Serbian political elites to avoid dealing with the question of responsibility and atrocities altogether. Not that this was unexpected – Serbian governments did virtually nothing to address this issue or to open a debate about the past at any level, managing to complete just about the bare minimum expected. For instance, this included the arrest and transfer of ICTY indictees accused of war crimes during the 1990s conflicts; an exercise that took until 2011 to complete. Successive Serbian governments, moreover, have been reluctant to engage in any formal acknowledgement of the atrocities of the 1990s, or pass laws to address their own, or their predecessors', complicity. The highlight of this lacklustre, government-led approach to the past is the declaration passed by the Serbian Parliament on 31 May 2010, which condemns the 1995 Srebrenica massacre. Of 250 members of parliament, 127 voted in favour of the declaration, whilst members of the right-wing Serbian Radical Party (SRS) and the Liberal Democratic Party (LDP) abstained from voting, which followed a deeply acrimonious parliamentary debate (see Dragović-Soso 2012).

To complicate matters further, the Serbian public sphere has since the 1990s been populated by vocal, often nationalist politicians, independent scholars, journalists or self-appointed 'experts' and partisan groups who claim to have superior knowledge of war crimes and the past (for instance, Ljiljana Bulatović, the biographer of Ratko Mladić, a former Bosnian Serb army general; indicted for the Srebrenica massacre; or the so-called 'Srebrenica Research Group') but whose main aim is to deny, actively and categorically, atrocities committed by the Serbs. Within this public sphere, the active revisionists have created a hegemonic discourse on denial of the past, whilst the NGOs have created a hegemonic discourse on confrontation of the past (c.f. Yerkes 2007:924). Most 'ordinary' individuals, however, would not align themselves with either view, and their non-conformity with either side of the polarised debate makes them almost invisible to broader debates about the past.

In this book, I illustrate some of those voices that do not belong to either vocal group. I do not concentrate on the NGO-led activist debate which has been very well covered elsewhere (e.g. Fridman 2011). I also do not concentrate on the 'active deniers', such as Bulatović, since this extreme view has long formed the focal point of analyses on Serbia and its past (see e.g. Ramet 2007). Rather, I turn to the 'underneath' of the immediately visible discourses (Ferme 2001) primarily to get away from what I believe has been an over-emphasis on both the public deniers and the activists, and to move away from the analytical insights that can be the only result of these narrow frames: that some Serbs deny war crimes, and some work actively to combat this. Instead, I suggest that there is much analytical value in examining the narratives that do not easily lend themselves to categorisation, for the reasons given below.

Confronting the past, when considered at the level of government or NGO activity, entails practical elements. On the political level it is relatively clear what confronting the past might entail, given that there are limited things governments can do – laws can be passed, memorialisation activities and sites funded, initiatives about the past endorsed, apologies issued (see e.g. Subotić 2011; Petritsch and Džihić 2010). Civil society, too, has a rich and diverse tradition of similar initiatives to draw on, since transitional justice projects have been implemented in a variety of settings, from Argentina and South Africa, East Timor and Sierra Leone, where it has played and active role in these processes (Humphrey and Valverde 2008; Kent 2011; Millar 2010). However, beyond this practical level, in which laws, trials and campaigns can be put into place, the understanding of what is generally meant by 'coming to terms with the past' is quite limited, and somewhat clouded by the inconsistent use of that phrase (for a discussion, see Dragović-Soso, forthcoming). Furthermore, even if the phrase were consistently used, it is not very clear how the practical mechanisms (courts, trials, campaigns) are intended to lead on to the metaphysical transformation (*'coming to terms with* the past'; the demonstrations of 'genuine transformation in popular consciousness' referred to by Dragović-Soso and Gordy 2010:193) nor what that might actually encompass at a societal level.

Serbia is often seen as a country that has demonstrated neither 'gestures of penance' nor 'genuine transformations' of popular consciousness (Dragović-Soso and Gordy 2010:193), and one which has failed to 'confront' its past and overcome denial (e.g. Beč 2005; Pešić, 2009). Whilst these sentiments are directed at both the Serbian public and government, there is a special emphasis placed on the former by domestic activists and non-governmental organisations working on these issues. On the one hand, whilst there is no agreement as to the scope of that process (see Dragović-Soso, forthcoming); on the other hand, it is often implied, and sometimes explicitly suggested, that this requires a 'breaking' of denial of past atrocities and silence about Serb responsibility inherent amongst the Serbian public (e.g. Fridman 2011). The suggestion is that only once denial and silence have been broken, would the Serbian public be able to come to terms with its past.

Certainly, the Serbian public, outside of activist and NGO circles, has not been very vocal or forthcoming to discussing the past openly, nor has it been receptive to local initiatives aimed at dealing with the past, such as discussions and campaigns publicising Serb-committed atrocities (Nosov 2005). Their silence and reluctance are interpreted as adversarial and negative, possibly filled with contempt or indifference (Beč 2005). Silence of the Serbian public, or their 'lack of reaction' (Fridman 2011) towards the violent past is also interpreted as a denial of the past. To corroborate this view, activists and scholars often point to a small set of surveys which, it is often suggested, seem to indicate a strong denial of the past and lack of desire to know about past atrocities (Dimitrijević 2008; Simić and Daly 2011). Faced with this state of affairs, civil society in Serbia continues to pursue projects aimed at exposing atrocities of the past, and attempting to get the Serbian society to engage with their initiatives. They seek an expression – public and unequivocal – of a mea culpa, whilst failing to recognise that there are many more elements to narratives and memories of the past. The past, which was violent, shocking and disorientating, produces narratives which are filled with ambiguity and contradiction (c.f. Smith 2004) and cannot be homogenised in the way in which transitional justice projects seek.

This approach to confronting the past derives form a narrow reading of transitional justice which relies on public testimony, narrative and visible action as an indication that the past is being dealt with in some way (c.f. Gandsman 2012). This narrow approach has been criticised for its oversight of alternative ways of confronting past violence amongst, in particular, non-Western communities (Millar

2012). Scholars drawing insights from communities in Sierra Leone, Rwanda and Argentina have pointed out that tensions exist between formal, organised, Western, truth-and testimony-based approaches to addressing past violence and communities which engage in non-verbal, or secretive or silent ways of dealing with difficult, brutal and violent experiences (Simpson 2008; Donnan and Simpson 2007; West 2003; Cuéllar 2005). Despite the constantly broadening view of transitional justice and critiques of its application (Millar 2012; Baines 2007; Shaw 2007; Miller 2008; McEvoy and McGregor 2008), this reflexivity has not reached transitional justice practice and discourse in Serbia. This book, therefore, goes some way towards addressing that research gap.

Main aims and approaches of this book

This book explores two main issues: first, 'ordinary' individuals experience of narrating, believing and keeping silent about violence witnessed in the 1991–1999 conflicts; and secondly, the tensions this may engender when they intersect with transitional justice mechanisms in Serbia. I argue that the narrow way of looking at the public's relationship with the past has created a framework which often excludes their voices. This book adopts a different approach. It does not assume the existence of a 'Serbian public', nor does it assume the existence of a 'confrontation with the past'. Rather, it takes an exploratory approach and considers how narratives about the violent past are manifest in private spheres, not immediately visible to, but not completely separate from the public sphere of deliberation and interaction (Johnson 1986). This approach is adopted partly as a result of the current focus of transitional justice in Serbia which aims to transform societal beliefs about the recent past, but without first engaging with them extensively and without considering how and where the society it aims to transform, is located and constituted. This book considers how knowledge about the past is discussed and embedded in some of those sites, such as storytelling, personal reflections and interpersonal interactions, located in the 'everyday' world (Mitchell 2011; Fox and Miller-Idriss 2008; Das and Kleinman 2001).

In this book, I take the approach that silence is not evidence of 'forgetting' about the past (Riaño-Alcalá and Baines 2011) and that it masks 'untold stories' (Simpson 2008). Importantly, this book follows Ferme in her assertion that 'the point is to understand how the visible world is … activated by forces concealed beneath the surface of discourse, objects and social relations' (Ferme 2001:2).

Above all, I consider how some of those 'untold stories' are shaped by past violence. Transitional justice, especially in the Serbian context, often ignores that there is a problematic relationship between *knowing* the facts about violent events and *speaking* about them (Daniel 1991; Das and Kleinman 2001; Scarry 1985a and Scarry 1985b). Following Daniel (1991), Das and Kleinman (2001) and Scarry (1985a and 1985b), I explore to what extent the ability to speak publicly, or at all, about human rights abuses committed against others in the 1990s, may be influenced by the horrific content of those crimes. Silences are created by an inability to speak (c.f. Daniel 1991), which transitional justice initiatives do not take into account, despite being heavily reliant on the ability and willingness of individuals to engage in public discourse about the past (c.f. Shaw 2007). Based on insights derived from Das et al (2001), Daniel (1996) and Scarry (1985a and 1985b) I argue that individuals in Serbia do not express beliefs and ideas about the past in the coherent and unequivocal ways in which transitional justice projects seek. Instead, they produce narratives which are fragmented, contradictory – containing both acknowledgement and denial – ambiguous, confused and impossible to quantify, generalise or homogenise (c.f. Smith 2004). The narratives presented here do not offer a coherent and singular view of the past and they do not illustrate a clearly recognisable 'denial discourse' or 'acknowledgement' discourse. Instead, they offer a range of divergent views and contradictory stories, in order to illustrate the range and complexity of stories about the past. Two dynamics, however, unify the diverse narratives here: they are marked with a profound inability to speak about the violence of the past, and are all subsequently invisible to the gaze of formal transitional justice initiatives. Therefore, this book can be read as a detailed case study into what happens to individuals' beliefs and narratives, when they are confronted with and asked to speak about, violent histories in which they, their friends and neighbours, may have been implicated (c.f. Daniel 1994; Daniel 1996; Scarry 1985a and 1985b; Das and Kleinman 2001).

In this book, I also illustrate how some responses to the past may constitute acts of resistance to the dominant narrative of confrontation created by the formal and civil society-led initiatives on confronting the past. Resistance, in this case, follows Scott's (1989) notion of the more insidious and 'everyday' types of resistance, which can be located in the creation of counter-discourses. I explore how, in the narratives presented, feelings of disenfranchisment from the broader 'confronting the past debate' – one which, according to the respondents presented here, does not take into account their views, beliefs and experiences – shapes counter-discourses which contain alternative (re)tellings of the past.

Lastly, this book adopts an exploratory approach to the idea of 'confronting the past'. It does not take for granted that such a thing as an explicit and clear 'confronting' or 'coming to terms with the past' exists, but rather, based on the research presented here, considers *what* this process might actually entail and how the current narrow adoption of this narrative might limit the analysis of individuals' beliefs and narratives about the past. The ways in which individuals and societies conceptualise their pasts – especially violent ones – does not necessarily correspond to the idealised vision that much of transitional justice literature and practice imagines, and in which the exposure of truth about atrocities automatically leads to acknowledgement and reconciliation (see Gibson 2006). This book aims to contribute to the broader field of transitional justice, particularly literature which considers transitional justice 'from below' (e.g. McEvoy and McGregor 2008); literature which considers localised interpretation of transitional justice (e.g. Ariazza and Roht-Ariazza 2008); tensions between formal and informal initiatives (Millar 2012; West 2003) and literature considering the silences and exclusions from transitional justice (Gandsman 2012; Riaño-Alcalá and Baines 2011; Miller 2008; Simpson 2008; Donnan and Simpson 2007). As Kelsall (2003) argues, there is not enough empirical research into how transitional justice is received by, or has impact amongst the audiences it targets; hence this book presents a detailed case study which makes a contribution to that research gap. It also aims to make a modest contribution to literature which explores the less visible impacts of violence on communities, social relations and language (Das et al 2001; Daniel 1996; Scarry 1985a and 1985b).

The book contributes some thoughts which will serve as a further deepening of those themes and questions; it does not present concrete or final answers. Hopefully, it will illustrate that, despite the current normative policy framework of the idea, 'coming to terms with the past' in its broadest sense has to take into account the tensions and contradictions which coexist in individuals' and societies' relationships with the past (as outlined e.g. by Smith 2004). Contrary to the policy-based practice currently in place, it should not indicate an aim or an outcome, and it should certainly not be the pursuit of coherent, singular discourses, where regret and acknowledgement of atrocities are clearly stated. Rather, 'coming to terms' with the past should be understood in all its messiness and complexity (much like any discourse, cultural or social practice). It ought to be understood as a discursive and/or enacted practice where denial and acknowledgement of atrocities coexist, as do expressions of revulsion, regret and questions about the past.

A note on methodology

This book is located at a convergence of fields and disciplines. It aims to contribute to the field of transitional justice, where studies of 'confronting the past' are located, but it also brings this field into dialogue with the fields of cultural studies and ethnography, with their concerns about how realities and meanings are produced (Du Gay et al. 2001). The field of transitional justice is quite interdisciplinary, and has its origins in human rights practice. However, one of the claims of this book is that the narrow methodological focus of transitional justice, as applied in the Serbian context, does not take into account the social and cultural dynamics which may determine the course and practice of 'confronting the past'. Specifically, not enough attention is paid to all the spheres through which societies and cultures are constituted. For that reason, and in order to radically rethink the understanding of the complexities of what 'coming to terms with the past' might entail, this book draws on the methodologies used in cultural studies and ethnography, and is influenced by the constructivist and 'poststructuralist concern with discourses (ways of representing and talking about phenomena) and their role in the construction of practices and concepts of reality' (Lupton 2006:2), and more generally, language as the 'medium through which meaning is constructed' (Du Gay et al. 2001:13).

This concern is exceptionally important, since, as I argue in Chapter Two, much transitional justice practice as well as the idea of 'coming to terms with the past', rely heavily on the use of language through its testimony-based approaches, but do not give enough analytical importance to the relationships between language and violence (e.g. Daniel 1996 and 1991). Transitional justice as applied in Serbia's case, relies also on essentialised and fixed approaches to truth and knowledge, without taking into account how individuals and societies actually construct, understand, acquire and view knowledge about the past.

As this book is a study 'from below', it is grounded in the discipline of cultural studies which is concerned with how cultures are lived and how meanings are made (Du Gay et al. 2001; Johnson 1989; Johnson et al. 2004). It is a part of the 'linguistic turn' (Barker and Galasinski 2001:2), and is 'an interdisciplinary field in which perspectives from different disciplines can be selectively drawn on to examine the relations of culture and power' (Barker and Galasinski 2001:25). It is also an interdisciplinary field 'where certain concerns and methods have converged,' bringing an 'understand[ing of] phenomena and relationships that were not accessible through existing disciplines' (Turner 1996:11) Unlike sociological research, it is not attached to the notion of 'population', and 'attitudes, opinions [...] behaviours' (Gray 2003:94). Rather, it produces rich studies which 'tap into cultural structures and formations' and view their subjects as 'socially and culturally shaped' (Johnson 1997:468 in Gray 2003:94).

In its attempt to explore and understand complex, multi-layered and often contradictory narratives about the wars and atrocities of the 1990s, this book employs an ethnographic approach. Using participant observation, field notes and interviews, ethnography is primarily concerned with the 'description of cultures' rather than seeking 'universal truths' (Hammersley and Atkinson 2004:9–10). The aim is to produce 'detailed accounts' of lived experience, beliefs and social rules (Hammersley and Atkinson 2004:9–10). It is, therefore, post-positivist and interpretative.

Importantly, in the spirit of such research, this book does not aim to make absolute conclusions, but rather to explore possibilities of interpretation since 'our ethnographies can only take us to resting points that are not endings but openings to new issues that require continuous working through' (Das and Kleinman 2001:26). Clearly, the focus in this book is on the qualitative, and it includes 'engagement in the lives of those being studied over time' (Davies 2005:5).

The focus in this book is on how individuals might express their ideas and beliefs about the past through narrative. Narrative, in this case, is understood as 'a story, and stories tell about things that have happened or are happening to people' (Berger 1997:4). This book focuses on narrative for several reasons. First because the ethnographic observation carried out for this work highlights that for this particular group of respondents narrative is perhaps the main site through which they express their own ideas about the conflicts. Indeed, the narrative-based approach is also pursued in transitional justice, particularly through e.g. testimonies at Truth and Reconciliation Commissions (TRCs) (see Hayner 2011). Secondly, and importantly, the focus on narrative stems from the notion that violent events have a direct impact on the ways in which individuals speak and name (or do not name) such events (see Scarry 1985a), and since 'even the process of naming violence presents a challenge' (Das 2003:293).[4]

The narratives include a set of thirty-six semi-structured interviews, collected during an ethnographic study, carried out in Belgrade between autumn 2005 and the beginning of 2007. They are in-depth, with the majority lasting well over two hours. These interviews supplement, and are part of, ethnographic observations recorded at the same time, as well as informal and un-recorded conversations. The sample is small, but having outlined the premise of cultural studies above, it should be clear that quantity does not have much relevance in research where the purpose is a description of cultures (see Hammersley and Atkinson 2004). These individuals, whose background is provided in Chapter Four, are what may be described as the 'ordinary' part of the Serbian public; they are not activists, politicians or intellectuals (usually the key subjects of much research on Serbia). My aim was to gather accounts from the sections of the Serbian society which are usually disengaged from public initiatives or interaction with researchers and analysts, or what Baines, in another context, labels 'everyday people' (Baines 2010:413). Other than that, there were no limitations as to who would be included or excluded, since this research was carried out on the premise that everyone has a story to tell about the war, the 1990s or the atrocities, and no one's account was more or less valid than anyone else's. Thus, the group of individuals presented are from a mix of socio-economic and educational backgrounds, and from a wide age range (the youngest participant is eighteen, the oldest eighty-two) as detailed in Chapter Four. I accessed this group through contacts I had prior to my arrival in Belgrade, and got to know others through 'snowballing.' But, it is also important for this research to highlight that most of these respondents are known to each other, which adds an interesting angle for the analysis of how stories circulate within a social setting.

This book cannot possibly present all the narratives collected in their full scope and multiplicity, and so the most illustrative extracts and accounts are selected and highlighted in the text. It follows Malkki's (1995:51) assertion that the researcher should not act as an investigator, 'piecing together evidence' and constructing a case like a 'police detective,' to create 'the whole picture'. Rather than pursuing 'extraction of truth for its own sake' and the 'blind accumulation of "data"', she urges selectivity since this is what allows us to gain access to 'those very partial vistas that our informants may desire to share with us' (Malkki 1995:51). I also focus on the certain motifs and explanatory strategies – silences, absences, secrets, denial, victimhood and conspiracy theories – partly because they are often seen as symptomatic of failures of 'coming to terms with the past' (e.g. Matić 2001), but also because they recur frequently in the collected narratives.

Lastly, it is perhaps pertinent to mention a few points about bias and reflexivity. Researchers in the social sciences, particularly in fields such as cultural studies and ethnography, have long highlighted the importance of self-reflexivity, and of accounting for one's role and position within the research so as to demonstrate where particular readings of research material may derive from (see e.g. Gray 2003 111–112; Skeggs 1995; Davies 2005; Hammersley and Atkinson 2004:16–17). Moreover, since '[a]ll researchers are to some degree connected to, a part of, the object of their research' (Davies 2005:3), I am compelled to disclose a few details, all the more so since, during the many years I have been presenting on this topic, I have more often than not been asked to declare my ethnic background. I suppose that in certain ways this may influence how the research presented here is perceived – I have no control over such assumptions being made, nor is ethnic background going to be the only possible factor affecting how this research is understood. There is an infinite number of variables from my background which may lead certain audiences to perceive bias in this study and I cannot possibly account for them all.

In his book on memory and the Irish Troubles, Dawson writes that whilst growing up and watching the news about Northern Ireland, 'I came to recognise a disturbing sense of their being something to do with me' (Dawson 2007:xvii). My own research trajectory followed a similar pattern and the same sense of the Balkan conflicts being 'something to do with me'. I was born in Sarajevo, with one side of the family from Serbia and the other from Bosnia. Leaving Sarajevo in 1992 as a child meant that the conflicts were always somehow present, but also distant (at times literally; since my family spent some years in South East Asia). In 2005, as a new PhD student at the University of Birmingham, I left for Belgrade with a vague notion of researching nationalism or national identity but without any clear idea as to how or why, other than intending to learn more about this part of my past. But the more time I spent in the field with my ethnographic observation, the less interesting and relevant nationalism became, and the more certain themes and patterns emerged: there were silences and evasions at any mention of the conflicts and atrocities of the 1990s, as well as the visibility of something which might be identified as denial. Intrigued, I chose to focus on this as my key area of inquiry. It is around about this time that debates about confronting the past became pertinent – Serbia had just had its Stabilisation and Association Agreement (SAA) talks with EU suspended as it had failed to hand over Ratko Mladić and the remaining fugitives to the ICTY.

In an article following the arrest of Mladić, journalist Ed Vulliamy describes the silence surrounding war crimes that he came across whilst researching in Serbia (Vulliamy 2011). I also located silence, but a silence which eventually made sense: silence about war crimes and the violent past had specific locations, but so did discussions about the same issue. Silences, furthermore, were not about an unwillingness to speak, but often about the inability to do so. In interviews, however, a dynamic opened up which I discuss in Chapter Five, and there was often a willingness to talk but a lack of articulation. But this willingness to talk did not come about as a result of turning up on someone's doorstep one day and asking about their views on Serb-committed crimes. Rather, it came about after a protracted amount of time in the field, which led to an understanding of where such narratives can be and are located – *not* in public. Perhaps my own background may have influenced the responses – Vulliamy is a foreign journalist, and I am both 'foreign' and 'local' but also younger and female. Perhaps this produced a perception of a less confrontational interview than one with a foreign journalist or research agency. This may have influenced the responses, but then again – it may not. Any one personal trait that may have influenced the course of one interview may have had no effect on another. Since we as researchers cannot be sure which part of our own story influences that of the respondents, I have named the most immediately obvious ones, as I am sure that readers and critics will locate others.

Finally, a note on terminology: Serbia and the former Yugoslavia in general, much like any other countries under analytical scrutiny, have been subjected to various politicised labels (see e.g. Goldsworthy 2005; Longinović 2011; Bjelić and Savić 2005). Those labels have often had an impact on how we understand and act with regard to those places.

Using the name 'the Balkans' is a case in point; as is the label 'ethnic conflict'. Both are reminiscent of early 1990s labels for the region and its troubles, and both have at times been problematised. Yet, both find their way into the title of my book. Both were included at the suggestion and then insistence of my publishers as a title that would resonate with a wider audience, but lest I be accused at a later stage of engaging in a study concerned with language and labelling of violence, but being at the same time neglectful of my own title, I must point out two things. If I am asked to label the conflicts of the 1990s, I am genuinely at a loss to find an appropriate label, as are my respondents (as discussed throughout the book). As problematic as this term is, 'ethnic conflicts' always finds its way into usage, despite my agreement with Mueller (2000) that this is a problematic term which masks a number of other dynamics. For want of a better word, I often use this one, since, after all, much about those conflicts was expressed in ethnic terms, and much confrontation about the past is likewise expected to be premised on the ethnic – that 'Serbs' will acknowledge atrocities committed against ethnic others. Whilst the respondents in this study sometimes used ethnic categories such as 'the Serbs', they are not the most dominant frame through which the conflicts were understood. Likewise, phrases such as 'ethnic' or 'ethnicity' were rarely used. Both categories are problematic and the view I take towards these is that they are socially constructed (see e.g. Barker and Galasinski 2001). However, the conflicts themselves were expressed ethnically, particularly by elites of Croatia and Serbia insofar as much insistence was made on notions of belonging, territory, culture, religion and language (see e.g. Dević 1998). In the conflicts, concepts of ethnic belong were, according to Jansen (2002:86), 'essentialised'. In this book, I also agree with Jansen (2002:86), who suggests that not recognising the usage of 'ethnic' in this context would be disrespectful to people 'of all nationalities who had been victimized because of those labels'.

As for 'the Balkans', as much as that term has taken on negative connotations, it is one that resonates with the ethnographic reality of the study, since it is a term frequently used by my respondents to refer to the region in which they live.

Structure of the book

Chapter Two sets out the theoretical framework for this book. It begins by outlining some of the key ideas in transitional justice, and highlights a number of limitations of this approach and its way of understanding the idea of 'coming to terms with the past'. This chapter also outlines the ways in which the practice of transitional justice has been used in the Serbian context, and the resulting conclusions it makes.

Furthermore, the chapter outlines the key theoretical insights which lie at the core of this book: following the works of Taussig (2004; 1984), Daniel (1991), Scheper-Hughes and Bourgois (2004a), Das et al. (2001), Das and Kleinman (2001), Humphrey (2002) and Scarry (1985a) and (1985b) amongst others, it draws on the ideas that violence affects societies and individuals in such a way that it 'unmakes worlds' (Scarry 1985b), and that societies living in spaces affected by violence have to find ways of integrating past violent events into 'known cultural terms' (Daniel 1996:208). That process may include narrative strategies such as silence, denial or the creation of 'alternative discursive spaces' (Chuengsatiansup 2001:63).

Chapter Three offers a very brief summary of the conflicts, war crimes and the 1990s in general. For readers with prior knowledge of the area this will chapter will not offer anything new, but for those unfamiliar with the region, it will put into perspective some of the events discussed by the respondents throughout the book.

Chapter Four then moves into a discussion of how the 1990s were lived and experienced by the respondents. The chapter also introduces some of the respondents themselves and gives brief backgrounds and short descriptions. This forms the first of the chapters founded on ethnographic investigation, and it starts to introduce some of the themes which will meander throughout the book, such as how the experience of the 1990s shapes ideas and narratives about the conflicts.

Chapter Five introduces the themes of knowledge about atrocities, and silence surrounding them. It discusses the silences which often surround the conflicts and atrocities, and presents ethnographic observations on this issue. It begins by considering how the respondents interacted with information about and media representations of the conflicts, and asks what was known and when. The chapter suggests that the media and official information channels were not and are not the only means of obtaining information about war crimes committed by Serbs, but that there also exist informal ways of obtaining such knowledge, through rumours and stories told by refugees, demobilised soldiers and paramilitaries. The existence of this knowledge, rather than its absence, the chapter argues, is what gives rise to numerous silences and evasions surrounding the questions of wars and atrocities. The chapter then unpacks some of the themes which often accompany those silences and phrases most frequently used to describe the wars and atrocities, such as 'horrifying' (*užasno*) and 'terrifying' (*strašno*). In so doing, it explores to what extent knowledge of 'horror and terror' creates and perpetuates silence – is there an unwillingness to discuss these issues partly because they are too disturbing and difficult to narrate? To complete this analysis, the chapter also considers the questions of 'hidden knowledge', reflecting on the narratives of the younger respondents who reveal much of what lies behind the silences and euphemisms of the older respondents: war volunteers, the dead, the missing, the traumatised – stories of horror which exist within families and communities but are rarely spoken about.

This question of difficult narration is considered in the context of transitional justice projects, and the logic which seeks an exposition and 'public-isation' (Johnson 1986:52) of past violence. Given that these narratives of 'horror and terror' belong firmly in the private domain, and are rarely discussed even between family members, is there much sense in treating the absence of such narratives in the public sphere as a symptom of failure to come to terms with the past?

Chapter Six then takes up the theme of denial as it is manifest in the narratives. It begins by highlighting two issues: that denial is not the main component of (m)any narratives of atrocity and war, and it is not categorical in the sense that there are attempts to negate the existence of events. Rather, denial often concerns the denial of responsibility, and is sometimes the product of an inability to comprehend the magnitude of atrocities. This is seen in the numerous contradictory narratives, where atrocities are both acknowledged and denied; or where regret or knowledge are expressed but responsibility by a person or persons is doubted. Denial discourses, in other words, are not impermeable or something that requires breaking, since they already include interactions with other discourses. This chapter discusses to what extent the production of such narratives may be due to revulsion that, as one respondent put it, 'a man could do something like that', and to acts of distancing oneself from those atrocities. As well as constantly reiterating their own moral boundaries ('I would never do such a thing'), respondents employed different levels of denial and distancing from atrocities for different actors according to their perceived moral positions. Therefore, the 'I' together with the familial – cousins, friends, brothers drafted to fight – is excluded from possible perpetrators, whilst 'the Generals' such as Ratko Mladić occupied much more ambiguous positions. On the other hand, the 'reprobates', 'drunks' and 'criminals' who volunteered to fight were blamed for everything from stealing, murder and rape to causing the wars.

Thus, denial is often found in narratives which act as a sort of mediation on issues, and which go back and forth between ideas – did it happen? How? – in which respondents claim they believe one thing in one sentence, and something completely different in the next. For this reason, I suggest that denial is not to be understood together with silence as a 'evidence' in the 'failure to confront the past' debate, because denial is never singular, categorical nor clear, nor is it ever the only narrative device found in these accounts. Nevertheless, the chapter argues, it does exist, but the diluted, confused and often rambling form in which it appears should be seen as an insight into a complex reality, rather than a unit of measurement for a process that is not easily quantifiable in the first place.

Chapter Seven considers the respondents' understanding of victims and victimhood. First, it discusses the interesting dynamic of accounts of conflict in which 'all normal people' are identified as victims of the war, regardless of their ethnicity. This is also reflected upon through a consideration of how difficult it is at times for respondents to recognise and discuss that something may have happened to their 'ethnic other' friends – both real and conceptual – caught up in the violence. The chapter also discusses a neglected aspect of debates on coming to terms with the past: that the NATO air strikes of 1999 perpetuated and reinforced the production of self-victimising narratives amongst the Serbian public since they experienced this event as victims. A question of physical manifestations of victimhood – the dead, the disabled – is also considered before the chapter moves on to discuss the question of resentment inherent in most victimhood narratives. There is much resentment over the perceived lack of acknowledgement of Serb victims of war, as well as of NATO, and a perceived bias of the ICTY. The chapter suggests that these victimhood narratives lead on to resentment partly due to the marginalisation of these voices and exclusion of certain experiences as 'valid' points of discussion in debates about confronting the past. For instance, there is a strong perception that not only are Serb victims of the war not acknowledged, but also that these victims are simply 'not important' in the question of confronting the past. This, the chapter argues, creates 'alternative discursive spaces' (Chuengsatiansup 2001:63) in which the theme of 'Serbs as victims' is frequently discussed as a way of redressing the perceived injustice and imbalance.

This chapter closes with a discussion of how victimhood is to be understood in transitional justice, which operates along clear divisions between victims and perpetrators (Sriram 2007), but does not account for anyone who may fall outside of these categories. How are we to account for societies who *feel* victimised but have no way of engaging with dominant discourses about the past? How can different vantage points from which the past is addressed, be reconciled in such projects?

Chapter Eight continues the theme of marginalisation and 'alternative discursive spaces' (Chuengsatiansup 2001:63) by considering in detail an interesting dynamic in accounts of war and atrocity – the existence of conspiracy theories in which actors such as the USA, the CIA, NATO and the EU are blamed for the conflicts, the break-up of Yugoslavia and the bias of the ICTY. Interestingly, this identification of external culprits is accompanied by very infrequent mentions of 'ethnic others' as perpetrators in the former Yugoslav conflicts.

The trope of conspiracy theory as a way of understanding the conflicts and recent history highlights the themes of marginalisation, disenfranchisement and perceived exclusion from mainstream accounts of the past, as well as a lack of agency and control over certain political developments. The chapter argues that the presence of such understandings of the past should not be seen as a failure of confrontation by a public ignorant of the political facts, but rather read as an insight into a complicated web of problems: the inability to comprehend and take on board what happened in the 1990s and how it happened, and anxiety about and fear of constant existential uncertainty. In this way, conspiracy theories can be read both as a way of denying responsibility for the conflicts and atrocities, and as discursive sites of resistance and attempts at subverting the dominant narratives about the past. Given that many conspiracy theories are concerned with the key tool of transitional justice in the Balkans, the ICTY, the chapter considers how and why individuals attempt to discredit such projects through acts of narration.

Finally, taking into account the complexity, richness and contradictions of accounts about the past, the ways of talking, omitting and denying, or ways of re-creating histories through subverted narratives which constantly appear, disappear and appear again, leaving nothing categorical, unified or concrete in any of the reflections presented here: how might we think of 'coming to terms with the past'? In this book, I aim to illustrate that the process of facing and confronting can also include aspects traditionally seen as negative, such as silence, denying and distancing, because acts of violence are hardly ever 'understood unproblematically but are surrounded by cultural elaborations and preparations, which focus the mind away from the idea of violence as a simple, natural expression of individual aggression' (Sorabji 1995:82). Thus, the act of acknowledging atrocities is not a linear exercise (see Cohen 1995), but rather a process filled with uncertainty, and one which meanders between horror, revulsion, disbelief, evasion, acknowledgement and the search for perpetrators as a way of making sense of the violent past.

Based on these insights, the book concludes by asking the following questions: given that regret and acknowledgement of atrocities are often expressed implicitly, or through more subtle discursive tools than denial or self-victimhood, what exactly then can be demanded from those requested to come to terms with the past? What kind of acknowledgement and what kind of narrative about the past is 'good enough' to be labelled as a successful act of confrontation? This book closes with some open-ended reflections on this theme, and suggests that transitional justice projects and literature need to have a much broader view of the complexities involved in an act of confrontation, however defined.

CHAPTER 2

CONFRONTING VIOLENT PASTS

Introduction

The phrases 'coming to terms with' and 'confronting the past' are used frequently to refer to tasks which societies emerging from violent or repressive histories, must complete. 'Coming to terms with the past', as Misztal suggests, has emerged as the 'grand narrative of recent times' (2003:147). Many of the themes which this book deals with, such as acknowledgement and/or denial of atrocities and genocide, are implicitly connected to broader debate about confronting the past. Moreover, confronting the past is seen as a crucial task which Serbia, but also other countries emerging from periods of violence and oppression, must carry out. But, what does the phrase actually mean, and what kinds of activities does it entail?

This chapter examines the field of transitional justice, as a key framework that gave rise to debates and narratives linked to confronting the past. Transitional justice mechanisms, legal processes and campaigns have also been applied in Serbia so that perpetrators of crimes in the 1991-1999 conflicts can be tried and held accountable and society be able to confront this past.

This chapter outlines some of the foundations in transitional justice and considers how its key principles have been applied in Serbia. It gives a very brief overview of how civil society activists in Serbia have carried forward key transitional justice campaigns and how they present the ordinary public and their role within debates regarding confronting the past. The Serbian public is generally seen as silent in debates about atrocities and genocide, and this silence is usually interpreted as denial or a lack of knowledge. This rest of this book offers a detailed case study of these dynamics, but before doing so, the last part of this chapter offers some theoretical insights which can help shed light on this silence and what it may conceal.

The chapter highlights that transitional justice frequently neglects the relationships between language and violence – a key aspect of this book – and suggests, following Daniel (1996) and Scarry (1985a and 1985b), amongst others – that the causes of silence may lie in the *nature* of the violence that audiences are requested to speak about. The lack of focus by transitional justice on the ways in which violence shapes language (Scarry 1985a and 1985b), has resulted in the neglect of individual and societal responses to violent pasts which are complex, diverse, contradictory and often do not conform to activist debates about confronting the past.

Transitional justice and 'confronting the past'

Transitional justice is a relatively new field of inquiry, with a growing body of scholarship, and here I will offer only a short overview in order to highlight how the key concerns of this field have been applied to Serbia's case and how this influenced the development of ideas inherent within the notion of 'confronting the past'. In its original conception, according to Lambourne (2009:29), transitional justice was used by Kritz (1995) to refer to societies in transition from undemocratic to democratic regimes. According to Lambourne, one of the term's first usages in relation to 'goals of reconciliation and peace-building' was by then UN Secretary-General Kofi Annan in 2004 (Lambourne 2009:29). As Hayner (2011:8) notes, there is an increasing expectation for accountability, since legacy of mass violence 'cannot simply be buried, and must somehow be addressed'. Importantly, as Vinjamuri and Snyder (2004:346) argue, during the emergence of this field, 'normative positions of scholars' have influenced the development of literature where 'scholarship, practice, and advocacy are deeply intertwined.'

As Nagy (2008) points out, the view of transitional justice has widened from its earlier usages and both narrow and broad definitions are still used (Sriram 2007:582), and it is the narrower interpretation of transitional justice which is often located in Serbia. According to Nagy, the narrow view can be attributed to scholars such as Teitel, who see transitional justice as 'the view of justice associated with periods of political change' and reflected in 'primarily legal responses that deal with the wrongdoing of repressive predecessor regimes' (Teitel 2003:893 in Nagy 2008:277). This narrow view has been broadened by e.g. Roht-Arriazza (2006), Mani (2007) and McEvoy and McGregor (2008) as well as criticised by a growing number of scholars for its exclusions (Miller 2008) and Western-centric practice (Millar 2012). For Roht-Arriazza, transitional justice is 'that set of practices, mechanisms and concerns that arise following a period of conflict, civil strife or repression, and that are aimed directly at confronting and dealing with past violations of human rights and humanitarian law' (Roht-Arriaza 2006:2 in Nagy 2008:278). Mani's focus is on a holistic approach and on 'restoring justice within the parameters of peacebuilding' (Mani 2007:17 in Nagy 2008:278). Thus transitional justice carries with it the implication of something broader and transformative – it assumes that proceedings such as war crimes trials will *lead on* to something (e.g. Dragović-Soso, forthcoming).

In order to achieve these objectives, transitional justice frequently employs mechanisms such as legal proceedings, notably war crimes trials or truth and reconciliation commissions. In general, as Crocker (1998:486) argues, the tools of transitional justice are expected to take into account a set of objectives which include, for example, platforms for victims, ascription of responsibility and also investigations to establish facts and importantly, 'promotion and elevation of public deliberation about what happened, who was responsible, and how society should respond.' Thus 'public deliberation' is seen as a priority since citizens 'can enter into a give and take ... so as to arrive at a democratic decision that all can live with, even though all do not agree with it' (Crocker

1998:500). I will be returning to the *public* aspect of transitional justice later on in this chapter.

Thus transitional justice has a clear practical aspect, and is often the preferred policy choice of international and/or Western organisations and donors involved in transitional societies, including the World Bank, the UN and NGOs such as Amnesty International and Human Rights Watch (Sriram 2007:583). Partly due to this, and the mechanisms which transitional justice has tended to favour in the past, the process has been criticised for its apparent over-emphasis on 'legalised accountability', particularly of the Western kind (Sriram 2007:588). The establishment of the ICTY in 1993, to prosecute individuals for war crimes, fits within this policy preference pattern.

This emphasis on Western 'legalised accountability' should make it apparent that transitional justice is also built upon a number of normative assumptions (see Kaminiski et al. 2006). On a practical level, transitional justice is *about* the past, or more specifically, a *working through* the past' (Kent 2011:4, added emphasis), since the tools and mechanisms it employs are particularly suited to examinations and reassessments, such as testimonies presented at trials of truth commission hearings. The idea of working through the past has been raised by a number of scholars since the end of the Second World War, though perhaps most memorably by Theodor W. Adorno in his 1956 essay (Adorno 1986). Whereas Adorno and intellectuals such as Primo Levi (1986) were more concerned with the philosophical aspects of this question, transitional justice seems to have adopted 'coming to terms with the past' as a practical concern. Transitional justice envisages certain transformative powers often implicitly attributed to its mechanisms: according to Kent (2011:4), there is an assumption that 'settling accounts' through institutionalised and legal means, societies will be able to 'come to terms' with and transition to stable democracies or at least experience a change in social values (see e.g. Subotić 2011).

How does the legal and practical implementation of transitional justice lead on to the more metaphysical concerns, and transformation? Very little in way of definition or clarification as to how this might work in practice has been said. This extrapolation is also noted in a some activist approaches, particularly in Serbia, where a number of

NGOs work to expose facts about the past, with the very specific aim that this will transform society's values (see e.g. Helsinki Committee for Human Rights, n.d. a and b).

Some scholars have attempted to clarify matters. For instance, Petritsch and Džihić (2010:18) suggest that there are different 'modes of confronting the traumatic past' which include the legal and cultural. The legal mode focuses on bringing 'perpetrators of criminal deeds to justice and hold[ing] them legally, and, in the end, morally accountable for their criminal actions' (Petritsch and Džihić 2010:18). The cultural approach includes 'a set of cultural practices of remembrance, representation and commemoration' and 'the focus here is on the attempt to come to terms with a difficult past by implementing various cultural strategies and means of expression like novels, films, music, performances, monuments or museum exhibitions' (Petritsch and Džihić 2010:18).

Furthermore, Petritsch and Džihić suggest that the delay in this process is due to 'conflicting issues of statehood' in Bosnia and Kosovo, problematic state building, poor leadership and misuse of the past by political leaders (Petritsch and Džihić 2010: 20–21). According to the authors, governments and citizens in the region do not have a high regard for 'facing the past' since there is a lack of trust in politics and states and a feeling that their group is under threat (Petritsch and Džihić 2010:21). Thus, the authors suggest, 'the majority of citizens', do not believe that the process will yield personal benefits and hence 'they thus stick to divisive narratives and self-victimisation' (Petritsch and Džihić 2010:21).

Anchoring the process of facing the past to external factors works up to a point, but it also suggests that whatever confronting the past might be, for citizens, it is always 'somewhere out there' and is contingent predominantly on political conditions favourable to the operation. To suggest this ignores individual agency and the complex interactions and positions towards official or external narratives and processes which individuals may possess. An individual's relationship to politics and leadership is not always singular, uncritical or linear, nor is it guaranteed that they would respond favourably to governments sympathetic to confrontation projects. To assume a direct correlation between government initiatives and a personal/societal facing of the past also risks overlooking the importance of decisions and understandings about the past reached by individuals on the basis of their own personal experience, witnessing and informal knowledge.

There is also a lack of coherence across the literature on transitional justice – particularly in the Serbian context – as to what 'facing/confronting/coming to terms with the past' is *exactly* (c.f. Dragović-Soso, forthcoming), and how we are to know when it has been reached, given that we are frequently told that it has not. For instance, noting that 'Serbia has not overcome its past' Pešić (2009: 180) notes that:

> Facing the past ... is not a shallow act of accepting the 'guilt' for the crimes committed ... but rather it is a process of coming face to face with our past crimes committed in the name of the Serbian nation.

It is noted further that the process of overcoming the past means a rejection of 'destructive politics' and insisting on ICTY prosecutions, and 'a psychological-moral sense of shame for the atrocities committed, as well as genuine empathy for the victims of crimes' (Pešić 2009: 180). In 'coming to terms with the past', as in transitional justice, there is an assumed relationship between truth (knowledge, facts about the past) and 'coming to terms with' it, as well as reconciliation (Gibson 2006). Thus the *relationships* between the mechanisms of transitional justice and its broader aims of what is clearly a 'societal' or normative transformation (c.f. Gordy 2005) are not really explored or explained. Hence, 'coming to terms with the past' (and its many variations such as facing, confronting and dealing with it) which is *nested* within the idea of transitional justice, seems to have broken loose and taken on a life of its own. It has, in Serbia's case, become everything from a concept, a narrative and a framework which underpins much discussion about transitional justice. In Serbia in particular, 'to come to terms with the past' is often applied in such a way as to suggest that this process is something to be measured, reached or captured.

Coming to terms with the past, nevertheless, usually implies that what has to be confronted is the truth about the past, one often unpleasant or violent, or both. This adds another layer of complication to the idea. As McAdams points out,

> '[I]n principle, nothing seems more straightforward than telling the truth. But in practice, even the most generous observer will admit that this is not an easy assignment' (McAdams 2011:305).

Furthermore, Lambourne argues that 'truth' is 'often interpreted as the finding of a single truth of what happened, who was responsible and why' whereas it can be seen as factual, forensic, personal, social, healing or restorative truth (Lambourne 2009:39). Complicating matters further, as McAdams puts it succinctly, is that 'no one would want to put themselves in the absurd position of claiming that just enough truth has been realised, but not too much' (McAdams 2011:305). Yet the current approach to confronting the past, usually via truth and justice, attempts to expose 'truth' to societies in the expectation that reconciliation will be reached. Gibson (2006:180) notes that 'truth and reconciliation' is more aptly described as 'truth → reconciliation' based on the idea that 'a society cannot reconcile itself on the grounds of a divided memory' (Zalaquett 1997:13). Hayner, however, concedes that in South Africa it was 'clear to all that ... coming to terms with the past with decades of abuses would take much longer than a few years, and much more than speaking the truth' (Hayner 2011:31–32).

Many assumptions rest on the idea that entire societies can reach an agreement on concepts such as 'the past', or 'the truth', and that 'confrontation' is a clearly defined set of objectives which needs to be followed. This is clearly impossible, as divided responses to landmark truth initiatives such as the South African Truth and Reconciliation Commission demonstrate (Hayner 2011:31). Whilst anthropologists have long pointed out that pasts are contested and difficult and post-conflict lives and societies are messy, fragmented and contradictory (see e.g. Das and Kleinman 2001), the legalistic origins of transitional justice have perhaps helped develop a narrow idea of 'confronting the past', ignorant of those anthropological complications, at least in Serbia's case.

Transitional justice initiatives and confronting the past in Serbia

Whereas scholarship on similar issues in Bosnia, Kosovo and Croatia is very varied, rich and detailed, covering a vast number of topics and populations (e.g. Nettelfield 2010; Haider 2009; Sivac-Bryant 2008; Zambelli 2011; Pavlaković 2010; Lamont 2010; Djurić 2010; Schwandner-Sievers and Di Lellio 2006; Schwandner-Sievers 2007; Idrizi 2007), transitional justice research on Serbia is much narrower, dealing predominantly with macro-level issues including cooperation with the ICTY, civil society and collective responsibility (e.g. Spoerri 2011; Subotić 2011; Subotić 2009; Simić and Daly 2011; Peskin 2008; Ostojić 2011; Clark 2009; Fridman 2011; Gordy 2005; Nikolić-Ristanović 2002b; Kandić 2010; Orentlicher 2008; Jalušić 2007; Nikolić-Ristanović and Hanak 2006). Certainly, this is in part due to Bosnia, Croatia and Kosovo's much more direct experience of warfare and their much clearer links to the post-conflict, transitional justice process. Serbia, on the other hand, is subjected to the same transitional justice mechanisms (e.g. the ICTY, domestic trials and recent campaigns for a Truth and Reconciliation Commission), but the literature and practice of transitional justice which address Serbia and its public focus on a much narrower set of problems. It forms an impression that Serbia's transitional justice problems are much more straightforward than those of Bosnia, Croatia or Kosovo – 'all' Serbia has to do is 'just' confront the past.

Much of the literature focuses on why there has been no confrontation, with the past, or suggests that there is not, whilst considering Serbia's other problems (e.g. Jalušić 2007; Subotić 2011; Clark 2008). Similarly, Serbia is often accused of failing or of having failed to confront its past or to begin a process of confrontation (see Pešić 2009). For instance, when asked in an interview, how Serbia is working on 'the process of facing the past,' prominent activist and head of the Helsinki Committee for Human Rights[1] NGO Sonja Biserko stated that:

It has not even been possible to start the process, despite the fact that many groups and individuals have worked on it ... through conferences, panels, printing publications ... As a state and a society, Serbia has not been engaged in the process at all. (Sonja Biserko in Helsinki Committee, n.d., a)

Furthermore, literature on Serbia also considers the question of responsibility and guilt quite extensively (Gordy 2005; Clark 2008; Subotić 2011). Gordy (2005) considers to what extent guilt can be addressed through cultural forms such as literature. Clark, for instance, discusses whether there is any weight to the argument which sees Serbian society as collectively guilty; and discusses whether collective responsibility might be a better term instead (2008:82–98). Subotić (2011) discusses the extent to which Serbian citizens can be seen as responsible for the mass atrocities of the 1990s, based on the idea that they either supported the regime or failed to distance themselves from it. Subotić writes that, since the state is the 'agent or representative of its citizens':

Citizens can also be held responsible for agreeing to and materially supporting – for example, through taxation – state policies that produced mass atrocity. These citizens, even in democracies, have either allowed these policies to progress, or have failed to stop them. They can be held morally culpable because they failed to disassociate themselves from such criminal practices. They bear societal responsibility for mass atrocity. (Subotić 2011:160)

Subotić (2011:161) identifies mechanisms which governments and society can implement ('memorialisation days, truth commissions, research organisations, investigative reports, education reform and media analysis') to facilitate a 'systematic addressing of societal, norms, values, beliefs and practices.' This is slightly problematic as it presents 'society' as homogenous and fixed, and does not take into account differences of opinion between social groups. It also neglects that dissatisfaction with a regime does not always translate into the kind of visible protest action that analysts can easily quantify (c.f. Scott 1989), or in the case of Serbia, were safe to carry out during the Milošević era (as detailed in Clark 2008:93).

In order to address questions of accountability, guilt and facing the past a number of domestic civil society initiatives have been implemented. In the absence of any real government engagement, NGOs, often working within a human rights or anti-war framework, have campaigned tirelessly on behalf of victims of Serb aggression, as well as engaging in awareness-raising initiatives. The most prominent and active of the NGOs are Women in Black, the Humanitarian Law Centre (HLC), Belgrade Centre for Human Rights, Youth Initiative for Human Rights YIHR and the Helsinki Committee for Human Rights. Many of the NGOs operated in the hostile domestic environment of the Milošević regime, continuing their work in the sluggish post-Milošević governments not receptive to transitional justice. These NGOs have carried out a large amount of work that is both directly and indirectly related to transitional justice, such as establishing victim centres (Nikolić-Ristanović and Hanak 2006) and centres working on documentation of the conflicts, such as the efforts of the 'Dokumentacioni centar Ratovi 1991–1999' (Documentation Centre Wars 1991–1999).

Many of the initiatives are dedicated specifically to eradicating denial about the past amongst the Serbian public through uncovering truth about the past, and inviting participation from the public, through talks, discussions and other campaigns. In 2005, for instance, the Helsinki Committee published a book entitled *Srebrenica: from Denial to Confession*, for which it stated that it 'contributes to the facing up to the past and catharsis of the side that has committed genocide (Helsinki Committee 2005). This complements the work of the ICTY which is similarly concerned with establishing facts in order to combat denial (ICTY, n.d., b).

Further well-known examples of projects aimed at the public have included the YIHR Srebrenica campaign, in which the NGO put up billboards around Belgrade and sent postcards to private addresses on the tenth anniversary of Srebrenica. The postcards and billboards contained black and white images by Tarik Samarah, some of which alluded to corpses (for an overview of the campaign see Nosov 2005).

In general, YIHR's aim for its transitional justice programme is 'to build new generations who will, through their actions – civil activism or through work in institutions – influence the change in the relations of their respective states toward the recent war past' (YIHR, n.d.).

In the same vein, one of the most prominent NGOs working on such projects, the Humanitarian Law Centre (HLC) led by Nataša Kandić, places a particular emphasis on 'public information and outreach', pointing out that it is 'combating war crimes denial among a public reluctant to face the truth about the past and advocates the need to face the legacy of grave and systematic human rights abuses in the times of armed conflict' (Humanitarian Law Centre, n.d., a).

The current focus of the HLC's work is a regional initiative towards organising a truth commission, abbreviated to RECOM[2], created to advocate the establishment of a regional commission for truth-seeking about war crimes and other serious human rights violations committed in the recent past. At the time of writing, the RECOM coalition includes over 1500 civil society organisations and 155 individuals from across the former Yugoslavia (HLC n.d., b). The initiative has had significant domestic and international support and has held extensive consultations across the region with local activists, victims' groups and others (RECOM, n.d.). Writing about the RECOM coalition, Kandić notes that:

> This is an extrajudicial mechanism for establishing the facts about war crimes and the victims of such crimes with the potential to bring people closer, help them reconcile and spread the area of shared political interests among nations ... this is the first regional initiative dealing with the past based on the facts presented by the victims of war crimes. (Kandić 2010: 233–334)

Covering all the main aspects of the NGO and intelligentsia-led debate about the past is simply not possible due to lack of space (but for an overview see Dragović-Soso, forthcoming and Ostojić, 2013). One important event must be mentioned however, as it highlights the opacity and limitations of the idea of confronting the past, even within the circles which are leading this public discussion. In 2002, a debate took place between intellectuals and practitioners. The debate was protracted, but according to Dragović-Soso (forthcoming), it can be summarised as follows: the intelligentsia and practitioners were split over the liberal media's reporting on the ICTY and whether it reinforced public resistance to facing the past. The division also involved the scope of facing the past: should acknowledgement of the past include only crimes perpetrated by Serbs (or also those of others); as well as whether such a facing ought to be discussed in terms of Serbs' collective responsibility for war crimes (Dragović-Soso, forthcoming).

Despite failing to articulate exactly what a confrontation with the past entails, activists and literature on Serbia nevertheless operate on the common assumption that uncovering and establishing facts leads de facto to reconciliation and/or 'combats denial' (Fridman 2011). Whilst it is extremely important for such information to be uncovered, it is also important to be wary of assuming a relationship between the establishment of facts and reconciliation and coming to terms with the past, since the relationship between knowledge and acknowledgement is neither clear nor linear (Cohen 1995).

Empirical limitations

Empirically, therefore, confronting the past is a virtually impossible process to track and measure (since this is really an idea without a research agenda, a coherent methodology or theoretical consistency), and furthermore, there is no agreement as to *who* can judge *when* a society has succeeded in coming to terms with its past. Despite this, numerous studies have either made assumptions about Serbia's failure to confront the past, or relied on attitude-measuring surveys (e.g. Petrović 2005). It has been commented, for instance, that 'the Serbian public largely refused to believe that Serbs had committed war crimes, and they blamed other nations and ethnic groups for starting the war' (Subotić 2009:367). These observations are based on survey results which indicate that in 2005, '81 per cent of respondents answered that Serbs suffered the most during the Yugoslav wars and 74 per cent believed that Serbs committed the fewest crimes of all ethnic groups in the former Yugoslavia,' and that in 2006, '64 per cent of respondents believed that facing the crimes of the past is important, but of these respondents 35 per cent believed this is important in order to vindicate the Serbs from false accusations of war crimes' (Subotić 2009:368).[3]Another observer, relying on a survey, noted that in Serbia, 'many people, whilst admitting that the army killed thousands of Muslim Bosnians in Srebrenica, argue that what happened was not a mass crime but rather a legitimate defense of national interests' (Dimitrijević 2008:10).

Other observers draw on another survey carried out by the daily *Blic*, just before the Serbian parliament passed a declaration on Srebrenica in 2010 (Simić and Daly 2011). The authors note that of 1000 citizens polled, 21% respondents would support the declaration, whilst 46% would support a 'single resolution that would condemn all crimes committed in the former Yugoslavia', and that

> Public opinion in Serbia remains divided. Although a minority accepts and recognizes the Srebrenica massacre as genocide, most do not. Many citizens and Serbian parliamentarians believe that the Serbian politicians and military officials who have been accused of war crimes are national heroes. (Simić and Daly 2011:6–7)

Furthermore,

> The survey included the question, 'What is your view of the crimes against Bosniaks at Srebrenica in 1995?' The results show that 55 per cent of respondents said they believe this was one crime among others, 'the magnitude of which has been intentionally overstated by our enemies and the media.' The crimes at Srebrenica were denied or perceived as invented by 7 per cent of respondents, while 22 per cent said they had no views on them. (Simić and Daly 2011:7)

Despite acknowledging that the survey had a small sample, the authors 'believe that it gives a valid impression of feelings that Serbian citizens have about war crimes committed by Serbs in general' (Simić and Daly

2011:7). It is not my sole intention to engage in methodological arguments, but two points need to be made. First, relying on surveys to gain an insight into complicated belief systems is limiting. Secondly, surveys, in general, can be phrased in such a way to find exactly the kinds of answers they are looking for, and the question regarding the media and Srebrenica is a case in point (would the result have been different if the question was split into two or three, e.g. Was it a crime? One crime amongst others? Did the media overstate its importance?). Notably, surveys can 'fish' for certain kinds of answers, and in this case it is apparent that they did not ask the respondents to reflect on whether they regret that Srebrenica happened, or express sympathy for the victims. Other than indicating that 'opinion is divided' which can be said about most issues, it does not actually help us gain an insight into the more important parts of this dynamic: why do those 55% believe that? What differences of opinion are there within the 55%? Who are the 55%? What about the other 45%? How and in what context do they reach this opinion? And, if this means that society is not ready to face the past, what percentage in each group is required in order for a conclusion to be made that it has?

This approach to belief and confrontation with the past does not capture the complexity and the broad range of relationships and narratives about the past. This has also led to a problematic production of knowledge, in which researchers continue to make claims on part of 'the public' and 'the society' without engaging with their beliefs and experiences in any meaningful way. In my critique of this issue, I wish to avoid replicating the Mundy-Strand debate on civil war in which Strand (2011) issued a rejoinder to Mundy's (2011) paper offering a deconstructivist critique of positivist, quantitative approaches to studies of civil war and thereby resulting in a disciplinary cross-purpose discussion. My concern is to demonstrate not that this approach is necessarily wrong, but rather that it lacks reflexivity and critique and can be over-simplified, in that it makes generalised claims about behaviours and beliefs which are hence presented as rather straightforward problems.

In such research, and in the way it tends to be used, extrapolations are made which use the numbers of people knowing about or denying events (without defining these broad concepts) to make normative claims about societies failing to confront the past. Of course, the fields of history, memory studies and anthropology are much more aware of such complications, but it would appear that 'confronting the past' and alternative, qualitative methodologies have not yet converged in the case of Serbia, to the extent that they have elsewhere (e.g. Baines 2010; Shaw 2007; West 2003). Above all, the most problematic issue here is that surveys treat opinions and attitudes as fixed, or as something which can be found and exposed. In this book I aim to counter that problem by situating the captured narratives in their broader context of lived experience and beliefs about a number of issues, in order to demonstrate where such opinions and ideas are embedded, and how they are shaped by social and personal relationships.

'Remaking worlds' after violent pasts: Violence as a 'counterpoint to culture'

Crucially, transitional justice often neglects the relationship between violent pasts and the ways in which audiences speak, or do not speak, about violent events, or the ways in which their ability to speak is affected by the nature of those events (see e.g. Kidron 2009). Given that the practice of transitional justice also includes discursive elements (testimony, confession, trial and public debate), this is quite a significant oversight. This book's approach is strongly influenced by literature on the anthropology of violence (e.g. Scheper-Hughes and Bourgois 2004a; Das and Kleinman 2001; Daniel 1996; Malkki 1995; Daniel 1991; Taussig 1984). As a result, it suggests a shift in focus for current interpretations of the problem of Serbia and its past. As this book discovers, the content of the recent violent history has a particularly disturbing resonance for many individuals who find it difficult to verbalise and accept the scale of horror and atrocity they 'distantly' witnessed (c.f. Humphrey 2002). The often-forgotten issue is that 'coming to terms with the past' actually requires audiences to actively engage in and talk about not just atrocities in the legal sense of the term, but atrocities in all their horror – murder, rape, death.

In asking people to confront the past, transitional justice often treats 'the past' as an unproblematic issue, at least in the Serbian context, insofar as it assumes that audiences ought to be able to talk about the past publicly just as soon as they are aware of the facts about atrocities. When we demand that those confrontations be made, we must also ask what is being confronted. Is there anything in that particular content that makes certain pasts all the more difficult to confront? Thinking about such issues yields a whole new set of reflections and potential analyses.

Transitional justice operates on the assumption that dark aspects of the past must be uncovered. But, elsewhere, scholars have suggested that there exists a range of issues that people tend not to want to know, or turn away from – these are atrocities and generally, other peoples' suffering (Cohen 2001). Rather than facing, a common impulse vis-à-vis violence is to *turn away* (Cohen 2001). Some of the events at the core of what is being confronted are so horrific that they are often described as 'unspeakable' (Orentlicher 2007:15; Hayner 2011). This rather complicates the issue of reckoning with the past. If they are *unspeakable,* how do we anticipate that they will enter public discussion? I pick up this point throughout the book, and demonstrate that, frequently, a vast number of these crimes are *literally* unspeakable or inexpressible (Daniel 1994; Daniel 1996).

Thus, in transitional justice projects in Serbia, 'coming to terms with' is almost entirely disembodied from 'the past', and there is almost no discussion amongst current initiatives and scholarship as to how the content of the past may bear relation to how it is processed and understood, nor how it is culturally shaped. As Kent suggests, instead of searching for a 'grand narrative of forgiveness and redemption,' we might look to Das and Kleinman's 'small local stories' that illuminate how communities are 'experimenting with ways of inhabiting the world together' (Kent 2011:5–6; Das and Kleinman 2001:16).

This book argues that, because of the nature of what individuals and societies have to confront, the process of understanding and coping with these facts, and eventually incorporating them into one's beliefs and a society's culture (c.f. Daniel 1994), are long, drawn out and difficult, often featuring processes which the works above have deemed as 'failures' to come to terms with the past, such as denial or believing in conspiracy theories, or silence (Kidron 2009).

Much anthropological or critical literature considering the effects of violence on communities invokes violence as something which unravels or undoes daily lives, beliefs, cultures and identities (see e.g. Das and Kleinman 2001). But, since much of transitional justice is about victims or perpetrators, there is an inherent assumption that 'distant audiences' (Humphrey 2002:x) such as Serbs in Serbia, are somehow not affected by the horrific events, or that being a witness has no effect on individuals and societies. They are assumed to be unmarked and un-traumatised by this witnessing, and hence the only obstacle preventing them from confronting the past is their own obstinacy or wilful ignorance.

These audiences, however, may undergo difficulties following the witnessing of violent histories. Those difficulties and coping practices may not be immediately visible or apparent, and can be best observed in the realm of 'everyday life', which is often 'taken for granted', or seen as 'uneventful' (Das and Kleinman 2001:1), but is often 'the site of many buried memories and experiences' (Das and Kleinman 2001:4). Das and Kleinman (2001: 1–3) point out that, following violence and suffering, attempts to restore 'normal' everyday lives are made. But, they also ask an important question: how do communities '"cope" with – read, endure, work through, break apart under, transcend – both traumatic violence, and other, more insidious forms of social suffering?' (Das and Kleinman 2001:3) This book attempts to illustrate some of those dynamics, and presents the narratives which follow as a detailed case study.

It should also not be assumed that, in coping with such transitions, violence will be the subject of open conversation, or expressed clearly and easily, since there is a strong relationship between violence and language. For instance, Elaine Scarry (1985a) urges critical thinking and reflection about the ways in which we write about war, suggesting that although it is 'too self-evident' that 'the main purpose and outcome of war is injuring', this fact often 'disappears from view simply by being omitted' (Scarry 1985a:1):

... one can read many pages of an historic or strategic account of a particular military campaign, or listen to many installments in a newscast narrative of events in a contemporary war, without encountering the acknowledgement that the purpose of the event described is to ... alter the surface, shape, and deep entirety of the objects that human beings recognize as extensions of themselves. (Scarry 1985a:1)

A number of critics have urged us to think about the ways in which acts of violence – war, torture, massacres, genocide – are presented and represented, and how they are expressed in language and culture (Scarry 1985a; Sontag 2003; Sontag 2004; Daniel 1996; Taussig 2004). The relationship between violence and language is extremely important in this case: beliefs and perception are often, though not exclusively, externalised through language. Denial, acceptance and belief about war crimes are expressed most often through conversations, stories, writing, confessions, witness testimony, speeches or the media. It is precisely because violent events are frequently labelled 'the unspeakable' that we must consider in depth the reasons for their unspeakability. For this reason, rather than forgetting the violence of war, it is useful to centralise it, because treating violence critically, or as a central object of our investigation (e.g. Scarry 1985a, Daniel 1994, Taussig 1984 and to an extent, Sontag 2003), allows us to observe the ways in which these horrifying acts can 'make' and 'unmake' worlds (Scarry 1985b).

This book considers the effects of violence on a group of people who occupied ambiguous positions during the former Yugoslav conflicts but for whom violence of the 1990s 'unmade' worlds (Scarry 1985b). From the narratives presented here, it appears as though much of this group is grappling with its own understanding of categories of victims and bystanders, or with the idea of their own possible complicity, given that they were physically distant from the front lines and the battle but never completely removed from it, since the violence of the 1990s also spilled out into their own lives. Following Sontag, the point made here is that such violence, when observed 'second hand' still affects individuals profoundly, since watching brutal events can leave behind unexpected effects and strong reactions (see Sontag 2003; Humphrey 2002). It is difficult to watch, view or know about an act of violence against another human being without this provoking a reaction, such as redefinition (Tromp 1995:126).

The notion of redefining or reframing violence can be seen in several anthropological works, in particular Daniel's assertion that violence as a traumatic experience is a 'counterpoint to culture' (Daniel 1996:208), and Taussig's claim that 'cultures of terror' are often mediated through narrative (Taussig 1984:467), which have their 'own vocabulary' (Perera 2001:157). For instance, Perera writes that the Sri Lankan violence between 1988 and 1991, 'introduced altered meanings of words' such as terror, torture chamber, kidnapped and the disappeared into 'journalistic and popular discourse' (Perera 2001:157). Whilst such words were 'not new to the Sinhala language' they came to be 'used with substantially altered meanings, specifically marked by the experiences of terror' (Perera 2001:157).

As Daniel argues, attempts at 'labelling' violence fail, because violence is an event in which 'there is a certain excess' and one 'which often cannot be understood in known cultural terms' (Daniel 1996:208). Culture, in this case, can be seen broader as 'a description of a particular way of life, which expresses certain meanings and values, not only in art and learning but in institutions and ordinary behaviour' (Williams 1961:61). Importantly, culture is 'connected with the role of meanings of society' enabling us to ' "make sense" of things' (Du Gay et al. 2001:13). Furthermore, as Taussig suggests, terror is a 'sociological fact and a cultural construction' (Taussig 1984:468); that is to say, whilst violence occurs, what sense is made of it and how it is talked about largely depends on societies, groups and contexts. Therefore, violence and war are inevitably mediated or culturally (re)constructed, sometimes so that a horrific event may be explained or explained away, precisely because most of the time, violent events are seen as unacceptable and a breach of most groups' moral boundaries (c.f. van Dijk 1992). Crucially, as Bar-Tal reminds us:

> Physical violence against human beings requires an explanation for those who carry it out as well as its victims. It stems from the

basic need to live in a meaningful and predictable world, as well
as in a just world. (Bar-Tal 2003:83)

This assertion is echoed by a number of authors. For example, in his
meditation on violence and identity, Sen points out that 'central to
leading a human life ... are the responsibilities of choice and reasoning'
and violence counters that (Sen 2006: xiii). The underlying assumption
of both Bar-Tal and Sen is that human beings construct what Verdery
(1999) calls 'ordered worlds', which can easily become disrupted by
something that lies outside of most groups' norms, values, and order.
This, of course, is also related to Giddens's notion of ontological security, a 'person's fundamental sense of safety in the world' which helps
them 'avoid existential anxiety' (Giddens, 1991: 38–39).

Violence, especially if directed at civilians, can throw the 'cosmos
out of joint' (Verdery 1999:115), since the taking of human life falls outside of most social norms, even though acts of violence and war are not
'exceptions' but 'rules' in human societies (Krohn-Hansen 1997:233).
Krohn-Hansen argues that acts of violence can be seen as part of the
everyday, as 'practises and meanings which belong to (in the sense of
being both products and producers of) a cultural, social and political
logic'; but even so, even if violence does, in certain contexts, become a
part of the everyday, there is no reason to assume that it becomes any
more acceptable (Krohn-Hansen 1997:233). However, the (re)presenta-
tion, (re)construction and mediation of this violence, either by individuals, or by media or political leaders becomes a key strategy before,
during and after conflict, and each party has its own reasons for doing
so: politicians and leaders need to legitimise their rule, the media supports (or opposes) the leaders, whilst most individuals need to find a
way of understanding the loss of life and the ensuing chaos. As Girard
succinctly notes, '[v]iolence is frequently called irrational,' yet 'it has its
reasons ... and can marshal some rather convincing ones when the need
arises' (Girard 1977:2). Importantly, as Humphrey argues:

Atrocities horrify and terrify by producing wounded and mutilated bodies as political signs and victims. Torture, rape, mutila-
tion and massacre are acts of excessive violence whose effects flow

from the production of horror in victims and witnesses ... Atrocities confront individuals with an existential crisis of the self and the need to make sense of the world. This unanchoring moment of horror is the 'space of terror'. (Humphrey 2002:1–2)

This effect of violence also affects the process of memory and remembering. Memories of violence 'resist symbolisation' (Krstić 2003:5), because the added dimensions of remembering atrocities (Lorey and Beezley 2002:xxvii) are bound up with traumatic meanings. The lack of processing of the event at the time of its occurrence (Caruth 1995), results in the mediation narratives which I have recorded here: the unresolved aspect of the trauma, whether a rupture in meaning (Eyerman 2002) or a physical trauma, mean that these events are often still 'going on'.

This book downplays the issue of collective memory as a crucial frame of reference precisely because of this added layer of complication: events are not 'just' remembered but they are not considered to be 'over' (Dawson 2007), since most of the narratives, or large proportions of them are expressed in the present tense, or a mix of tenses. For the respondents, much of this is still going on.

In addition, studies of memory are chiefly concerned with two things; according to Schwartz:

> The first relates the discontinuities of the past to an on-going constructive process motivated by the changing concerns of the present. The second approach draws attention to continuities in our perception of the past and to the way these perceptions are maintained in the face of social change. (Schwartz 1991:222)

This is particularly the case with conceptualisations of collective memory (e.g. Halbwachs 1992) which examine the relationships between past and present, and between individual and collective memory (see Olick and Robbins 1998). In this book I acknowledge that memory is involved in the narratives of conflict, and that 'it is in society that people normally acquire their memories' and 'in society that they recall, recognise, and localise their memories' (Halbwachs 1992:38). However, the narratives here, being so often expressed in the present, and often being concerned with events that are still taking place (such as ICTY trials), would not benefit from analysis through a (collective) memory framework. Moreover, as will become apparent throughout this book, not all the narratives contain attempts at recollection; some are chiefly concerned with countering the hegemonic narrative of confronting the past, and often are implicitly about the past, but in fact do not narrate events which happened, focusing instead on the act of resisting and subverting.

Lastly, as other works have considered the question of memory and confronting the past in Serbia (e.g. Dragović-Soso 2010), my aim for this book is to consider a different framework. What does confrontation with the past look like, if the violent aspect of that past is viewed as central to the analysis?

Based on these insights, this book analyses some of the narrative strategies which appear throughout respondents' interviews and ethnographic observations. In order to make sense of the narratives of conflicts and atrocity collected throughout this research, this book works with the following assumptions. Taking Daniel's assertion that violent events are a 'counterpoint to culture', and that violence 'unmakes' words (Scarry 1985b; Nordstrom 1995: 131), the narratives presented here are seen as attempts at 'remaking' such a world (Das et al. 2001). My underlying point is that the brutality of the 1990s has left audiences without the tools – discursive, conceptual – with which to make sense of the scale of horror that took place. As a result, they have devised their own narrative strategies to cope with, understand and make sense of that violence.

CHAPTER 3

A SHORT SUMMARY OF EVENTS: THE 1990S CONFLICTS, WAR CRIMES AND NATO AIR STRIKES

This chapter familiarises readers with some of the key events of the 1990s referred to in this book and mentioned by the respondents interviewed. For the sake of brevity, this chapter will not focus on covering the break-up of Yugoslavia in any great detail, which is discussed in a vast and notable literature (e.g. Ramet 2004a; Ramet 2004b; Judah 2000; Popov et al. 2000a; Allcock 2000; Magaš 1993; Silber and Little 1996) nor the circumstances and developments of each war. This chapter concentrates on the events directly related to this book, that is certain atrocities, such as the Srebrenica genocide, the siege of Sarajevo, ICTY indictments, NATO air strikes and the death of Milošević, primarily because they are the key events in the backdrop to Serbia's recent history and were crucial components of the stories told by respondents in this study. The focus is also on the Milošević-era media and their representation of war and atrocities, as this was a source of wartime information for the respondents, as well as for the Serbian public in general. The key aim is to provide a frame of reference for their narratives which follow later in the book.

The Milošević era, 1987–2000

The reign of Slobodan Milošević formed the main backdrop to most of the events considered in this book. Slobodan Milošević consolidated his political career when he became President of Serbia in 1989. It has often been debated whether Milošević was indeed a nationalist and whether 'the War of Yugoslav Succession had an ethnic character' (see e.g. Ramet 2004a).

However, as Ramet argues, whatever Milošević may have believed privately, he still 'used the propaganda apparatus at his disposal to stir up nationalist passions and used those nationalist passions to motivate Serbs for war' (Ramet 2004a:756). Indeed, whether or not he truly believed in 'Greater Serbia', his regime still created a context in which history and national mythology were used to explain and frame contemporary events, and which produced only two available categories of political identification – 'patriot' or 'traitor' (Bieber 2002:104).

A summary of Milošević's rise to power is given by Ramet (2004b), who sees 1987 as a turning-point. At a meeting with Kosovo Albanians and Serbs in Priština,[1] Milošević uttered the famous line which echoed throughout his rule, telling local Serbs that '[n]o one will dare beat you.' (Ramet 2004b:770) Most infamously, in 1989, Milošević presided over a 600th-anniversary celebration of the Battle of Kosovo in Kosovo Polje. His speech alluded to various threats to the Serbs (Ramet 2004b:770). Most critics see this speech as pivotal in the Yugoslav crisis: it marked the start of Yugoslavia's descent into war, as well as providing a visible starting-point for new political discourses of fear and nationalism which characterised the years ahead.

With collaboration from the nationalist writer Dobrica Ćosić and other influential intellectuals, he also began to support the revision of Serbia's borders (Ramet 2004b:770), in order to incorporate the Serb-inhabited areas of Eastern Bosnia and Croatia. The pan-Serb movement, which Milošević supported at the start of the 1990s, was threatened in 1993 when he fell out with Radovan Karadžić, leader of the Bosnian Serbs; the Serbian media began to vilify Karadžić (Bideleux and Jeffries 2007:252).

The break-up of Yugoslavia and the wars in Bosnia and Croatia

The break-up of the former Yugoslavia, and the wars which followed, occurred on Milošević's watch.

The break-up of Yugoslavia commenced in 1991 with Slovenian independence, and reached its crisis point with the Croatian declaration of its independence, which eventually resulted in a war between the new Croatian army and the remains of the Yugoslav People's Army (JNA). Months before Slovenian independence, in March 1991, the Serb minority in the Croatian Krajina region had declared its own independent 'republic'. Republika Srpska Krajina (RSK) was never internationally recognised. Croatia's independence was recognised on 15 January 1992, by which time a third of Croatia's territory had been occupied by the JNA and Croatian Serb rebels, with serious damage to many Croatian cities. A UN peacekeeping force (United Nations Protection Force, UNPROFOR) was deployed in Croatia in 1992, by which time war had broken out in Bosnia-Herzegovina. The war in Croatia culminated in 'Operation Storm' over several days in early August 1995, part of a Croatian Army offensive to recapture Serb-held territory.

The many complicated issues in Bosnian politics and society were finally externalised at the first multi-party elections in November 1991, where the nationalist parties rose to prominence: the Party of Democratic Action (*Stranka demokratske akcije*, SDA), led by Alija Izetbegović; the Serbian Democratic Party (*Srpska demokratska stranka*, SDS), an offshoot of the Croatian Serb party, led by Radovan Karadžić; Croat nationalists were represented by a branch of the Croatian Democratic Union (*Hrvatska demokratska zajednica*, HDZ). Most of Bosnia's electorate voted along ethnic lines and the majority of the seats were won by the nationalist parties (Silber and Little 1996). Tensions rose after the elections, and Bosnian Serb leaders threatened to form a Serb Republic should Bosnia gain independence. The Republika Srpska (RS) was declared on 9 January 1992, with the Bosnian Federation's independence being declared on 1 March. By the end of February

1992, the first serious fighting in Bosnia had broken out in Bosanksi Brod, and by 2 March tensions had also escalated in Sarajevo. After a Serb guest was shot at a wedding party, Momčilo Krajišnik (the Serb Speaker of the Bosnian Parliament) called it 'a great injustice aimed at the Serbs' (in Silber and Little 1996:205).

The wars seem never to have had popular support among the public. There were mass demonstrations in Sarajevo and in Belgrade, whilst desertion from the army or dodging the draft for the Croatian war was not uncommon (see Miličević 20006). Magaš and Žanić (2001:xxiv) note that 'contrary to the way they have usually been portrayed by the Western media, most Serbs had never given much (if any) support to the "Greater Serbia" programme.'

Whereas the war in Croatia was fought between the newly-formed Croatian army and the remainder of the JNA, predominantly Serb and controlled by Belgrade, the JNA had pulled out of Bosnia in 1992, leaving the Bosnian Muslims (Bosniaks) and Croats to fight against the newly-formed army of the RS (*Vojska Republike Srpske*, VRS). Official Serbia's involvement had always been suspected, however. In 1992 the UN imposed sanctions on Serbia on suspicion that it was assisting the Bosnian Serbs, and in 1995 Slobodan Milošević signed the Dayton Peace Agreement on behalf of the Bosnian Serb side. The effects of sanctions were grave (see Gordy 1999; Judah 2000), and resulted in economic difficulties and shortages. Numerous anti-Milošević demonstrations and some specifically anti-war ones took place throughout the 1990s, and various anti-war groups, such as the Women in Black, protested throughout the wars.

War crimes in Croatia, Bosnia and Kosovo 1991–1999

The wars in Croatia and Bosnia were marked by 'twin evils' which would later become their landmark. The first was the proximity in which the wars were fought – often between former friends and neighbours – being very often localised in this way (see e.g. Bax 1997). The second was the brutality and the level of violence, resulting in a large number of war crimes, crimes against humanity and genocide. The full list of cases brought against the perpetrators of these crimes is on the website of the International Criminal Tribunal for the former Yugoslavia (ICTY), set up in 1993 with the purpose of prosecuting these crimes, deterring others and contributing to peace and justice on the territory of the former Yugoslavia (see e.g. Clark 2009). Here, however, I will recount some of the cases which are most relevant to this study, namely the siege of Sarajevo, the 'marketplace' massacres and the Srebrenica massacre and genocide. This is therefore not an exhaustive account, but focuses primarily on events which the respondents and I discussed most frequently.

The siege of Sarajevo lasted from 1992 until 1995 and the ICTY has raised several indictments, including that of Ratko Mladić (General of the Bosnian Serb army, the VRS), on this charge. During the siege, civilians were trapped in the city, and were subject to mortar and sniper attacks. In particular, three such attacks have become infamous, due to their brutality and to the fact that they were blatant attacks on civilians.

The three massacres included the 'breadline massacre', on 27 May 1992, with twenty civilian fatalities and 100 wounded. Two subsequent attacks occurred in markets, the first at Markale in Sarajevo, in February 1994 (sixty-eight fatalities and 200 wounded civilians) and the second on 28 August 1995 killing thirty-seven civilians and wounding eighty. All three massacres were denied by the Bosnian Serb side, and all were subject to exhaustive UN investigation (see Rusek and Ingrao 2004:837).

After several contradictory investigations, Markale was examined in the light of new evidence at the ICTY trial of Bosnian Serb General Stanislav Galić. The second marketplace massacre, again denied by the Bosnian Serb side, resulted in an 11-day NATO bombardment of Bosnian Serb positions, as soon as the initial forensic report concluded Serb responsibility (Rusek and Ingrao 2004:847). By this time the VRS had already besieged and attacked all of the designated UN 'Safe Areas' – Goražde, Tuzla, Žepa, Bihać, Sarajevo and Srebrenica.

Other war crimes committed during the Bosnian war included concentration camps, massacres, executions and the pillaging of towns. These were perpetrated by all three sides and some were committed by paramilitary troops. To a lesser or greater extent, paramilitary units 'are routinely deployed by governments to preserve plausible deniability and to cloud the issue of command and control' (Amanpour 1999:267–268) and in Serbia they are often blamed for the worst atrocities of the conflict. One of the most prominent units, the Serb Volunteer Guard (the 'Tigers') was headed by the Serbian criminal Željko Ražnatović Arkan. In April 1992, it committed one of the first atrocities of the Bosnian war by occupying the Bosnian town of Bijeljina, having recently carried out the same operations in Vukovar, Croatia (Malcolm 2001:236).

Paramilitary organisation was not confined solely to former criminals like Ražnatović. Vojislav Šešelj, already a Serbian Radical Party (SRS) leader when the Bosnian war began, formed his 'self-styled "Četnik" army' (Malcolm 2001:226). The word 'Četnik' refers to Serbian royalist forces, fighting against Josip Broz Tito's Partisans, and Croatian nationalists, known as Ustaše in the Second World War. Both words, Četnik and Ustaše, later came to be used to refer to all manner of Serb and Croat nationalists respectively, frequently being used as derogatory labels. Vuk Drašković, now one of the most prominent Serb politicians, attached a paramilitary unit ('Srpska garda') to his Serbian Renewal Movement (Srpski Pokret Obnove, SPO) (Danas 2004). Šešelj is currently on trial at the ICTY, partly on a charge of financing and organising a paramilitary unit (see ICTY, n.d., c).

Forced population displacement and the pillaging of smaller towns and villages were not uncommon during the Bosnian war, in particular in Eastern Bosnian towns of Zvornik, Foča, Goražde and Višegrad. The towns' Muslim populations were either killed or forced to leave, and they then sought shelter in the Bosnian Federation or enclaves in the RS; according to Malcolm (2001:237), '95% of the Muslims of Zvornik, Višegrad and Foča fled their homes by the end of April [1992]'. In turn, displaced Serbs who had been forced out of, or fled, their homes in other parts of Bosnia settled in the towns and villages of RS. Ethnic displacement in Croatia and Bosnia was accompanied by the destruction of religious and cultural monuments. The most notable incidents of the latter included the destruction of the Mostar Bridge and the siege of Dubrovnik, as well as the destruction of mosques and churches all over Bosnia. There were also concentration camps, in places such as Prijedor, Ovčara, Trnopolje and Omarska (see Vulliamy 1999:102–106).

In 1992, executions of Bosnian Serbs took place in villages around the small eastern Bosnian town of Srebrenica and the village of Bratunac. There was also a Muslim attack on the Serb village of Zalažje on 12 July 1992, in which at least forty local Serbs were killed (Duijzings 2007:153), and another Muslim attack on the Serb village of Kravica (in the vicinity of Srebrenica) on 7 January 1993, where 46 people were killed. In 2006, the ICTY found that murder and cruel treatment of Serbs detained in Srebrenica occurred between 24 September to 16 October 1995, and 15 December to 20 March 1993, by the Bosnian Military Police of the Srebrenica (ICTY 2006). Naser Oric ́, one of the leaders, was indicted but later acquitted of charges of direct involvement, although he was judged to be guilty of failing to prevent cruel treatment and murder. He was sentenced to two years' imprisonment but released for time already served (ICTY 2006).

In 1995 the Srebrenica genocide took place, in which more than 8,000 Muslim men and boys were killed by Serb forces. A number of facts have been established by the ICTY convictions of Dražen Erdemovic ́ and Radislav Krstic ́ and reports carried out by the UN and the Dutch and RS governments (Duijzings 2007:146). The town, a designated UN safe area, was hosting thousands of refugees from neighbouring villages and towns, as Bosnian Muslims fled from the advancing VRS. Srebrenica was shelled and besieged by Ratko Mladic ́ and the VRS between 9 and 10 July 1995. After warnings, the troops failed to withdraw by 11 July, and by 12 July the women and children were separated from the men and deported. More than 8,000 Muslim men were killed. Some of the men were executed in villages around Srebrenica, and some attempted to flee to nearby Tuzla but were executed en route (see Vulliamy 2005). Many attempts were made within official Serbia and RS to reduce or dispute the numbers. Ratko Mladic ́ and Radovan Karadžic ́ were indicted for genocide in Srebrenica in July 1995, together with eighteen others. There have already been three guilty pleas, and three convictions with nine others awaiting trial. Specifically, on 2 August 2001, Bosnian Serb military commander Radislav Krstić, a key actor in the massacre, was charged with and convicted of aiding and abetting genocide, and is serving a 35-year sentence.

As of May 2012, the ICTY has indicted 161 persons for violations of international humanitarian law, committed on the territory of the former Yugoslavia, and sixty-four of those have been sentenced (thirty-six of those have already served their sentence); thirteen have been acquitted, thirty-six have had their indictments withdrawn or died; thirteen had been transferred to domestic courts, whilst sixteen are currently on trial. Notable cases include the guilty plea of Biljana Plavšić, former president of Republika Srpska. On 2 October 2002, Plavšić pled guilty to persecution of Bosnian Muslims and Croats in thirty-seven municipalities in Bosnia, between 1992 and 1995 (ICTY 2002). On 27 January 2004, Milan Babić, former President of RSK, pled guilty of participating in a campaign of persecutions against non-Serbs (ICTY 2004). Former president of the self-proclaimed Republika Srpska, Radovan Karadžić was arrested in Belgrade and transferred to the ICTY on 30 July 2008. He was a fugitive for thirteen years. He is charged with, amongst other crimes, genocide against Bosnian Muslims and other non-Serbs, in Bosnia (ICTY 2008).[2] In 2009, the ICTY delivered a judgement for crimes committed by Serbian forces against Kosovo Albanians in 1999. Nikola Šainović, Nebojša Pavković and Sreten Lukić were sentenced to twenty-two years' imprisonment; Vladimir Lazarević and Dragoljub Ojdanić were each sentenced to fifteen years' imprisonment (ICTY 2009). All were high ranking police and army officers.

On 15 April 2011, Croat army general Ante Gotovina (tried together with Ivan Čermak and Mladen Markač) was sentenced to twenty-four years imprisonment for crimes against humanity, comitted against Krajina Serbs between 1991 and 1995 (ICTY 2011) but this was reversed on appeal on 16 November 2012. On 26 May 2011, Ratko Mladić was arrested in Serbia and later transferred to the ICTY. He was a fugitive for some sixteen years. This was followed by the July 2011 arrest of Goran Hadžić, the last remaining fugitive.

The media and war crimes

The Milošević regime exerted control and influence over most of the mainstream media throughout the 1990s, partly in order to suppress dissent and partly in order to represent a particularly distorted picture of the conflicts. That representation relied on political framing of the wars as self-defence, and ultimately acted to normalise and, in some circles, garner support for the war (Skopljanac-Brunner et al. 2000). Drumming up support in this way, or at least leading the public to believe that the wars in Croatia and Bosnia were somehow unavoidable or acts of self-defence, was necessary for Milošević at the time, since his regime 'lacked political and moral legitimacy' and relied on the use of 'the power of symbols' (Pavlaković 2005:4).

The mainstream Serbian media presented a factually inaccurate picture of all the 1990s conflicts. Thompson (1994) describes how, in all three republics, print and broadcast media reporting on specific events was predominantly concerned with creating one-sided versions of the wars which cast one's own nation as the central victim. Thompson (1994) states that Milošević and his regime seem not to have orchestrated direct propagandist programmes, but did take legal and illegal actions to control the media and its content. Supposedly oppositional radio stations were denied frequencies, and a court ruling forced the independent stations B92 and Studio B off air for 30 hours to stop them covering an opposition rally in March 1991 (Thompson 1994:59). Journalists and other staff were also purged to make space for Milošević supporters, forcing others to either collaborate or resign. During the wars, the most powerful media were newspapers such as *Politika* and *Večernje novosti*; both were pro-war and pro-government, with *Novosti* as the more extreme (Thompson 1994:64). The other main communication channel was Radio Television Serbia (*Radio-televizija Srbije*, RTS). Its flagship evening news, *Dnevnik 2*, was watched by vast sections of the population, who received an hour or more of supplementary war reporting every night during 1991 (Thompson 1991:84). Most of the mainstream Serbian media at the time took a pro-government, pro-war stance, except independent dailies and periodicals (*Borba, Vreme, Republika*) or radio stations such as B92.

The pro-Milošević media's version of the wars was framed within what Žanić (2007) calls the 'folklore matrix' and can also be conceptualised as national mythology (Čolović 2002). Representations of 1990s wars relied on heroic epic language and images (Žanić 2007:23), but also on mythical narratives of heroes and martyrs (Čolović 1996, 2000, 2002). As fighting broke out in Croatia, *Politika* carried stories of the 'Ustaše' and references to World War II. The following headlines all stressed the perceived (Croat) threat: 'The entire Serb people has been attacked', '1941 started with the same methods', 'Genocide mustn't happen', and a report stating that 'scenes from fifty years ago were repeated when Croatian *Ustaše* attacked the Serb people' (Thompson 1994:72). *Politika* 'supported the war in Bosnia from the outset' (Thompson 1994:81) and continued the same way, giving 'every possible credit and the benefit of every doubt to the Serb side without argument or examination.' (Thompson 1994:80) In May 1992, it ran a series of WWI propaganda posters such as 'Serbia needs your help' (Thompson 1994:80–81). Its reporting of the incidents in Zvornik (where Serb soldiers and paramilitaries attacked the Bosnian Muslim population) suggested that Zvornik Serbs were under attack, with headlines such as 'Muslim extremists attack Serb municipality Zvornik' and 'Defenceless people kept hostage by Green Berets'; the same went for attacks on Foča, Višegrad and Bijeljina (Thompson 1994:85).

Dnevnik's coverage was different only in the imagery it used – or, rather, did not use. Images of victims and fighting were conspicuously absent (until the attack by Muslims on the Serb settlement of Skelani), and landscapes and (unacknowledged) archive footage were used instead of real footage (Thompson 1994:94). In addition, *Politika* did not cover the Srebrenica massacre in July 1995, and what little was said suggested there had been 'an evacuation' of population from the town. The use of images of landscape and archive footage instead of images of actual fighting, battles, dead bodies or the brutality of war (unless referring to Serbian victims of Croat or Bosnian violence) omitted or obscured Serb activities and crimes. (Thompson 1994:105). Denial tactics were employed to avoid covering incidents such as the three-year siege of Sarajevo and the Omarska concentration camp (Thompson 1994:105), yet:

> RTS's masterpiece omission, however, is more than the sum of its parts. It has constructed a version of reality in which Serb forces never attacked Bosnia, never slaughtered scores of thousands of its people and displaced scores of thousands more, never besieged its cities and towns and never laid waste to its village. (Thompson 1994:110)

The Serbian media's war coverage was thus highly theatrical and manipulative, offering an 'illusion that everything is normal' (Popov 2004b:15) – or at least, as 'normal' as it can be at times of war, which is to say, that it represented accepted and 'desirable' notions that 'we' are not the perpetrators, 'we' are simply defending ourselves. Žanić points out that the media are comparable to myth because 'they define and reinforce […] moral, aesthetic and cognitive structures that acquire their legitimacy simply by being repeated in text after text, in programme after programme' (Žanić 2007:14). Thus, even though little direct propagandist manipulation took place, the media acted to misinform and reconfigure the boundaries of reality.

Overall, the dominant representations of the war in Serbia were very close to a Baudrillardian 'simulacrum', as the audiences received images mediated to a point at which they became 'speculative, to the extent that we do not see the real event that it could be or it would signify' (Baudrillard 2001:27). The coverage was over-stylised, representing events that did not necessarily exist, for example a war in which no bodies of others were to be seen (c.f. Thompson 1994). Such a war can be best described as 'promotional, speculative, virtual' (Baudrillard 2001:30), and its coverage as 'trompe l'oeil' (Baudrillard 2001:62).

Kosovo war and NATO air strikes 1999–2000

The post-war period between 1995 and 2000 was characterised by increasing opposition to Milošević and popular discontent. When the wars began, resistance to Milošević had predominantly been the domain of a 'consistent liberal critique articulated by such people as Žarana Papić, Sonja Liht, Vesna Pešić, and Sonja Biserko [NGO and feminist activists]' and an 'inconsistent anti-war critique, associated with such opposition figures as Vuk Drašković and Zoran Djindjić.' (Ramet 2004b:772) The post-war period also saw growing populist mobilisation against Milošević especially as he stifled domestic opposition and alienated nationalist supporters by reverting to his rhetoric of socialism (Bideleux and Jeffries 2007:254).

The NATO air strikes were a low point for Milošević's regime, and precipitated the end of his rule. The existing tensions between Serbs and Albanians in Kosovo escalated in 1997, after protracted repression of Albanians in the then province, which then prompted attacks by the Kosovo Liberation Army (KLA). This led to a spiral of violence, initially between the Serbian Police and military and the KLA, but spreading also to civilian populations. Milošević received his first warning from the international community on 5 October 1998, by which time approximately 800 people had been killed, and 30,000 people (15% of the population) had been displaced (Bideleux and Jeffries 2007:541).

Milošević's final warning to stop the Kosovo violence came on 24 September 1998. Air strikes began on 24 March 1999, but the process leading up to them was complex and prolonged, since the Western powers involved faced divisions and disagreement over the right course of action (Dannreuther 2001:20). The air strikes targeted Serbian military and strategic positions in Kosovo and Southern Serbia. Their last phase concentrated on Belgrade, and several city-centre buildings were targeted (the Interior Ministry, RTS headquarters, SPS headquarters, power stations and others), and the Hotel Jugoslavija in New Belgrade. The Chinese Embassy in Belgrade was damaged during the New Belgrade air strikes. The air strikes ended on 10 June 1999, when Milošević finally signed a peace agreement which resulted in the withdrawal of Serb forces. The UN Mission in Kosovo (UNMIK) was set up and took over temporary administration of Kosovo (see Dannreuther 2001:26), until Kosovo eventually proclaimed independence from Serbia on 18 February 2008.

In the subsequent presidential elections on 24 September 2000, it was clear from early on that Milošević was attempting to falsify the results (Bujošević and Radovanović 2003:5). Although Vojislav Koštunica had won the election, and crowds immediately began celebrating Milošević's defeat, Milošević did not concede. One opposition leader, Zoran Djindjić (president of the Democratic Party, DS), called for a general strike, which commenced on 29 September across the country and included many workplaces, schools and key services. Milošević maintained the ideological stance he had held before and during the air strikes, again accusing the opposition of being NATO-led (Bujošević and Radovanović 2003:7).

On 6 October Milošević appeared on television and finally conceded the presidency to Koštunica. In January 2001, Djindjić became Prime Minister of Serbia; a move seen as seen as Serbia's long-awaited emergence from isolation, and its move towards Europe and international cooperation. However, Zoran Djindjić was assassinated on 12 March 2003, and Serbia appeared to be returning to another period of isolation and nationalism, particularly after the conservative Vojislav Koštunica became Prime Minister of Serbia 2004.

Milošević's ICTY trial

On 28 June 2001, Djindjić's new government delivered Milošević to the ICTY making him the first (former) head of state ever to be handed over to an international court (see Bideleux and Jeffries 2007:287). The Milošević trial, lasted more than four years and was televised in Serbia. Although the Milošević trial was predominantly concerned with war crimes in Kosovo (1998–1999), the original indictment was amended in November 2001 to include for genocide against Bosnian Muslims. Milošević first appeared in court on 3 July 2001 without lawyers, and the trial opened on 12 February 2002. Refusing to enter a plea, he claimed that the ICTY was a 'false tribunal', that the indictments against him were 'false indictments', and that the trial aimed 'to produce false justifications for war crimes NATO committed in Yugoslavia' (Bideleux and Jeffries 2007:287).

Milošević died in 2006 before the end of the trial. Although he died from health complications, his death was presented as suspicious in Serbia. In the week after his death, most newspapers, especially tabloids, ran front-page headlines such as 'Milošević poisoned', 'Milošević murdered by The Hague' and so on (e.g. *Večernje Novosti* 2006a, 2006b, 2006c). The death was reported mainly within conspiracy-theory parameters, and his subsequent, posthumous popularity owed much to this coverage (Stanić 2006):

> [Milošević's] death, for which perhaps 90% of the population believes The Hague Tribunal, an institution accused of power and injustice (usually a synonym for 'anti-Serbdom'), is responsible, does not lead to forgetting, but rather a loud silence ... That silence was so loud the day after [Milošević's death] that Vuk Drašković had to, almost with disgust, remind [the public] of Milošević's misdeeds. (Stanić 2006:13)

On the day of his funeral, the SPS and SRS held a joint 'funeral service' in front of the Parliament building in Belgrade. Newspapers suggested that the attendees were largely SPS and SRS supporters, and that the SRS was using the rally to win over SPS voters. Several motifs from recent years were juxtaposed: attendees carried Milošević's pictures alongside those of Mladić, Karadžić and Šešelj, with inscriptions such as 'Serbian heroes'. Several blocks away, at Trg Republike, Belgrade's main square, a counter-rally was organised via an anonymous text message which had circulated around Belgrade in the preceding days and was published in the independent newspaper *Danas*. The rally, which aimed to gather anti-Milošević supporters to celebrate the 'end of an era', numbered only a few thousand attendees, mostly in their twenties and thirties.

The research for this book (autumn 2005 until start of 2007) was carried out in the context of an ever-increasing isolationist and nationalist rhetoric at a political level, and the sense of political optimism following the fall of Milošević seemed to have disappeared. In 2006 the initial negotiations for Kosovo's future status began between Belgrade and Priština (for an overview, see Weller 2009) and the increasing likelihood of Kosovo's independence cast a very heavy shadow over

Serbia. In addition, the Stabilisation and Association Agreement with the European Union was suspended in the same year, pending Serbia's full compliance with the ICTY. Some changes were noted only in 2008, with the departure of Koštunica's DSS from government, and Serbia's reorientation towards Europe. From 2008, Serbia's foreign policy prioritised European integration, but also, Kosovo. This, and other changes, led to the eventual arrest of the four remaining ICTY fugitives: Stojan Župljanin on 11 June 2008 in Belgrade; Radovan Karadžić in Belgrade on 21 July 2008; Ratko Mladić on 26 May 2011 in Lazarevo, Serbia and Goran Hadžić on 20 July 2011 in Serbia. All have been transferred to the ICTY.

CHAPTER 4

'THAT WAS JUST NOT NORMAL': THE 1990S AS A DECADE OF SICKNESS, INSANITY AND HORROR

Introduction

In an attempt to understand narratives about the past, and how these present a confrontation with the atrocities of the recent conflicts, it is important to consider how individuals experienced the 1990s. Most of the time, literature concerned with confrontation with the past does not explore this in any depth. Yet the ways in which the past was experienced will inevitably determine how its different aspects are viewed and discussed today. Thus, in asking a society or community to 'confront the past' it must not be assumed that 'the past' is viewed from some neutral vantage point (a version of this statement is to be found throughout a multitude of memory studies scholarship, such as Connerton 1989; Halbwachs 1980). Likewise, it must not be assumed that a confrontation with atrocities – acknowledgement, expressions of regret, public discussion – will be divorced from the broader experience of the time in which they occurred.

This is especially important because the 1990s was a particularly turbulent decade in Serbia. Not just in terms of politics, but socially too, as living conditions deteriorated and all kinds of crime, violence, spousal abuse increased (Nikolić-Ristanović 2002a; Clark 2008:35). In an excellently detailed chapter on this issue, Clark quotes filmmaker Janko Baljak: 'War and weapons that arrived in the capital, as well as the large number of refugees and all sorts of war syndromes, made Belgrade the "Chicago of the '90s" (Trbić 2000 in Clark 2008:34). Furthermore, 'the nation's health ... greatly suffered as a consequence of poor nutrition, inadequate medical supplies, overcrowded living conditions and stress' (Clark 2008:36). As a result, psychological health also deteriorated, and the sedative Bensedin became the best-selling medication in Serbia during the Milošević years, with estimated 50,000 packages being sold monthly in Belgrade (Clark 2008:37; Vasović 2000). Hence, for someone living in Belgrade, the 1990s would have been shaped by these turbulences, as well as the conflicts which were occurring at the same time.

Furthermore, one of the arguments that this books makes is that the individuals presented in this study are still attempting to 'come to terms with' the experience of the 1990s, not just the question of atrocities. One trend, which emerged quite strongly amongst almost all respondents – and by their own admittance – is an inability to comprehend what actually happened in the 1990s in their entirety. For them, atrocities were often seen as inexplicable; especially considering the level of brutality involved (this is discussed in the following chapter), but the breakup of Yugoslavia and the fact that the wars occurred in the first place remains just as unexplained. 'The past', or more specifically, 'the 1990s' remain a site of unanswered questions, and many of the narratives presented here can be viewed as attempts to answer and make sense of at least some of those.

'Diagnosing' the past

How, then, did this decade look from the vantage point of the respondents in the study? The first feature of the 1990s is that everything that was experienced at that time seems to have been lumped together into one box of 'really ugly memories' (as stated by one of the male respondents). This includes experiencing the wars – predominantly at a distance – hyperinflation, shortages, watching war coverage on television, atrocities and later on, NATO air strikes.

A relatively small set of words is used almost constantly to describe the 1990s, the conflicts and atrocities: these are rarely separated in respondents' accounts. This included 'horror', 'horrifying', 'terror', 'fear', 'terrifying'[1] and phrases indicating sudden catastrophes, illness and incomprehension. For instance, reflecting on the wars, one of the younger respondents, Ivan, said that 'To this day, I still don't get it'; whilst Miroslav, an older respondent, points out that for him 'those wars, they were total horror, a cataclysm' and that they were the result of 'stupidity'.

The second feature of these experiences is that the decade is frequently described as something that was simply 'not normal'. The use of this kind of language indicated that, above all, the 1990s were extremely disorientating for those who experienced them in Serbia, and of course, in the rest of the former Yugoslavia. This is how anthropologist Marko Živković describes that time:

> When I returned to my native Belgrade in the summer of 1993 after four years spent abroad, I was struck by how 'opaque' the situation seemed not only to me but to other 'natives' who lived there continuously. My own society became almost as unfamiliar to me as it might have been for an outsider. Milošević's Serbia was a place undergoing traumatic change and experiencing what is, by any standard, a high level of general turmoil. (Živković 2001:168)

Milošević's Serbia was 'an extreme situation' in which, according to Živković, 'a great deal of what has previously been taken for granted by the majority of people is thrown out of kilter' (Živković 2001:168). In addition, 'the ability of almost everyone in Serbia at that time to figure out the social landscape was severely impaired,' since:

> That landscape was populated by government ministers, central bank governors, directors of big firms, regional bosses, Socialist

Party functionaries, generals, prophets and pundits, influential writers, opposition leaders, police chiefs, criminals-warlords – 'businessmen' – and the mysterious State Security Service. How much power, influence, and autonomy all these actors and institutions actually had was far from clear, yet it was important to figure out in the world in which nothing seemed to be stable, rational, or what it was supposed to be. (Živković 2001:177)

Added to this general turmoil – which in Serbia, as Živković notes, was often described using the metaphors of 'jelly', 'slush' and 'mud' (Živković 2001:168) – was the further complication of several wars, all of which started quickly and often against expectations. Furthermore, everything collapsed at the same time: borders, known political systems, the country/countries, standard of life, friendships, companies, morals. On the one hand, people had to deal with a quite incomprehensible event – war, which by their own admission no one really understood – and, together with that, a real existential crisis which was accompanied, at times, by sudden poverty, physical or psychological illness and broken relationships. Thus, the experience of the 1990s represented a break with 'normality' on multiple levels. In a sense, the unfolding events at times must have seemed like a reflection of personal traumas. Things that were once unexpected, suddenly occurred (the breakup of Yugoslavia, war); and occurred in the most brutal way possible (violence, which by any account was horrific).

All the changes of the 1990s produced a kind of disorientation which, to paraphrase Verdery, reordered 'meaningful worlds' (Verdery 1999:35), or which could be understood as Daniel's 'counterpoints to culture' (Daniel 1991).[2] They produced a 'disorientating' type of change in which 'people of all kinds [can] no longer count on their previous grasp of how the world works' (Verdery 1999:35). In accounting for the disorientating post-socialist change, Verdery suggests that people, 'whether consciously or not', become 'open to reconsidering (either on their own or with the help of political, cultural and religious elites) their social relations and their worlds of meaning' (Verdery 1999:35). This is the type of change which destabilises even the most routine knowledge and belief, the 'what goes without saying'

(Bourdieu 1977:167). These kinds of disorientating events undermine 'the everyday life-world', 'fundamental assumptions and expectations regarding the nature of the world and the individual's position within it' (Kulyk 2006:283). Similarly, Verdery argues that 'such moments lead to reconfiguring one's world' since '[i]n moments of major transformation, people may find that new forms of action are more productive than the ones they are used to, or that older forms make sense in a different way' (Verdery 1999:34). This latter point is not to be underestimated, because the impact of the events of the 1990s on individuals was so profound that they still struggle today to understand what happened – a dynamic examined in the following chapter as well as throughout this book.

This is also reflected in the language used to describe that period. As well as the use of 'terror' and 'horror', a surprising number of medical and psychiatric phrases emerge in the accounts presented here. Using the language of pathology, respondents describe that decade as 'not normal'; it was 'insane' and sick'; the war was 'insanity'. Belgrade was a 'mad house', people who went to war were equally 'insane', 'lunatics', 'drunks' or 'mad'; atrocities committed were also 'sick' and not committed by 'normal people'. Or, as a respondent mentioned once, things in Belgrade had become so desperate that 'We have a saying here: "who hasn't gone crazy yet, is not normal"'. 'Gone crazy' is how both politicians such as Milošević and his wife ('she was an insane woman') and people subjected to their rule were described.[3] According to Greenberg, engagement in discourses of 'abnormalcy' and pathology also suggests that '[a] desire to be "normal" points to the experience of chaos in Serbia and a breakdown of the disciplinary mechanisms that produce regulated and reliable subjects who can translate desire into action' (Greenberg 2011:97).

This kind of language, which included metaphors that e.g. Belgrade was a 'mad house', and the 1990s were 'sick', reflected just how 'out of the ordinary' the events of the 1990s were, but also give an indication that the search for other kinds of descriptive language had failed (this is discussed in the following chapters). Metaphors, importantly, are 'not neutral' and according to De Leonardis (2008:34) tend to hide as much as they reveal. Furthermore, De Leonardis, drawing on Lakoff

(1991) suggests that the ways in which metaphors produce meanings 'requires that a given domain of experience be understood in terms of a quite different domain of experience' (Lakoff 1991:217 in De Leonardis 2008:34). Medical metaphors, which have been used extensively in world politics and history, (see e.g. Szasz 2001), establish a 'homology between biological disorders and social disorders' (De Leonardis 2008:39).

Moreover, 'illness and disease are debilitating states' and 'serious illness and death are strange, mysterious, frightening and *unexpected* events' (Lupton 2006:1, original emphasis), and so reliance on this kind of language also suggests an experience of pain and discomfort. But medical references to the past, attempts to 'diagnose' it, also suggest an attempt to make sense of, and find answers for, those events of 'madness', since after all, medicine and psychiatry are attempts to find rational solutions to sometimes disturbing and incapacitating illnesses. After all, as Lupton points out, 'medicine, or the faith in medicine, is a creed' (Lupton 2006:1). Secondly, this attempt at pathology can be understood as specific positioning of oneself towards the past, (a point I pick up in Chapter Seven) whereby the respondents are almost adopting the position of a physician who makes declarations on what went wrong, rather than that of the patient or the disease itself which may be a *part of* what had gone wrong. This is carried out in a manner not dissimilar to that suggested in Parson's Sick Role, where the sick role assigned to the past, and by extension one's own role in the past) is seen in passive terms (Parsons 1975). Using this vantage point distances one from the events in question. This is one of the first hints of the self-ascription of a passive role in recent history that, together with the self-ascription of victimhood, will become quite a visible trope during the course of this book. Interestingly, whilst the respondents often assign themselves passive roles in this way, they themselves are not passive, but are constantly engaged in creating narratives and re-examining ideas about the past. This use of medical metaphors should also be considered together with the physical manifestations of the idea of victimhood which I discuss in Chapter Seven, in which respondents discuss the visible consequences of the wars, and express their shock and regret over the large numbers of the wounded, disabled, the sick and the dying.

These indications that the past was experienced as difficult, uncomfortable and incomprehensible are important because it is in this context that narratives and ideas about the war and war crimes emerged – giving way to attempts at 'making sense of things', but also denial and conspiracy theory as a way of 'shaping reality' (Bock-Luna 2008:190) and managing marginality, uncertainties and fears. The respondents' backgrounds are crucial, as their responses to the wars, war crimes and atrocities ought to be understood in the broader context of their experience of the 1990s, something they frequently drew upon (also in Clark 2008).

When respondents highlight their experiences of the 1990s, most often this period is seen as something that required an effort just to survive[4] and struggle through, amongst a number of existential and personal problems. For most, this period was filled with uncertainty – most of which has not yet disappeared, even after the fall of Milošević. Whilst Serbia has moved on, politically and economically, most lives remain where they were interrupted in 1991. For most of these respondents, the stagnation brought on by the 1990s is still in place, as they struggle to find work, travel and generally emerge from the lower economic status they found themselves in and the isolation that Serbia was plunged into for almost two decades.

For this segment of Serbia, the brutality of war and the inconceivable stories of the 1990s were played out on television sets in their living rooms as well as through less visible, yet intimate connections. In the 1990s, most routine and ordinary acts of day-to-day life in Belgrade were interrupted and imposed upon by bloodshed across the border, but also by fear of mobilisations, talk of over flowing hospital wards and neighbours who joined paramilitary groups. The disruptions to normality and routine also disturbed more ethereal concerns and challenged the belief systems of many respondents: for instance some turned to religion during the 1990s, whilst others turned away. Most started to question their belief in their leaders, the state, the army, friends and colleagues.

Conversations with respondents also revealed an ambivalent attitude towards one of the key actors of the 1990s – Milošević. Furthermore, as this chapter illustrates, those who supported Milošević did so only in the early years and their support wavered very quickly. After this period, almost all respondents entered a period during which they either withdrew their support for Milošević or approached him critically. Moreover, most of these critiques were expressed privately, rather than publicly – all respondents here almost completely withdrew from any kind of public engagement during the early 1990s. A number of respondents state that the economic crisis and wartime tragedies, together with the generally depressed mood of people, made many retreat into family life and keep company with like-minded friends, instead of actively engaging in public discussions, or expressing opposition to Milošević (even if they felt it).

For many, engaging in public life, discussions and expressing their opposition was made difficult due to what Gordy labels 'the destruction of alternatives', in which the regime of the 1990s shrunk the political and cultural spaces in which dissent could be expressed (see Gordy 1999). Discourses created around wartime events labelled all oppositional comments and viewpoints as those of 'traitors' and 'foreign mercenaries' (Kostovicova 2006:28).

Yet, for other respondents, the 1990s did not only 'destroy alternatives' (Gordy 1999) and make them retreat into private life, but also generated a sense of despair which in turn produced a kind of apathy towards the regime and a helplessness where most believed that no matter what they did the situation was completely beyond their control. In fact, it is precisely this helplessness and lack of control which characterised many of the respondents' experiences of the 1990s, as they felt that they had simultaneously watched the wars unfold without participating, and that they were somehow directly engulfed in it, especially at times when Belgrade was economically devastated and flooded with refugees and soldiers, and later, bombed. It is no surprise, therefore, that this perception of a lack of control over the unfolding events, together with the accelerated pace at which they happened, with one war following another and the country disintegrating within a few years, produced resentment, shock and horror that these things happened at all.

These motifs are the key features of almost every single narrative – even those respondents who were too young to remember the conflicts often spoke about confusion and revulsion at finding out the extent of the violence which had taken place. Many of these sentiments are not routinely expressed, but rather exist silently within private reflections, and are spoken about rarely and in very closed, anonymous and confidential settings, such as during interviews recorded for this research.

The respondents: who is 'the public' that needs to confront the past?

This chapter introduces some members of the usually anonymous and loosely defined 'public' or 'society' which frequently appears in discussions of transitional justice in Serbia. It is a group that occupies a curious role in transitional justice: it is both visible and invisible, in that we frequently hear about 'the public', but know little about it. It is also an audience at whom majority of transitional justice projects are directed, and an audience invited to participate in the public dialogue about the past. They are assigned subject positions (Das and Kleinman 2001:5), being the ones who must confront the past; but are usually rendered silent and invisible.

They are also often made out to be un-knowledgeable: refusing to engage with NGOs and their transitional justice projects, or to believe basic facts about the wars (see e.g. Orentlicher 2007). In general, they are seen as *recipients* of knowledge and facts about the wars. Having not had any direct experience (or so it is assumed), they are not seen as active agents and producers of knowledge about the conflicts.

They can be seen as part of Serbia's 'silent majority',[5] one which does not receive much academic attention; those who are often spoken about but do not often speak for themselves (Clark 2008:2).

That 'silent majority' is the focal point of this book. They did not fight in the wars, nor are they NGO activists; they are also not prominent media figures, nor are they outspoken anti-nationalist or nationalist intellectuals. Precisely due to this, such 'ordinary' individuals, who are out of the public gaze, are difficult to describe. Therefore, this chapter attempts to describe the respondents' location in Serbian society, their preoccupations and everyday concerns, by a way of introduction to the study's participants.

This is a study of a group of individuals who form a community of sorts, as some are known or related to each other, as there are several overlapping familial or friendship circles amongst the respondents. Therefore, the conclusions made here are relevant to this group and should not be extrapolated to 'society' or 'the Serbs'. It is not my intention to do so, and where I have made general statements, they are intended to apply to this group only. What, then, may be the merit of such an approach? I hope that by presenting the individual accounts in this book, I will demonstrate that narratives about the past are as individual as their authors; as are attempts to 'make sense' or 'confront' difficult questions. Of course collective beliefs exist; public, national or political discourses find their way to individual narratives, and so nothing is 'purely' individual or 'purely' public since these spheres are 'not sealed against each other' (Johnson 1986:52). At the same time, I hope that the complexity presented by the narratives here highlights that generalisations about denial risk oversimplification by smoothing out all the nuances, contradictions and rough edges of narratives about the violent past. My aim is to present a range of these narratives by drawing on insights collected from this group of respondents.

The following section is an introduction to some of the key respondents in this study, and presents a selection of their experiences of the 1991–1995 conflicts and NATO air strikes. The events presented here are those which respondents themselves isolated as significant and formative experiences for them in the 1990s, or incidents from that time which they found particularly striking. Here, I concentrate on the 'key' respondents, whose stories were particularly interesting or illustrative of that period (this is mainly due to constraints of space, since including such narratives from all respondents would not be expedient). Whilst I do not discuss all of the respondents' experiences, some elements presented here are common to all participants in this research: no one had participated in the fighting or had personally been physically afflicted by war-time violence. However, all kinds of loss are common to all participant and associated with the 1990s, whether that was friends killed in the conflicts, friends lost due to un-bridgeable political differences or marriages which ended during this time. Others had lost jobs, opportunities, schooling, and/ or suffered ill-health.

My time in Belgrade was spent with several families and close-knit groups of friends. Their ages ranged from sixteen to eighty-two, and their backgrounds were varied: some had arrived in Belgrade a few years before to attend university, whilst some had been born there, and yet others had arrived in the 1950s through to the 1970s from other parts of Serbia to study or work. What they all had in common was that they were – for want of a better word – ordinary. It is a group best described not by who they are but according to what their daily concerns are (Brubaker et al. 2006:206). Their lives and their concerns did not stand out from the lives of most of the population, and they revolved primarily around family and social life, work or education and usually, making ends meet.

A number of important works have studied in great detail the chaos which Serbia experienced during the 1990s, and have given precise chronologies and statistics (see e.g. Ramet and Pavlaković 2007; Clark 2008). The aim of this section is to present this part of history as experienced and narrated by the respondents presented in this study.

'It's all becoming quite exhausting'[6]

Rada,[7] fifty-four, and Mladen, fifty-six, in many ways typify what can broadly be called middle class Belgrade. Rada was born into a family of *Beogradski starosedeoci*, the 'Belgrade old-timers', families who could trace their presence in the city several generations back. This was often seen as a distinguished position to hold, differentiating the old-timers from new, mainly 'provincial' arrivals who populated the city after the Second World War, and later, Serb refugees from Croatia, Bosnia and Kosovo. The old-timers saw themselves as guardians of sophisticated urban values. Their animosity towards the newcomers (mainly concentrated in the New Belgrade part of the city), led to various urban legends: Rada told me that the 'provincials' initially emptied their rubbish bins out of the window of New Belgrade social housing tower blocks, and used bathtubs as planters. A kind of snobbery developed around New Belgrade: it was built across the river, on a flat plain that used to be a part of the former Austro-Hungarian Empire, and Rada's eighty-two-year old mother Emilija, like many of her contemporaries, still referred to it as 'Hungary'.

Rada and Mladen epitomised the left-of-centre values and lifestyles of the generation born in 1950s Yugoslavia – the generation that in many ways benefited materially from the Communist regime. They were both university educated and held economics degrees, finding employment in a state owned company as soon as they had graduated. In the 1970s and 1980s they travelled widely around Europe, and they had at least two holidays a year – like many of their generation, they lamented that such things were so easily affordable and doable at the time, something that their children's generation were not likely to experience.

Travel and the loss of mobility was something all generations felt bitter about. Emilija told stories of travelling to Timişoara, Romania, with her husband, whenever they felt like visiting a particular restaurant – they would drive out there after work, and return to Belgrade in the early morning of the following day. She told stories of coachloads of Bulgarian tourists visiting Belgrade and staying in a hotel near her apartment, and how the day after Bulgarians left, shoe-shops in her neighbourhood would be left without stock. Now the previously 'poor' countries of the former Eastern bloc are part of the EU, and she, like many others, finds it inconceivable that they need visas for Hungary. Moreover, in the 1990s, the family, like everyone else in this study, found themselves with no goods to buy, much like the Bulgarians and Romanians they used to feel rather sorry for during the Communist era.

Rada, Mladen and the widow Emilija captured the essence of what is means to be educated, cultured and middle class in post-1990s Belgrade. More often than not it meant holding a poorly paid job, thanks to the economic crisis which has engulfed Serbia ever since the 1980s. They only managed to survive because they had bought their properties before the 1990s. Above all, being middle class in Belgrade in the present day often meant the erosion of a comfortable lifestyle that was enjoyed once, not too long ago.

For example, Rada and Mladen could no longer afford to purchase books, go out, or take holidays, despite having two incomes. In many ways, their lives stopped in 1991. This is Rada's description of the last sixteen years of their life:

> For the last sixteen years, life is all about fighting every single day for survival. You can keep your spirits up, just about, sometimes I succeed, sometimes I don't. It's all becoming quite exhausting. You have no idea what the next day is going to bring, or if you will be here or not. Everything around us – it just doesn't inspire confidence, that things will be better. So, you have to carry on, put pressure on yourself to keep going. Sometimes you fall down, sometimes you get really depressed, and when you see that you are stuck there, you have to really pull yourself up, because you know that after depression, what follows is real, physical illness. And you can't allow yourself that in this particular time, in these awful conditions. And that's how days pass by, months, years.

The majority of Rada and Mladen's information about the war came from their regular news-watching, and crucially from their conversations with a family of Bosnian Serb refugees who had escaped to Belgrade. The family, from the Sarajevo neighbourhood of Ilidža, were living in an nearby apartment, whose owner had retired to the countryside and allowed the refugee family to live in his home. This was not an uncommon story in Belgrade. Various families offered whatever help they could, as the state could not provide adequate support for the large numbers of refugees living in Serbia during the 1990s. Some were exploited by unscrupulous landlords, whilst others had managed to come across genuine goodwill and were housed for free.

In 1991, when the army was carrying out mobilisation for the war in Croatia, Mladen had the luck not to be drafted, and between 1992 and 1995 he helped deliver aid in Republika Srpska.

Rada had been critical of Milošević ever since he came to power; she was angry at the Kosovo rally in 1989 because 'it was not the right thing to do to trample all over Kosovo Polje just like that. It is holy ground.' Mladen, on the other hand, supported Milošević in the early days but eventually changed his mind. The whole family took part in the 5 October 2000 demonstrations, with the exception of Emilija who was never quite sure what she thought of Milošević, but was grateful that during his regime 'at least the pension arrived on time.'

They stayed at home during the air strikes of 1999, with Rada giving up on the shelters after a few days. Emilija saw the NATO air strikes as 'nothing' compared to the German bombardment of Belgrade in WWII.

'Tell your children not to say their names in public'

Ana, fifty-three, is a divorced mother of three grown-up children, and is a close friend of Rada and Mladen's. She is unemployed, having been made redundant in 2000 when the state-owned bank she worked for was privatised. In the 1980s, however, Ana and her husband enjoyed a comfortable middle-class life, in which she socialised a great deal and had many dinners and parties with friends, as well as two holidays a year. This stopped abruptly in the early 1990s, when her salary was often not paid, or was inadequate for basic provisions. In the late-1990s, she also divorced from her husband, whose alcoholism had progressively worsened. According to Ana's daughter, the husband had, under unknown circumstances, been in Bosnia during the war, in the capacity of either a photographer or cameraman, but this was not discussed as the former husband was generally not mentioned.

Today, Ana's main source of income is her mother's pension, which is supplemented by odd jobs such as babysitting. Her three children are all at university and live at home with her. She lives in New Belgrade, in a new, low rise apartment block populated with military families who were dispersed there through various employee housing schemes.

Ana's mother, Danica, 74, was born in Montenegro. She frequently mentioned not being a Communist sympathiser, because Communism 'destroyed the farmers and the peasants'. She recalled many WWII stories, such as the time when she and her siblings had got lost in the woods and stumbled across Italian soldiers. One pointed the gun at them, and the other stopped him and waved the children away. Danica's village in Montenegro was destroyed during the war and her family constantly moved, finally settling in Serbia. As schoolteachers, she and her husband worked in Bosnia and Germany.

Ana spent the war years in Belgrade. Because her block of flats was populated with military families whom she met with socially, Ana heard a lot of stories and rumours related to the war, some of which I recount throughout this book. They formed a large proportion of her information and knowledge about war events.

In 1991, Ana's Bosnian Muslim friends living in Belgrade, were dismissed from their jobs as engineers at a state-owned company, with no explanation. Their children were the same age as Ana's children and once, in 1993, she took all of them to the bus stop where they caught public transport for school.

Ana said that the horror of the 1990s had struck her for the first time one day when she was putting both the families' children onto a crowded city bus. In 1993, as inflation was rising, public transport was in chaos, and was virtually not running. The children often had to walk several kilometres to school. On the days that the bus did arrive, it was so crowded that children had to squeeze in and stand at the open doorway. The neighbour's son shouted for his brother: 'Mirza! Mirza! Hold on!' At that point, several people shouted obscenities. Ana was terrified, and afterwards went to see the boys' mother. She said, 'Tell your children never to mention their names in public. Everyone will know they are Muslims, someone might do something!' The friend thanked her and said that this never occurred to her. Ana replied that it had never occurred to her either, but that Belgrade was starting to resemble a 'madhouse' (*ludnica*). Though Ana and the family continued to be friends, one day the family had abruptly left Belgrade and Ana never managed to find them.

Incidentally, Ana was a strong Milošević supporter when he first came to power, because 'he said something that I was so proud to believe in, so proud to say finally, openly, I am a Serb', but just a few years later she attended every major demonstration against him. On 5 October 2000, she 'was choking on tear gas just like everyone else in Belgrade,' but after that 'nothing really changed'. Danica on the other hand was a supporter of Radovan Karadžić, and thought he was a capable leader, 'better than Milošević, better than any of these others we had'.

For Ana, the brutality of the various Yugoslav wars was brought home when a family of Serb refugees from Bosnia turned up in their suburb. The family of eleven members had arrived with only a few suitcases. Ana, who herself was living on a minimum wage, helped the family out by giving them the keys to her late father's unfinished house, which was being built in a village near Belgrade. She never charged them rent, and as Ana's family could not afford to finish building the house, the eleven members are still living in the only habitable space, on the first floor, amongst bare walls and little furniture.

'Sinking and sinking'

Katarina, fifty-three, and Stevan, fifty-four, are next door neighbours and close friends of Rada and Mladen. They are educated to high school level, and moved from Montenegro to Belgrade when they were twenty years old.

Katarina was always a housewife, bringing up the two daughters, whilst Stevan worked as a builder. Katarina was very interested in my project. She was very talkative and was very keen to talk about 'how things were before all this started.' The family did not have any friends or relatives in Bosnia and Croatia, but Katarina was deeply affected by the wars. She said that she still felt the loss of her 'republic', the former Yugoslavia: 'We had everything then, mountains, the seaside, a very nice life. At one time, it's all yours, and then it was gone.' What disturbed her most about the wars was that she saw pictures of children refugees on the news. She said that she could not bear to watch these images, and in the 1990s often left the room while husband watched the news. This is how she described the 1990s:

> At first, when Slobodan Milošević came to power – it was all –
> look, how nice he is, what a clever man, and someone normal, after
> Tito.[8] I don't mean that Tito was something – we lived really well
> during that time, but after him, there were these, I don't even know
> what their names were. The presidency, people from all republics,
> and then comes along one Serb, rises to the top, with ideas, he
> promised things, and the first year he was in power everyone was

all, wow, just delighted. [In Kosovo Polje 1989]... when you see all those people who turned up, and this anonymous man, but everyone is shouting in support for him: 'Sloba, Sloba!⁹' but he was completely unknown. He turned up – I had no idea who he was. When he had that meeting in Belgrade, I watched it on TV and, you watch, he is decisive, nice, promising. But later, you see that things are different... But people didn't care, they just cared that they had a leader, but all that is a consequence of Tito's time. Because Tito was a leader, and people didn't understand what Tito's rule was all about. And then, when the war started in Bosnia, and then you see that, and then you see that you are living worse than before, then, you see there is nothing in the shops, you go to the supermarket and wait in the queue for milk for hours. You wait for bread for hours. In the shop, there were only tins. Inflation! And you see that you are just sinking and sinking. You work all month for one Deutschmark, for five marks. And then you realise. Then you start thinking how to survive. When you see, people are all left without work, no one has anything, people smuggling all over the place, cigarettes, foreign currency, I mean, chaos. There was no petrol. Really – a catastrophe. And then after that comes the bombardment. It was not nice. It was a disaster. Really... when you realise that he is destroying you and that you are just going backwards. More and more unemployed people. Black markets are booming. People had cigarettes [for sale] on these cardboard boxes. Then, a bit further away, people with petrol. You go to the market, and what you can get for one mark in the morning, in the afternoon, you can't.

Stevan also admitted that he is often nostalgic for the old days. He was, he said, shocked when the wars started, and could not understand them then or now. He thinks the only outcome of the wars was that some people got rich whilst others became poorer. Stevan's example of this was their well-off neighbour, who ran a funeral parlour and was 'a nice man'. But Stevan did not like the fact that the man had made his money during the war, when, according to the neighbour, he had been called out frequently by Belgrade families to pick up

bodies of the dead from Bosnia and Kosovo. It is said in the neighbourhood that the undertaker had picked up Milošević's casket when
it arrived in Belgrade, charging double his usual rates – despite the
rumours that many local undertakers had offered this service for free.
For Stevan, the 'Gravedigger' epitomised everything that was wrong
with the current state of affairs in Serbia: that people had become rich
only through death and destruction.

For Stevan and Katarina, the real shock, as for many, came during
the air strikes in 1999, when they were in such disbelief over what was
happening that at first they simply stood still, looking at each other
when the first air raid siren sounded. But later, this turned to panic,
and soon Katarina learned to keep a 'shelter bag' with the basics packed
by the door. This happened only after a bomb exploded close – or what
seemed close – to the family's apartment block. Later, Katarina said,

> We learned that the kinds of bombs they were using were new,
> powerful ones. Our shelters, which are really basements, are nothing
> for the kind of technology they have. They said on the news that the
> bombs could dig themselves so far in the ground that there is no
> shelter in Belgrade that could save you if one hit your building.

The anti-Milošević family

Gordana, fifty-four, was a university friend of Rada's and their families
were close. She is divorced and lives with her mother, Natalija, eighty-
two, and son Slavko, 22. Gordana was a journalist for one of the large
Serbian dailies, but left in the early 1990s to become self-employed.

The 1990s were a difficult time for her because she was going
through a divorce and had serious health problems. The family spent
that entire period – as well as the NATO air strikes – in Belgrade,
even though they had the option of leaving for the family's weekend
cottage in the countryside where it was safer. Gordana refused – 'they
will not make me a refugee in my own country.'

During the conflicts, Gordana said she watched the state news rather
than the BBC, which she had on cable (she was fluent in English), even

though she knew 'what kinds of things were going on at *Politika* and RTS.' Some of her colleagues were being made to leave, or were resigning because, 'certain stories were just not being published. You would file something and someone would call you aside and say, things are not really like that'. This was an allusion to attempts made by some reporters to publicise atrocities committed by Serb soldiers; they were routinely silenced.

Slavko said he started reading and learning about the wars only recently, after he travelled to Sarajevo with a group of friends for a concert. He suddenly realised that 'when you meet someone on a street in Sarajevo, you actually have no idea if some Serb did something to that guy's family.' He studied engineering, and had 'no friends who were interested in politics', but on his own attempted to read about the war where he could. Although he discussed politics in general with his mother, he did not talk about the wars themselves for fear of upsetting her. Gordana, despite health problems, took part in demonstrations against Milošević. On 5 October 2000, her whole family went to the protest together – even her mother, who was already elderly.

Natalija came from a wealthy family whose property was confiscated during the Communist period. But even so she rarely spoke about this, and expressed her vengeance towards Milošević instead. She was a Djindjić supporter 'from the start' and believed that no one would be able to lead Serbia in the same way. During my visits to the family, Natalija rarely left her room due to a worsening health condition. On the day that I recorded Gordana's interview, she insisted leaving her room to have her story recorded too. Although I told her this was not necessary, she said she could stay up for twenty minutes for something 'so important'. In the end, her recorded interview was over an hour long, and she said that she was glad that someone would finally get to hear what she thought of the 1990s, which were 'a disaster'.

'War is a horrific thing'

Mirjana, sixty-two, lives alone in a large apartment in New Belgrade. She is the aunt of one of my younger respondents, whose extended family I had got to know well. She is retired, having been an accountant for a state company for her entire working life. She was very active, and was always travelling abroad with her pensioners' club to historical sites of interest. Her home is filled with books and paintings.

Her grown-up children live in the United States. Her daughter emigrated in the early 1990s, and then sponsored her brother and paid for his education so that he could escape from the draft in 1999, upon completion of his army service in 1998. Mirjana attended his army swearing-in ceremony and recalls a particular moment that horrified her. The ceremony included the new soldiers swearing that they would give their life for their country. She could not reconcile herself to this after the ethnic conflicts. She thought that 'war is a horrific thing'. Mirjana experienced a deeply unsettling time in the 1990s when her son had been conscripted into military service. It made her extremely unhappy that he might become 'cannon fodder', and after he finished his service she urged him to emigrate, because there was danger of the draft when the first rumours of air strikes emerged. This incident is discussed later on, in Chapter Six. During the early stages of this, she helped hide one of her son's friends from the mobilisation teams that were looking for him. She did this even though she knew it 'it was illegal, an offence, and I could go to jail for harbouring a "deserter" '.

In the first months of the air strikes, she managed to travel to France. She was deeply offended by what she read about Serbia in the French press: 'there were stories that Serbs had cleansed villages of thousands of Albanians, which is ridiculous. There is no village in Kosovo which has more than ten or twenty houses!' One day, she was on a bus in Paris, reading a story about the air strikes, when a Colombian tourist in the seat next to her started chatting. After a friendly conversation, the Columbian woman asked Mirjana, 'Is it true what they are saying about the Serbs?' a comment which angered her. She replied, 'Well, is it true what they say about you and drug smuggling?' After a while, she returned, overland, to Belgrade, and stayed there for the remainder of the air strikes.

'I couldn't comprehend there would be someone crazy enough to take us to war'

Mara, sixty-two, and Jovan, seventy-two, are retired. Mara worked as an accountant at a state company and Jovan was a civilian engineer working with the JNA. Mara was Mirjana's cousin, and the two lived only streets away from each other. Mara and Jovan spent all of the 1990s in Belgrade, and did not leave during the air strikes. Their three grown up children had emigrated during the 1990s and settled in the USA and Canada. During the ethnic conflicts, one of their daughters and her two children were living with them, and Mara's most horrific memory of that period is the shortage of milk, at which point they became concerned for the children's health:

> I will never forget that. When we had to survive the inflation, when I felt that personally. When I had to give my grandchild a five million dinar note to buy a yogurt and a bun. I was crying. I was walking down the street and I was crying, because I couldn't even buy bread. I had to go to work and I had to stand in line to buy things, because the children couldn't do it. I stood in a line, my grandchild was born in '91. Then I had to start making my own bread, because the union gave us some flour and later sugar. And we made things with that sugar and flour, and water and oil. The simplest things, women exchanged recipes. But in the shops it was just sad. There was nothing. Nothing until the union got us that flour.

This daily struggle to obtain the most basic goods was a leitmotif of 1991–1995 Belgrade, and affected all my respondents. The family managed to survive – like most others – only because they had some connections or relatives in the countryside, where owners of smallholdings managed to produce their own meat, vegetables and dairy products. Time and money permitting, Jovan would visit his distant cousins in eastern Serbia from time to time, bringing back bags of cheese and ham. They were preoccupied with looking after the grandchildren and working at the same time, and Mara did not follow the war developments closely, whilst Jovan did.

His biggest regret was that people had no say in the wars. He knew a bit about the Yugoslav economy, and knew it was in trouble long before this was publicised. He is still confused because, 'I couldn't comprehend there would be someone crazy enough to take us to war.' Jovan attended the first anti-war protests in Belgrade. He said that in that demonstration he found himself standing next to a young man called Zoran Djindjić.

'Have you forgotten Milošević and 1993?'

Svetozar, seventy-six, is a widower and lives next door to Branka, also a participant in this study, whose family called him 'granddad'. When I met Branka's family, she introduced me to Svetozar as someone who 'would be perfect for your project because he loves talking about the past, and loves history.' In all our meetings, Svetozar was very friendly, and chatted a lot about the 1990s, which he saw as 'catastrophic'. Svetozar came from a poor family from a village in southern Serbia and came to Belgrade as a young man. Eventually, he made his way up to a managerial position in a company which distributed heavy machinery throughout former Yugoslavia. During the 1970s and 1980s, he travelled around the whole country with his amateur sports club. But his fondest memories are of serving in the Yugoslav army, a service which he completed in a barracks in Kosovo, sometime in the 1950s. He remembered this as a time in which strong friendships were formed, mostly with non-Serbs serving in the same barracks, and days off when the soldiers went to Priština. He had fond memories of his Kosovo Albanian friends and the times they spent drinking in local bars, but due to age, distance and politics they had lost touch over the years.

When the crisis in the country began to be felt in early 1990, he could not comprehend the secessionist politics 'it was all one country, and now they're saying there is an embargo on Slovenian products! Can you imagine what that meant? We couldn't work, couldn't produce anything – we needed Slovenian machine parts!' Svetozar supported Milošević in 1989, and with several friends, went to the Kosovo rally. He liked the atmosphere, and the fact that so many Serbs from all over Yugoslavia had congregated in one place. Speaking about the trip, Svetozar says:

I was ready to put both hands in the fire for him [Milošević]. We fell for his stories. Then '89 came and that 600th anniversary [of

the Kosovo battle]. And at first, I said, bravo! Well said. [...] We
were guests, in one village, right next to Priština. On our way
there, there were Albanians shouting things at us, rude gestures
and they were spitting at the bus. I said to the driver, hang on,
stop here so we can show them! He says, it's all in vain, man!
As soon as you stop the bus they run away. But in that village,
they [Kosovo Serbs] greeted us like brothers, really well, they
were so happy that we were there. They said, brothers, you have
arrived! Happy, they were crying. Then they put up the Serbian
flags, there was music. They said we want to sing some Serbian
songs with our brothers. Well that was before the talk. We
went a day early. We hoped things would change for the better.
But nothing changed for the better [...] But then I came back
to Belgrade and I realise, he's removed Saša, I can't remember
his last name, and then he removed others from government too
and removed [Ivan] Stambolić and put him up as a director of
some bank. I said, what is this man doing? He's cementing his
position! Fine, but I don't like him anymore. Then his politics
just became crazy.

Svetozar said he is at present one of the few people in his pensioners' club who is unequivocally critical of the former leader. One day,
in 2006, he complained that his seventy-year-old friend had recently
said, 'things were never as bad as they are now with these democrats!'
Svetozar shouted, 'I told him, what are you talking about? Have you
gone crazy? Have you forgotten Milošević and 1993, when you had to
stand in the supermarket queue at dawn, just to buy a litre of milk?
And then the next day, the same thing, to buy a second litre?'[10]
   Svetozar went to his pensioners' club every Saturday, where he and
his friends had dinner and listened to a small local band singing folk
songs. Milošević's funeral in March 2006 took place on a Saturday and
Svetozar, whom I saw several days later, was visibly annoyed: the club
had cancelled the music for that Saturday out of a sign of respect for
Milošević. He thought this was a disproportionate reaction because 'people die every day'. He reported that a lot of his friends did not come to
the club that day because they had stayed at home to watch the funeral,

which, together with the rally organised by the SPS, was televised. When members of the club asked if the manager could put on the television so they could watch the funeral too, Svetozar went home in protest.

'A normal life'

Miroslav, fifty-four, and his wife Svetlana, forty-two, both teachers, are close friends of Rada and Mladen. They lived in New Belgrade. They have a fifteen-year-old son, whom Miroslav thought was 'becoming a nationalist' when he saw him wear a T-shirt bearing Ratko Mladić's image. Both parents reprimanded him, but Miroslav said, 'he is a teenager, he doesn't care. He's doing this as some kind of reaction, some kind of trend with his friends. He just has no idea what it all means. For him it is a phase, like with music.' They drew the conclusion that the teenager did not actually know much about Mladić, or who he was, but that he assumed him to be some kind of counter-cultural figure. They were certain that his behaviour was something he would grow out of as, according to Miroslav, this kind of activity seemed to be a trend amongst certain groups of teenagers, born after the war, who had no clear picture of what had actually happened. Nevertheless, Miroslav, a frequent demonstrator against the Milošević regime, was aghast.

In his student days, Miroslav travelled around Yugoslavia and was friends with progressive musicians and artists. When the wars started, he was worried that he may be drafted, but this never happened. During the 1990s, he was an outspoken critic of Milošević, and was suspended from his job when a new school director, a Milošević sympathiser, was appointed. He eventually got his job back but never toned down his opinions on the war and Milošević. In 1999 he made it clear to his colleagues that he would not fight if he was recruited. During the late 1990s, Miroslav received many offers to travel and visit friends abroad, but he had problems being granted visas, to the point that he eventually gave up.

Svetlana admitted she was not as politically involved as Miroslav. After the NATO airstrikes she said she 'completely retreated into family life' and refused to engage in any kind of political debates with friends, to the point that she 'hardly knows who is who in what party' and what was going in present day politics. She was not sure if she voted in the last election, or in fact, which last election – there had been too many, and they had all blended into one. She was tired of wars, and 'just wanted a normal life.'

Escaping the draft

Nevena, thirty-eight, is a friend of Rada and Mladen's. She works in public relations. Her father, Nikola, seventy-four, is an integral part of the family and helps support it. His pension is generous by local standars – before retirement he had been the manager of one of the largest hotels in Belgrade. Nevena's brother Mirko, forty-nine, and her husband Ilija, forty-four, both used to be bar managers in downtown Belgrade. The bars which they ran were important meeting places for gangsters and criminals in the 1990s. Ilija recounted that it was normal that customers would arrive with entourages, guns, 'bodyguards' and what everyone suspected were stolen cars.

In 1991, Ilija received a notice drafting him into the war in Croatia. As the couple were expecting their first child at the time, Ilija was excused from duty; however, the weeks during which he attempted to negotiate his release from the draft were stressful and tense for the family. Nevena said that the first baby was born at the worst possible moment in history, in 1991, as they then spent the next ten years worrying about being able to afford food. She could not bear to watch the news alongside the burden of raising a child during this time.

Nevena's father, Nikola, was similarly appalled by the wars of the 1990s. He was born in a small village in western Serbia and remembers the problems that the village faced in WWII. There was a strong nationalist *četnik* movement in the village, whilst the neighbouring village was predominantly Partisan. He said that his memories of the end of the war and the tensions in the villages left him with strong anti-war views. He expressed strong support for Yugoslavia, and had friends in all the former republics. The loss of the country upset him, as did the violence of the war, against which he protested. During the early 1990s, he said that Radovan Karadžić and Ratko Mladić, and a

number of other political and criminal elites, often turned up at the
hotel he managed, where they would drink and gamble.

Not escaping the draft

Siblings Vanja, twenty-eight, and Petar, thirty-six, share a flat in
Belgrade, as Petar is currently unemployed. They have lived in
Belgrade most of their adult lives, and their parents are retired, living
in a city in northern Serbia. Vanja works for an international company
in Belgrade. She usually works from 8.30am until 9pm every day, and
on her days off is still expected to put in a few hours of work. Her
mother, who held a similar job in a state company in the 1970s and
1980s, worked only 8am until 4pm every day. She is appalled at the
amount of work young people are meant to put in today, but Vanja
accepted her workload as an inevitable transition to capitalism.

Petar has held several well-paid jobs at large international companies which set up business in Serbia after 2000. In his last job, he
was a manager, but had to resign after a number of differences with
the executive. After that, he found it difficult to get a job, because
looking for work in Serbia is 'impossible, since you only need good
connections and everything is already decided, interviews are basically
just a formality.'

Vanja 'hated politics' – her university education was delayed by a
year because of the chaotic situation in the 1990s, and the NATO air
strikes. Vanja's view of the 1990s was that the problems were caused
by 'lunatics' and that Serbia is run by 'old men'. Vanja took part in the
5 October demonstrations, but Petar did not, because by that point,
he had 'given up hope that anything would change'. He said that he
was angry; every time he voted, his votes were stolen or the election
was a 'farce'. He gave up voting and protesting as he had 'had enough
of demonstrations and standing in the queue to vote for nothing.' Petar
says that the 1990s were:

> Seriously difficult. Everywhere I went after that, people asked
> me – how did you manage to survive? All the time the same
> question, how did you manage to survive? It was impossible.

Impossible. But you learn ... If there had been no cheques and inflation, you couldn't survive. You go to the supermarket and all you see is a tin of sardines and a pot of yogurt. Nothing, literally nothing. Queuing up to buy flour. People stocked up, 200–300 kilos, in case you find nothing, you can bake bread. That's how it was. At the end of the month, your bills, if you wait until the end of the month you could go to the street, exchange 10 Deutschmarks and pay the bills.

In 1999, at the start of the air strikes, Petar was mobilised, and spent several weeks with an anti-aircraft unit near the Kosovo border. He said that the experience was 'a joke' and that he and the unit 'sat there for days looking at the sky. And then nothing. I went home'. Vanja, on the other hand, was 'terrified. You don't know where your brother is for weeks.' Earlier, in 1991, Petar was attending university, but had friends who were not, and they had to hide, so as not to be mobilised. Both Petar and Biljana, Vanja's close friend, and a respondent in this study, mentioned that mobilisation in smaller towns was a much more terrifying prospect because young men found it more difficult to hide – everyone knew everyone else, and in some cases, 'dodging the draft' was seen as shameful.

Friends who stopped calling

Branka, fifty-four, who works as an administrator in a state owned company, is a university friend of Rada and Miroslav's. She is divorced and lives with her son Filip, an architecture student. Branka's first indication in 1992 that anything was seriously wrong was the night she received a telephone call from a woman she did not know, a Bosnian Serb refugee who had got Branka's number from a mutual friend. The woman was frightened; she had fled from Sarajevo and did not know anyone in Belgrade. She asked Branka if she would be able to meet her at the bus station. Branka said:

It was the middle of the night, I had no petrol, but I got a friend over and we went, you just had to help whoever you could. The woman was completely terrified, who knows what had happened to her in Sarajevo. She stayed with us for two or three days and then left for Germany.

She said that at the time things were so out of the ordinary that one did not stop to think rationally:

> There I was, driving with my friend, driving through the city, completely deserted. In pyjamas and trainers. What am I doing? Who is this woman? But you only think about these things later. We helped, that was the most important thing.

Branka also had a friend in Belgrade whose husband was amongst the first to be drafted in 1991, and all she said about the experience is that the friend was not told where her husband was being deployed. They had no news of him for over a month, after which he finally returned. For some time after that he could not bear to have the lights switched off at night.

Due to the nature of her work prior to 1991 she dealt with business contacts in Croatia and Bosnia, where she also had friends. They all stopped calling very suddenly. She never knew whether they had disappeared, moved, or whether they simply did not wish to remain in contact. She often wondered how they had survived the wars in their respective countries. Branka knew several people who had volunteered for the war in Bosnia, but really did not want to elaborate on this. She stayed in Belgrade during the NATO air strikes, which she called, satirically, a 'reward' (*nagrada*), remarking that after all the events of the early 1990s, 'they just couldn't leave us alone.'

This episode of 'the friends who stopped calling' demonstrates the kinds of uncertainties and assumptions that many had to live with at the time. Most of the respondents here had friends in Croatia and Bosnia. Almost anyone who has directly or indirectly experienced those wars knows the creeping dread encountered when a friend's or relative's telephone suddenly goes unanswered. The unanswered call, or the absence of one, is full of terrible possibilities: death?

disappearance? And some clutched straws: escape, immigration, or just a dead phone line, or a friendship strained by political difference. Branka did not take action to find out, but did not articulate why. Whether she worried about what she might find out, or simply did not know what to say – either way, she has to live with that uncertainty which inevitably colours the ways in which the past is remembered, understood or talked about.

The war generation

Bojan, Biljana and Ivan, all twenty-seven, are close friends of Vanja. The group were students at the same time, and all except Ivan had recently left university. They were all teenagers just as the wars were starting, and so they represent a generation of young people in Serbia that has grown up with constant conflicts in the background. Being a teenager in the 1990s was difficult; according to Biljana, the only things that teenagers were concerned with – shoes, clothes and music – were virtually impossible to have at the time because no one could afford them. She said that as a teenager it was difficult to care what was going on with the wars, but at the same time it was unpleasant to grow up with violence and fighting constantly on TV. She does not have many recollections of the period, but remembers funerals of soldiers which used to take place every so often in her parents' small town in the south of Serbia.

Bojan was more engaged in politics. He tried to keep himself informed, because he saw war all around him – his parents, like Vanja's, lived in a small town, and he always saw soldiers walking around in uniform. Ivan, who also grew up in a small town, said the same. His town also hosted large numbers of Serb refugees from Bosnia. Ivan does not remember much of that period, but his cousin's draft for the Croatian war left a deep impression on him – this story is recounted in Chapter Eight. Ivan stayed with his parents in the town during the NATO air strikes, as it was deemed safer than Belgrade, but during his visit a local factory was hit. Bojan stayed in Belgrade during the air strikes, and recounted stories of parties. He said that amongst a certain section of young people there was a mood of 'letting go' because 'we were in danger, and there was another war, but people just didn't care anymore. There were no classes, nothing to do, nowhere to go, so we just partied.' Later, this group started taking part in organised anti-NATO protests, and then anti-Milošević protests.

Bojan and Ivan are also friends with Sanja and Novak, two other respondents in this study, who are older, but have similar backgrounds and shared similar war experiences. Novak shares a last name with a well-known convicted Serbian war criminal and often makes a joke out of this when introducing himself. Novak said that he was always politically engaged, even as a teenager, and constantly protested against Milošević. For him and Sanja, protests were a regular part of growing up, just as disturbances were a regular part of university life. Sanja was angry that her school and university life were so undermined by the 1990s and the sanctions; there was often no heating, no glass in the windows and no schoolbooks. Novak's parents 'made him go to the countryside' during the air strikes, whilst Sanja stayed in Belgrade, experiencing that period as 'a complete turnaround, a complete personal trauma.'

When Milošević died and the news of his funeral in Belgrade started to emerge, Sanja received a text message reading: 'Spring at the Trg [Republike]![11] Let's meet and say goodbye to Milošević forever! Bring a balloon. Meeting at 3pm. Forward this.' Shortly afterwards, Ivan also received the same message, and only a day before the funeral was to take place, a half-page advertisement appeared in the newspaper *Danas*, elaborating the text message. The meeting was a 'counter-demonstration' organised by an NGO. Sanja, Biljana, Bojan, Vanja and Novak decided to go, and I joined them. Petar 'could not face another demonstration'. We arrived at Trg Republike and a crowd had already started to gather. The attendees all carried balloons, and were predominantly young, with a few older participants. There were three or four policemen standing around, whilst the Milošević funeral rally a few blocks away was patrolled by riot police. A member of the audience stood up at the foot of the statue in Trg Republike and burned a photo of Milošević. Someone had put up a mock version of a death notice on a nearby post. It expressed delight at Milošević's passing, noting all the things he was leaving behind (i.e. Serbia's debts and the dead), and in place of those in mourning, it was signed 'Citizens of Serbia: Happy, Delighted and Lucky.'

As the group moved from Trg Republike to Kalemegdan Park to release the balloons, we noticed TV cameras and reporters; Vanja waved at them, but Biljana hid behind her friends, saying that she cannot let her grandmother see her at the demonstration.

'All this will cost us in the end'

Veljko, seventy-four, a widower, is Jovan's cousin. Born in a small village in western Serbia, he has lived in Belgrade since he was a teenager, doing odd jobs and working his way up to gain an education, eventually becoming an accountant at a state company. He built his own house in Belgrade, and lives there with his son and daughter-in-law. He spends his time reading, and has recently read both the Bible and the Qur'an, he says, 'out of interest'. He spent the 1990s in Belgrade, and during the NATO air strikes refused to leave his house, where he felt safer than in the shelter.

During the early 1990s he was 'shocked' at the behaviour of Serbian politicians, particularly after seeing a member of the SPS announce on television that 'killings of Muslims' had taken place. The shock was both from the phrase, 'killings of Muslims' and the fact that someone had been 'stupid enough' to say it on television. He did not support the wars, and in its early days, he and a few friends started writing a sort of improvised newsletter, in which they said what they thought of the situation – things, he said, which could not be printed in the newspapers. They distributed the newsletters around their state-owned company. The company director called Veljko in for a meeting to ask if he was behind the stories. Veljko replied that he always put his name on what he wrote because he was not ashamed, but that he was ashamed of the things he had to write about: 'I told him – all this will cost us in the end!' He incurred the wrath of the director, who was a Milošević supporter. Veljko told me this story twice, and both times he implied that 'what he had to write about' were the rumours of murders and those who 'boasted about them'. However, in our interview he said that he 'can't say now, for sure' whether he knew about war crimes at the time.

CHAPTER 5

'YOU CAN'T BELIEVE IT'S HAPPENING': KNOWLEDGE, SILENCE AND TERROR

Introduction

Discussions about the past, the conflicts or war crimes are rarely encountered amongst individuals in social settings. These are not issues which are discussed frequently, or in public, except by dedicated activists, intellectuals, a few politicians and some media. Throughout 2005 and 2006, through to 2007 when this research was carried out, several important events occurred. First, the now infamous 'Scorpions' tape was televised in summer of 2005, which depicted the execution of young Muslim men and boys at the hands of a Serbian 'special forces' unit, 'the Scorpions'. Commentators expected this event to be a turning point, after which Serbian society, being subjected for the first time to such a graphic and visual representation, would be able to confront the past (Zverzhanovski 2007). Then in February 2006 (false) rumours of Mladić's arrest surfaced, and later the same year Serbia's SAA agreement with the EU was suspended, due to its failure to comply fully with ICTY demands and hand over the remaining fugitives. During this time, until his death in 2006, Milošević was on trial. These are just some of the high-profile events which ensured that 'the past' or war crimes had an almost continual presence in the media. Whilst it is difficult to say exactly what kind of effect these events may have had on individuals and their relationship with the past, one observation at least can be made – these events did not prompt or facilitate dialogue in circles where it was not already happening. In social gatherings, for instance, there was virtually no mention of any of those issues, with the exception of the death of Milošević.

Amongst the respondents in this study, the wars are not frequently discussed for two main reasons. First, they no longer form a part of everyday life. Real day-to-day family or monetary concerns have far greater importance and inevitably displace concerns such as confrontations with the past or reflections on the violence of that era. It is important not to underestimate these issues. The society that we ask to confront its past is not made up of individuals who are free of other preoccupations. As Donnan and Simpson suggest in their study of Northern Ireland, individuals tend to subordinate their thoughts about violent pasts 'to quotidian demands' (2007:12); similarly with the respondents presented here, concerns about the past are de-prioritised since the demands of day to day life are at times overwhelming. Secondly, we cannot underestimate just how difficult this past was – and still is – for most of that 'distant audience' (Humphrey 2002: x).

Importantly, as this chapter will illustrate, what initially appears to be a silence, does not equate to a complete absence of engagement with the past (Donan and Simpson 2007). What *is* said and thought about the past is not always articulated publicly or in the way in which we might easily recognise as an engagement with the past. This chapter draws on the works of Humphrey (2002), Scarry (1985a) Scarry (1985b), Daniel (1995) and Scheper-Hughes et al. (2002) to argue that talking about violence – whether experienced or witnessed – is difficult because of what *is* known. Verbalising often painful topics such as murder and death is all the more difficult because images and knowledge of the atrocities committed in the 1990s are so closely enmeshed with individuals' own difficult experiences of that time.

Thus, the narratives in which respondents raise the question of war crimes are extremely complex and multi-layered. In most of these, there is often a rather large amount of what happens to be irrelevant information before 'the relevant' things start to emerge. For instance, even when directly asked about a particular event such as the Srebrenica massacre, most of the respondents spoke about all kinds of other things – the television, political parties, Yugoslavia, criminals etc. – before mentioning or referring directly to the event with which the question started. Direct references to war, war crimes and atrocities are often buried or wrapped in layers of other issues, which indicated two things: first, the issue of war crimes itself is very much bound up with other problems, such as the breakup of Yugoslavia, through connections which are made in the respondent's own logic. Second, that swaddling of very contentious issues in layers of other ideas about the past demonstrates a vulnerability where this subject is concerned. The subject itself is sensitive, and often quite painful – as many respondents stated directly – and it therefore takes some time to get to it. What this layering also reflected – intriguingly – is also the way in which certain events in the past, such as knowledge about war crimes, slowly started to seep out into the Serbian public. During the 1990s, in the midst of competing truths, propaganda and misinformation, certain kinds of information about war crimes in particular emerged with soldiers returning from the front, as well as refugees and other first-hand observers. It is often those first-hand accounts and rumoured atrocities and horrors that were heard personally, rather than from the media, that appeared to bother some of my respondents the most.

This chapter begins with a consideration of the question of *knowledge*: what did respondents know and when? Did they become aware of the atrocities at the time they occurred or much later? Knowledge about the past exists: it is rare to find someone who claims outright that they do not know what kinds of atrocities were committed by the Serbs during the conflicts. But 'knowing' is complicated: the narratives below suggest that knowledge about the atrocities has been acquired over the years, some during and some after the war; through 'official' and media channels as well as rumours and other kinds of informal knowledge.

The media and witnessing

The media, especially television, played a significant part in most respondents' experiences of the wars. Most had followed the news about the wars on television, becoming, to borrow a phrase from Humphrey (2002:x), the 'distant audience'. However, the media was only one source of information, which was supplemented through more informal channels, such as hearsay.

Those respondents old enough to have consumed the news demonstrated a relationship to the media that was *not* passive, nor straightforward. In assessing the media, respondents demonstrated a number of contradictions. First, events which they chose to discuss and present as evidence were often the same events which had been over-represented in the mainstream media in the 1990s. For instance, a shooting incident at a wedding in Sarajevo prior to the start of the war and incidents at Markale, Skelani, Kravice and Bratunac were mentioned as places where mass-atrocities had been committed against the Serbs. That the media representation of these events was factual and correct was never challenged. However, when discussing atrocities where large numbers of people were killed by Serb forces, respondents often pointed out that they could not have known about this at the time since only one source of information was available to them. Thus, pro-regime media was both taken as a source of news and criticised, as were foreign outlets such as the CNN and BBC.

Even though regime media was not trusted (see Gordy 1999), it appears that amongst my respondents its war coverage was often chosen over other outlets: for instance, respondent Gordana, herself a former journalist, told me that although she had the BBC and CNN at home from 1990 she did not watch them during the war. Her friend Rada elaborated that she felt the same way because those outlets' version of events consisted of 'all lies'. Whilst one gets the impression from Gordy's work that Belgraders who had moved from the provinces to Belgrade during the 1990s were those who rejected alternative media sources more readily (Gordy 1999), it is worth noting that all of my respondents had spent either all or most of their adult lives in Belgrade. It is difficult, therefore, to say conclusively that the preference of one media source over another was the result of educational or socio-economic factors.

Furthermore, it is pointed out that media choices during the Milošević regime could be summarised as 'the distinction between passive and active approaches to information – between the wish to be informed and the desire to inform oneself' (Gordy 1999:97). Gordy (1999:97) argues that those who were satisfied with regime-controlled media did not have the motivation to seek other sources. However, choosing the pro-regime media despite misgivings, can be accounted for though other factors, too. For instance, the alternative media, which depicted a much more realistic vision of the conflicts, was seen as much more intrusive, and its images as much more disconcerting, unsettling and shocking. One respondent, Petar, in his twenties at the time, pointed out that by watching the mainstream state media one watched 'battles', rather than 'atrocities' and crime. The Serbian pro-regime media allowed for a completely different type of viewing experience. It was the type of media that – as respondent Mladen noted – allowed one to 'get used to it, and after a while to stop noticing things.' It encouraged and facilitated passivity, but nevertheless not all viewers – and not all respondents in this study – approached it with complacency, either at the time or in retrospect.

Overall, however, it is difficult to measure in any concrete way exactly what was known about the war and war crimes and when, since respondents frequently contradicted each other (and themselves) as to what they found out about the atrocities and how much of this information came from the media and when. For instance:

> I am likely to read the newspapers only if they happen to be nearby. Now that my son has this business, I get the papers for him, and I might read the headlines while I wait for the work-ers to turn up. Back then, I avoided the newspapers, literally avoided them. I followed [Ivo] Andrić, who said to a young man he saw reading the papers, he said, 'why are you ruining your eyesight reading something that tomorrow will turn out not to be true?' That was my view of the press. I had a good reason for that. One day, I came across a very nice article in a newspaper about me – my name was there, the company where I worked, all these wonderful things I had supposedly done. But I never did any of those things that were written about me. They must have mixed me up with someone – no journalist had ever talked to

me or asked me anything. So there you go, I had read an article
about myself. There were all sorts of things. (Veljko)

No, we didn't know. What was known from the TV was if a
Serb … if something happened to him. Everything else, that was
covered up here, so that people wouldn't complain. No, no, all
that was revealed later. They released information according to
what suited whom. But, for example, what we saw was when all
the columns of refugees started from Knin. What you saw on TV
was what you knew. Except if you were there yourself. (Stevan)

Many respondents had made a strategic choice as to which media
they engaged with, in the act of witnessing distantly the conflicts
(c.f. Humphrey 2002). The extract below is from an interview with
Gordana, a former journalist who quit her job in the 1990s.

To be honest, I didn't know about Srebrenica. I didn't know that
was happening. Back then, when that was happening, our media
didn't [stops] – although we had cable, Sky News and BBC from
1990 – but we didn't follow it. So, I accepted everything critically. I didn't take the news for granted. To me it was perfectly
clear that it was impossible that only one nation was like that
because they all, Muslims, Serbs, Croats, all took part in atrocities. That was clear to me. But who took part in what measure?
We are the largest people, numerically speaking. So we may have
committed the most evil – it is possible. I do believe these latest
figures that the government of Republika Srpska issued, that
there were seven to eight thousand Muslims killed. Of course,
I am for the condemnation of all crimes.

[Later in the same interview]:
But to me it was clear, that … it was our fault. That what hap-
pened in Kosovo was, after all, horrific. That the police, or army,
or the paramilitary, that they were killing and raping women.
I saw that on the BBC, our media didn't show that. Those
Šiptar[1] women, children, old people. Was that genocide? I don't

go into that question. My level of information comes from the media only.

This extract highlights several dynamics. To the respondent, two things are 'clear' yet, at the same time, there is a level of uncertainty ('was it genocide?') for which the media is blamed. However, interestingly there is also a mention that 'our media didn't', before the sentence is stopped. Did not what? Presumably, given the context of the subsequent sentence, it did not show, for instance, the extent of death and destruction. This type of response is quite typical of many respondents who begin to formulate sentences before they abruptly stop, often just before something indicating one of the horrific aspects of the 1990s is about to be mentioned. By way of comparison, in her research with young intellectuals in Serbia, Zala Volčič (2006) comes across very vivid descriptions of wartime reportage. In the quote below, a media researcher from Serbia remembers the pictures:

> … war coverage usually portrayed a journalist who interviewed Serbian soldiers ready to make some patriotic statements to the camera … The scenes of mountains would be accompanied by a commentary that explained this was the place where Muslim mercenaries from all over the world were hiding … Generally … the reports from the war front were distasteful … it was like a media autopsy … they were showing atrocities committed to [sic] civilians … The camera penetrated into the details of the tragic victims … and showed mutilated bodies, remains of corpses, smashed heads, torn ears, eyes plucked out, pigs tearing parts off of human bodies, and flies eating up the flesh … (In Volčič 2006:322)

This is unlike the types of responses that emerged in the research presented in this book, where much of what the media did show was avoided in description. In addition to this, contradictions between respondents were quite common. For every respondent that mentioned that the media did not show atrocities, there would be another respondent who would suggest that it did. This emerged particularly clearly in the accounts of younger respondents, whose ideas about what was known and when were very different. For instance, Bojan and Marko, both teenagers at the time, said the following:

> I tried to keep myself informed as much as possible, I tried to imagine what it was like for someone living under siege, who can't even stick his head out of the window. [...] After the war, when I started travelling, I spoke to people from Sarajevo, who told me what it was like. How they had to make cooking oil, what they used for food, to survive, how they had to run across those streets, and how snipers were waiting for them. The majority [in Serbia] didn't know that; if they knew that, things would have been different. But we were besotted with war, that's how they wanted it to be, in this situation, when people have no job, nothing to live from. That was the tactic that the authorities had, I mean, that you make a man besotted with war, and he doesn't even think about anything else. And all people just want to survive. In that situation it is so easy to manipulate. And we were so isolated, with just that one television, and obviously when they said, they are doing evil things to us, we believed it. We couldn't judge, when we had that main source of information. Hm, from that side I think we are victims, but then again, at the end of the day, that can't be a justification for not knowing. A man has to find those things out. If not back then, then look, now, ten years later, now people can see what happened, they can start to look. (Bojan)

> Oh I think I knew then. I was reading all the time. Maybe I didn't know the exact details of what happened in Srebrenica, but back then we had *Naša Borba*, they had good reports. But I always had this principle, I have to know what we are doing, it is more important what we are doing to them, than they to us. So I always tried to find out, I hated Serb crimes, I tried to find out what they are doing over there. Especially, when you think about it logically, in terms of the army and artillery. Statistically at least it was always clear that the Serbs had the most military power and therefore, it is likely that proportionately we committed the most crimes. (Marko)

The media was also identified as the reason for adopting certain kinds of views, by both the younger and older respondents:

> I remember that RTS had these heartbreaking stories, like, I don't know, where a Serb soldier was killed, and Serb soldiers are dying and are being tortured, and I don't know, such and such things were happening. And you think, of course, those are horrific things, of course I would start hating the Croats! But you know then I was so young, I couldn't understand, but now I see just how strong the media was and how that was actually the greatest evil. (Biljana)

> They put on these tragic stories on the news, and even I, some-one who was protesting against the war, I still sat there staring at the TV and thinking, 'Yes! We have captured another village!' And in reality, it was some hamlet with two houses or a back of beyond hill no one had ever heard of, because everything that was happening in Bosnia was happening in villages. But people started to care, the propaganda made you care what we were winning. (Miroslav)

The respondents' critique of the news coverage of the conflicts thus made it easier to 'blame it on the media' (Volčič 2006) that things were not known but it also served as a convenient way of avoiding certain difficult topics. Since much of the media was not viewed in a favour-able light, discursively, it provided a subject which could be discussed in place of war crimes. For instance, this is how Jovan, who used to work in the military as a civilian engineer, talked about Srebrenica:

> About Srebrenica, I heard, much later, after all of that was over, so I don't remember, but I know what I later read in the press. Before the war I hardly ever read our newspapers, and especially not when Yugoslavia broke up. Before the war I read the Croatian press, *Vjesnik*. The *Vjesnik* that used to come out on Wednesday, and we'd receive it here by Sunday. So it didn't bother me to read something Croatian. I used to read it every single week. I also

read scientific journals, Slovenian and Croatian, it was relevant for my work. I had a subscription [all before the war]. So, it wasn't a problem for me to read the Croatian press, as long as they wrote well. And they used to write much better than our press here.

Avoiding the subject, evading questions or talking about something else entirely are common features amongst the older respondents in particular, and are discussed throughout the subsequent chapters. Here, I find it especially interesting that the issue of poor media quality in Serbia was used to deflect discussion of the conflicts. Such avoidances and contradictions are important as they illustrate that there is neither a clear cut nor a linear relationship with the media (nor any other official/dominant discourse on the conflicts).

Respondents also commented on their experience and knowledge of the 1990s, and compared it to the media narratives in such a way that demonstrated that for them much of the time the two realities converged (the media's and their own experience) as did the two temporal dimensions ('then' and 'now'; also in Jansen 2005). Here is one such extract, which makes use of the present tense to describe what happened 'then'.

First, you think, you can't believe it is happening. Then, as years went by, you see on the news, they say one thing, you see people who are dying. That was all somehow [stops]. On the news, they would put some really irrelevant news first, and then they serve you the rest later. But on the radio it was different, you know, you listened to different ratio stations, it was different, because on the news the main item would be, for example, something really banal, but people are dying, children are dying. (Katarina)

The additional importance of role of the media is in the way in which it facilitated the *witnessing* of atrocities. It allowed audiences to watch these as they took place; even though it attempted to cover up that they were indeed atrocities. As Sontag argues, the act of *watching* an atrocity requires a response from the viewer (Sontag 2003:16) and an active engagement or questioning (since pictures of human suffering

are hardly ever approached uncritically and passively) (c.f. Sorabji 1995).
The media coverage invited participation and so it created viewers who
were at once participants and 'distant audiences' (Humphrey 2002:x);
watching, reacting and responding, as the extracts above highlight. As
Humphrey argues:

> Media witnessing of atrocity is not merely the technological
> extension of our perceptual capacities, it conjures up a differ-
> ent experience. Meaning is shaped by the selectivity of cam-
> era, by the visual and narrative associations of the viewer, by
> the 'timelessness' of the moment, and by the illusion of greater
> understanding created by the prosthetic screen. However, the
> weakness of the image in intentionality also allows for a media
> experience which seeks narrative closure, a story to tie up what
> is seen. (Humphrey 2002:97)

Seeking 'narrative closure' and attempting to make sense of what was
happening on screen and then to reconcile it with one's own experience,
knowledge and other information acquired informally, is something
which comes across very frequently in the interviews collected here.
Humphrey also suggests that television 'allows the viewing of atrocity
between radically separated sites: the ordered and disordered' where
'the viewer watches in secure comfort ... via a screen which protects but
also prevents the viewer from comprehending the Other's experience of
pain and suffering' (Humphrey 2002:101). That appears to be the case
here only partially, since this audience watched the conflicts in some
degree of *dis*comfort (though greater 'comfort' than those on the front
line) and *in*security; two tropes which were constantly highlighted.

It was a situation which, to quote one of the elderly respondents,
made 'you feel like it's war, but you just don't see fighting anywhere.'
This comment came from an elderly respondent who had lived through
the Second World War as a child, but others too felt that war was not
just 'over there' but at home too – refugees had been turning up, and
were often in close proximity. In Emilija's case, for example, they were
next door; and Branka and Ana had helped refugees too. Then there
were all those who were drafted to fight, those who went voluntarily

and the sight of uniformed men in the city was no longer uncommon. Feelings of fear and insecurity were located in all kinds of situations. Ana illustrated how this anxiety permeated day to day situations: getting into a small car accident one night, on a rather empty stretch of road, she became frightened when two men in suits came out of the other, expensive car involved in the accident; 'They were DB! [State security] Assassins!' They may or may not have been, but for many the 1990s were the kind of time when all kinds of seemingly inconsequential events could be interpreted as sources of fear and insecurity.

For many respondents, the media stitched together these two realities. The fear and anxiety felt individually were articulated through horror on the screen, and the heightened feelings of insecurity placed the respondents both on the inside of the conflict and outside of it as the images and news became so closely tied up with their own experience. Seeing people dying on the screen could not be separated from the knowledge that one's friends in Bosnia or Croatia may have suffered the same fate; or that a conscripted friend may have been the ones doing the killing. This constant convergence of realities produced complicated subject positions towards the wars; especially evident in the later discussion of victimhood and marginality discussed in Chapter Seven.

'People talked': silence, rumours and informal knowledge

The opaqueness and deliberate misrepresentation of the conflicts by the mainstream Serbian media did not succeed in covering up the atrocities and the knowledge that civilians had been murdered and displaced, in part because a large amount of information was gathered through a number of informal channels. In general, approaches which suggest that the Serbian public was, and still is, under-informed about wartime atrocities because of the Serbian media, underestimate the importance of the acquisition of informal knowledge, gathered through rumors, hearsay accounts told by refugees and returning soldiers.

There is a particular phrase that I came across quite frequently. In attempting to find out how much the respondents knew about the wars and atrocities 'back then' or now, many suggested that they had 'heard things' because 'people talked'. The Serbian original, *'pričali su ljudi'*, suggests rumour and has gossipy undertones which are not easily translated into English. This phrase was often expressed in the past tense, and related mainly to the 1990s. Its frequency indicates that there was at one time a point at which *some* of the darker aspects of the past were talked about or rumoured, although they were not debated or discussed, but most often were communicated by being half-said, hinted or (over)heard. This information was often unpleasant and carried stories of who killed whom; on all sides. Serbs were not left out of this, and rumours of Serb-committed atrocities spread. Such stories emerged briefly and circulated before being silenced. Out of silence, more rumours would emerge (Feldman 1995:234); did it really happen? Did they really do it? Taussig writes about a similarly silenced or silent narratives his assessment of political terror in Colombia:

> I am referring to a state of doubleness of social being in which one moves in bursts between somehow accepting the situation as normal, only to be thrown into a panic or shocked into disorientation by an event, a rumor, a sight, something said, or not said – something even while it requires the normal in order to make its impact, destroys it. (Taussig 1989:9)

The displaced Serbs in particular, were an important source of such information. For instance, at some point in the 1990s Emilija used to have Serb neighbours who came from Bosnia. She mentioned them rarely; I initially heard the story from her daughter. I asked about the family in the interview, but Emilija was somewhat reluctant to talk about them, and mixed up two different families.

Q: Your former neighbours here, they came from Bosnia?
A: There was that. When that Zorica came here. When she came here [to the flat next door] they [owners of the flat] phoned and said, 'can you wait for her?' We did. She came from Sarajevo, and she was saying what was happening, and what is [*stops*]. That woman came here with just a handbag, she had nothing.

Q: Apart from her, did anyone else talk about the war?
A: No, no one.

Q: Back then?
A: Well. Sometimes it was talked about. When you remember something, like that. We had other neighbours, they were from Bosanska Dubica or Krupa,[2] I don't know. But they had a [*stops*], he had finished his studies, the family was very well off. They left [Belgrade] before the air strikes. He said a Muslim man came to them and said, like this: 'Get your family, your children and leave. I don't want to see you here in the morning. I, as a Muslim, will kill you.' So then they left, and they lived here.

The story was not forthcoming nor easily told, and a sentence was not completed, ('what was happening, and what is') but it was only later that I learned from the family the reasons for this. Emilija did not like talking about the family from Sarajevo because, according to her son-in-law Mladen, the story was horrific. What they learned from the Sarajevo family (Emilija's story had reduced this to just one woman, Zorica), is that in their Sarajevo neighbourhood of Ilidža, two men terrorised civilians. One was a Muslim and one a Serb. The Serb they called 'Četnik Ivan', and, according to the story he used to decapitate local Muslims ('one every day'), and display the heads on the hood of his car. Zorica's family had a teenage son who saw this, and after their escape to Belgrade the teenager became obsessed with violence. In 1998 the family moved to Germany where, according to Mladen, the teenage son was frequently in trouble for violent offences. Emilija did not talk about this because she found it very upsetting and deeply disturbing.

Emilija's account suggests one more issue: that there is something at the very core of such stories that is not openly discussed, or even articulated. That 'something' was the implicit knowledge that not only had someone died a terrible, brutal and often undignified death, but that, if the rumours were true, they died at the hands of Serbs. Rumours, particularly those of gruesome crimes, played a crucial role in shaping realities of war. As both Taussig (1984) and Krohn-Hansen (1997:234) argue: 'rumours and experiences of uncertainty, ambiguity, and doubt are, to a considerable extent, the very stuff out of which violent political histories are made' (Krohn-Hansen 1997:234). Furthermore, as Feldman points out, there is a very strong connection between silence, things which cannot be said because they simply cannot be described, and rumours:

> It is as if the first wound of violence, the initial and simultaneous damaging of individual bodies…effaces the social capacity for description. Things are thought but not said, and when speech emerges it is not from that aborted thought but from the intervening gap of the not said. Rumour begins at the borders of silence around the kernel of the absent event, the disappeared body, the silenced name. (Feldman 1995:234)

In this case, I would also argue that the *presence* of informal knowledge and rumour also reinforces the silence, because what most respondents came to know through informal channels is that the reality of what was happening was much worse than what was being presented. This related in particular to Srebrenica. Sanja, who was a teenager at the time of the conflicts, remembers rumours about Srebrenica – she learned about the event from the media around the year 2000 but by then, she said, so many rumours had circulated 'that for me wasn't a surprise, but you feel awful, you feel ashamed because you belong to those people, and you know there will be consequences.' Rumors, viewed from within Milošević's Serbia and the 'quagmire' of 'mud' and 'slush' which Živković (2001) so eloquently describes, only gave access to partial truths and partial understanding. Humphrey writes that 'the narration of rumour, seeking to give collective experience meaning in the absence of widespread social credibility, is constructed with damaged vision and voice' (Humphrey 2002:85). Similarly, in Serbia terrible things were suspected and heard; but they could be true, or they could be false, and the possibility of their truth often rendered them unspeakable.

Silence

The deeply disturbing nature of what became known, whether through the media or speculation and rumours, has left a legacy of silence that persists until the present day. In other words, a silence surrounds the atrocities of the past, not because they are unknown, but because they are *known*. Their content – of violence, atrocity, brutality – is partly what prevents their discussion.

A case in point is the infamous 'Scorpions' video, in wide circulation at the time that the research for this book was conducted. It did not provoke a discussion amongst my respondents, but rather, more silence. Most of the atrocities and horrors associated with that particular film had long been known or suspected. But the silence surrounding this issue is not indicative of a failure of confrontation with the past (as in e.g. Beč 2005); rather it is indicative of a deep horrification. Sontag writes that despite centuries of history and art 'representing atrocious suffering', 'there is shame as well as shock in looking at the close-up of real horror' as 'the gruesome invites us to be either spectators or cowards, unable to look' (Sontag 2003:37–38). Moreover, such images of 'hellish events', Sontag argues, are all the more potent when they are not professionally produced, but are amateur efforts (as the 'Scorpions' video was) (Sontag 2003:23–24). The images of horror, rather than prompting a discussion, can shock audiences into silence, as violent events break down words (Das 1995:184) since it is 'upsetting to have the opportunity to look at people who know they have been condemned to die' (Sontag 2003: 54).

This is not a uniquely Serbian phenomenon, and the answer as to why 'the Serbs' might turn away from such images should not be sought within other 'Serbian' problems such as voting for Milošević, or nationalism. The horrific images of Iraqi prisoners in Abu Ghraib, and their reception by British and American audiences, whose governments were involved in the Iraq war, are a case in point. The publication of these images did spark off a debate, but not one which was as society-wide as may have been expected. The problem also was that, as Bennett et al. (2006) argue, the press in the US was reluctant to label Abu Ghraib images as torture.

The authors argue that the leading national news organisations did not produce a counterframe to the Bush administration's frame of the event as 'abuse' (Bennett et al. 2006:467). Indeed, in Sontag's (2004) assessment of the same, she notes that 'the pictures will continue to "assault" us .... Will people get used to them? Some Americans are already saying they have seen enough'. Having 'seen enough' is precisely the phrase used by some of my respondents to describe their reactions to the Scorpions video and other images of atrocities.

When I asked respondents about the silences surrounding the atrocities, most of the time this question was met with no concrete response. Vanja, however, provided a possible answer. The war in Bosnia is not discussed in her family, she said, because 'it was gruesome'. Other respondents suggested similar dynamics:

> You know, you'd expect that all evil things in life will be forgotten. And so, these Serbian people, no matter how much they present us as insane, we're completely normal because we want to forget. We're completely normal because if anyone had gone through what we've gone through in the last fifteen years, they'd be the same. If someone is constantly bombarding you, constantly sending you back five or six years, when someone is constantly showing you pictures of corpses, murders, this and that. You have these political shows now and they talk about that all the time. Someone has decided that these people should not be left alone. (Petar)

> It's all over. At our family gatherings there were some arguments because of politics. There were some really big fights. And then I just said, enough! Enough of your politics! If we are here as a family then we won't talk about stupidities. Let's talk about our life, and our children. So not now. My whole family is mourning for Yugoslavia and everything that happened. (Mara)

> You know what, we talk about it less and less, because we have other problems, how to survive. But then you see something on television, and you start to remember everything and then you say – horror! God forbid it is repeated again. You know, you

remember all those people, when they came here from Bosnia, when they – I mean, that was just horrific … I want to forget everything, and I just don't want to remember, but now, I can't forget … You know what, I don't follow the news anymore. I'm just fed up with everything. I don't really bother with the news. The only important thing is that my children finish school. Sometimes I might read the newspaper from ten days ago. My husband and Mladen, they follow everything. I can't. I am just worried about how we will manage with money. You see. Every day the market just gets more expensive. (Katarina)

When we talk about it, it is often mentioned, but we don't just talk about the worst. We mainly talk about how nice things were before. I had a lot of friends in Croatia, in Bosnia. I used to holiday a lot on the Croatian coast, and there I met a lot of friends and colleagues. And we were always in touch, right up until the war, and after that, they don't call but neither do I. We talk about that less and less. Most of the time, we are just criticising those fools who started the war. It's not the people's fault. (Nikola)

These extracts illustrate that something terrible had taken place; there is a 'mourning'; and something was also 'evil' that should 'never happen again'. In Petar's interview extract someone is showing pictures of 'corpses, murders', but almost immediately, the rest of that formulation becomes 'this and that'. Before things are stated explicitly, they are very often replaced with words and phrases that seek to cover up that 'something', almost as if a plaster is being applied to conceal a wound.

Here is how another scene played out at one time during the research for this project. A news item about the Scorpions trial came up whilst I was talking to Ana and her daughter Tijana. Tijana, having been a child during the 1990s and not knowing much detail about that time, also did not know what the news item was referring to and asked Ana what it was all about. Ana stayed quiet. Tijana asked again 'Who are those men?' Ana remained quiet and then shrugged and said, 'it is nothing'. I found out from Ana's other, much older daughter

Iva, that Ana's discomfort may have been caused by something much more personal: it turned out that Ana's ex-husband, a man with whom she had not spoken for years, was in Bosnia during the war working as a cameraman. Her daughter, who told me this, had no other details – she had also not spoken to her father for years. But that piece of information hovered over the Scorpions incident. Ana knew her ex-husband was, according to her daughter, 'filming something'. In a perhaps disturbing parallel, the Scorpions incident had come to light because 'someone' had filmed 'something.' This illustrates one particularly delicate point about the 1990s – for rather a lot of people in Belgrade, the war was at times a bit too close to home (sometimes literally), since their own husbands, relatives and friends may have been implicated in various ways (see also Orentlicher 2007:21).

Ana's reluctance to discuss the war with her children is not unusual. Another younger respondent, Ružica, eighteen, the daughter of Rada and Mladen, complained that no one ever wants to explain anything when she hears similar items on the news. This is the case even though Mladen follows political developments in the region very closely and the family has several newspapers at home every day. The family had been very negatively affected by the 1990s – in addition to personal and mental health problems, one of their close friends was mobilised for the war in Croatia. The 1990s and the wars were difficult and rarely-discussed topics, since they were closely interwoven with personal tragedy and hardship. Ružica does not lack information about the wars nor the 1990s but does not understand their interpretations and implications:

> When I see some things in the newspapers I just read the headline and I don't read on. That war was something completely incomprehensible to me. Or when I see something in the news and I ask my parents, what is this? they are like, come on, it doesn't matter, I'll tell you another time.

> *Q: What kinds of things?*
> A: Well, for example, that Serbs are responsible for mass killing people in Croatia and Bosnia and in general that Serbs are guilty.

So I listen to that. And I listen to that and then another side of the story, and then I just don't know whom to believe. And then in the end, it just doesn't interest me anymore. I can't burden myself with that. But at school, we had some refugees but they never talked about that. I had for example a good friend from Bosnia, and I knew only that her dad died in the war, but we never said anything else about that. Now, it's like if we start to talk about it someone will say did you see this or that on TV and I just go, come on, leave it, let's not talk about that.

The situation is similar amongst young people and the lack of discussion of the topics within their own peer groups. Ružica's friend, the slightly older Filip, twenty-two, said the following:

If we talk about it it's all about should someone or other go to The Hague. Should this person go there, and Srebrenica, was that OK or not? Is it OK that all those people are talking to us about it, or not? Not really about the war itself. Because no one from my surroundings was – no one, no one. About The Hague, well some people are totally against it. I am somewhere in the middle, neither here nor there. But still, we have some people who say, it's normal, you have to prosecute, they weren't supposed to do those things.

Amongst both the younger and older respondents, wars were rarely discussed, even amongst the closest friends, despite the culture of relative openness that one finds often in Serbia. My respondents were not reluctant to talk, for instance, about topics that elsewhere could be deemed quite personal – salaries, health problems, relationships – and the absence of talk about wars in this open and talkative culture appears quite odd. However, this absence of wars in conversations occurs mainly in group situations, particularly between parents and their children. On the contrary, in much more private conversations, for instance, between only two people or in interviews carried out for this research, the respondents were surprisingly forthcoming. All generations, young and old, spoke freely about their thoughts and feelings about this period, however, the ways in which the older generation discussed this time was quite opaque and marked with evasions and metaphors as discussed thus far.

Re-examinations of the past, therefore, belong to a very private domain. Mostly, they are not discussed in arenas where judgements may be passed or contrary opinions may emerge. This is why interview settings, or discussions where there are only two people present, appear to be conducive to such discussions. Interviews act as spaces for re-examination and reflection, which most respondents had quite clearly been doing for some time, but not voicing their ideas openly in daily discussions with friends and family. The majority of stories were formulated as questions and inquisitions which, it often seemed, the older respondents had been asking themselves for a long time, in private, as the narratives very often spilled out, and kept unfolding, disconnected, with a sense of urgency and a need to bring up as many issues as possible – the shortages, the social crisis and the feeling of being consonantly horrified when hearing about the war. Some respondents, Jovan for instance, told me that they had never spoken with anyone else about some things they expressed about the war in their interviews with me. The interviews provided a space for discussion which many respondents told me they appreciated. For instance, after our interview, Ivan said, 'I have been waiting for years for someone to ask me about this. It's useless talking about things like that here. My friends have their own problems and they don't care.'

This private reflection is at odds with various NGO initiatives aimed at confronting the past, since their approach is founded on the attempt to make these kinds of discussions *public*. NGOs have at times been judgemental about the public at which they aim their campaigns, and as result, their approach has alienated much of their audience.

As several of the respondents here have indicated, the more they are 'told' (in their view) by NGOs to confront the past, the less they feel willing to engage in their projects (and not because they do not agree, but because they do not like being told what to do and how to do it). Writing about South Africa, Cuéllar (2005:161) notes that silences can also be 'reactive', formed 'against the intervention of "experts" and other intermediaries' an observation resonant for Serbia. Furthermore, keeping these reflections guarded against the public gaze serves a useful function. Analysing silences amongst Northern Ireland Protestants, Donnan and Simpson (2007:13) find that 'restricting the flow of information' in this way, allows individuals to be in 'control' of their feelings and the knowledge about violent events which they share.

As the rest of this book demonstrates, most of those feelings are still unresolved, and filled with contradictions, or opinions which do not align with, for instance, NGO campaigns. Leaving war discussions for private spaces is 'safer', since opinions and ideas will not be exposed to possible ridicule or judgement. Furthermore it is safer in the sense that subjects which provoke emotional reactions are in many ways difficult to discuss in front of others (for instance, a couple of the respondents cried in the interviews). In this way, things like news items about the Scorpions or NGO initiatives such as the Srebrenica poster campaign (see Nosov 2005) intrude into these silent spaces and demand attention. This clashes uncomfortably with the desire for privacy and the response is often a further retreat away from the glare of the public gaze.

Horror and 'all kinds of things'

Evasion of the wars was therefore twofold – individuals avoided talking about the atrocities of the past, except in interviews. Futhermore, there was often an avoidance in naming certain things. This frequently meant that war crimes, together with the 1990s and the wars in general were referred to as 'horror' and 'terror'. The motif of 'horror' is also located in oral histories collected in the volume by Rill and Šmidling (2010). In the volume, veterans and their families speak about their experiences and recollections of the 1990s. In this impressive collection of oral histories, two women from Serbia discuss their experiences of this time, particularly in regard to the mobilisation of their family members. In their recollections there is a frequent repetition of *užas* (horror) and the expression of incomprehensibility (see Rill and Šmidling 2010, pp. 222–243; 205–387).

In addition to the same frequent invocations of horror and terror, the narratives of my respondents, were quite vague at times and did not always address specific aspects of war (even if this was the original question), nor did they recollect events, incidents, dates and so on, but their narratives were marked by opinions, analyses, questions and resentment. Such eclectic responses and lack of linearity were primary indicators that the wars are still undergoing a process of mediation – most are still confused about what actually took place, not in the *factual* sense, but in a conceptual one. For instance, almost everyone I spoke to admitted that they are still unsure as to *why* the wars took place and often used phrases such as 'how can something like that happen?'. When attempts were made to address these issues, respondents used a number of evasive strategies, such as metaphors, so as not to speak directly of things like massacres. As Kerby points out, 'recollection ... is both selective and interpretative' (Kerby 1991:83).

These strategies resonate with Daniel's (1994:237) assertion that certain violent events are 'unimaginable', and therefore 'unspeakable'. For instance, as demonstrated in the extracts below, the openings of three interviews, the explanations often included significant evasions: that war was being spoken about is implicit, but quite often, even though 'war' was in the question posed, it made no appearance, discursively or conceptually, in the respondents' answers:

What I remember – first there was the break-up. That break-up [...] I think if politics hadn't been involved, if rule had been stronger [...] if they had been interested in saving the country, it would have been saved. But, if it hadn't been for stronger outside forces, it would have been saved without a problem. (Stevan)

I remember that no one asked me if we should go to war or not. Even today, I keep repeating that, because no-one asked me [...] I couldn't comprehend that there would be someone crazy enough who would take the country to war. (Jovan)

I feel so sad about it. I read what happened in Slavonija, what kinds of brutalities they carried out. I heard from people who were displaced. A woman who said her own godmother doesn't speak to her anymore, nor do the neighbours who were her friends. That is horrible! And all the destruction of houses. A house – gas, they close the windows and shoot a bullet with flames or maybe something else but the house burns down and everything in the house. Horror! We are relatively poor people, and what we have, we destroy. But what makes me the saddest is human victims. You can't make up for someone's life ... I'm really sad it all happened, that a brother could turn on his brother. Everyone used to live together, Serbs in Bosnia with Muslims and Croats, and suddenly, they took their guns out and started shooting each other. And those mass graves, and those murders, they really unsettled me. We really didn't need that. (Mara).

The news was available, especially the TV and radio. And the press ... You just read, and listened and crossed[3] yourself – even if you never crossed yourself, you did then, because you said, what is going on with us? We heard. We heard that there were all kinds of things. (Nikola)　.

At other times, there was so much evasion that it was unclear what the respondents were actually referring to. Imprecise, indefinite terminology was often used to refer to the war, which was frequently described as 'all that', 'this and that' ('ovo i ono'), or 'things that happened' ('stvari što su se desile'). Stevan, like Mara and Katarina, referred to 'that break-up', and Jovan remembered 'that'. Veljko called it a 'bar-room brawl', Mirjana a 'horrific and dirty game' and Petar 'general craziness'. As Sontag points out, in 'trying to comprehend "radical" or "absolute" evil, we search for adequate metaphors,' (1978:85) in order not to confront the 'absoluteness' of what the metaphor replaces. It is important to bear in mind that, as Das suggests, 'violence annihilates language' and 'terror cannot be brought into the realm of the utterable,' (Das 1995:184, in Humphrey 2002:9) and thus quite often the silence that is understood as an obstinate refusal to discuss atrocities committed against others is often an inability to, literally, *speak* about it (e.g. Das 1995; Daniel 1991).

In addition to the 'long-distance' terror (c.f. Humphrey 2002) that respondents found difficult to verbalise, there were also things which they observed much closer to home, that they found just as disturbing. The episodes do not relate directly to violence, but rather its outcomes, and they demonstrate another merging of wartime realities:

> You know what, I feel so sorry that all those things happened, and all those people of course, because ordinary people were not to blame for what happened to them, for the kinds of situations they found themselves in. And even in my family we had some things like that. If that happens to you, people simply just find themselves without anything, and then have to go to another city. Or when your loved ones disappear or get hurt. Simply, emotions are very high then ... One of my work colleagues, I remember, she even lost her flat in Belgrade. They had some kind of temporary accommodation, because her husband had gone to war. She was left alone with her child. One day refugees kicked her out of her flat. She was living in the corridor for two days, with her child! That refugee had some kind of connections, and so they were just kicked out. And her husband is on the front, fighting, total chaos! She told me that, and it's a very disturbing story. (Nevena)

> We listened about Markale. And then the murders of those soldiers, when they left the barracks in Sarajevo. Alija [Izetbegović] gave the order to shoot, so they killed them, doctors, everyone. They are going to Serbia, why are you shooting them? I don't know how many educated officers were killed. And those poor soldiers. The ones who were leaving the barracks. I can't believe it. That you kill people when they are leaving that territory. And that was one common army, Yugoslav. But now if you are a Serb, you have to leave. Although my husband's brother, he did not leave. He is a Serb, married to a Slovenian woman. He did not leave with the army. Because his daughter also says she is Slovenian, and the daughter had a Slovenian boyfriend, also in the army. So she said, what does it mean now, different army? What if

my boyfriend has to shoot at my dad? And then she was crying. But it's good that he stayed there. Because those who came [Serbs, who left army posts in Croatia, Slovenia and Bosnia and came to Belgrade] they are really suffering. There are people who still live in barracks and rooms. My husband said some refugees [military families] turned up at their office, they had nowhere to put them. Can you imagine, at the office, children crying, over there a woman cooking, and those people didn't even have anywhere to shower, just the office toilet. What suffering that was! The army couldn't look after its own people. (Mara)

There were so many things. What we lived through in ten to fifteen years, in some countries that would not happen in two hundred years. Here, there were so many examples and so many reasons why we resent the West. They very openly started to break Yugoslavia. Slovenia is splitting off with the support of the West and Croatia. So the West just keeps breaking and breaking us and we are supposed to bow to them. And wars are happening. You can't say that war is controlled. No, it happens, and in the minds of people, their consciousness is changing. Why would we go to war? But by the time you understand that for yourself, everyone has killed everyone else. War is something` when in your own head there is this strange situation, and an unpleasant situation in your everyday life. You start to think differently. (Mladen)

The converging of realities in this way, also demonstrates why the respondents did not approach the past through a predominantly 'ethnic' frame – wars produced a lot of suffering, everywhere, and to many respondents, it was *all* horrible and terrible. This diverges from transitional justice approaches in Serbia which highlight the need for the public to address and acknowledge the victims of other ethnicities. However, such differentiations were rare, stemming from a much more holistic view in which the wars affected 'all' of 'us', across the whole of the former Yugoslavia. In another study, McGrattan raises a similar issue with regards to Northern Ireland, pointing out that ethnic framing within transitional justice oversimplifies and disregards the complex identities and experiences of violence, since not all individuals would necessarily nor primarily, have experienced the conflict as 'ethnic' subjects (McGrattan 2009). Furthermore, it is difficult to negate that some things, which were observed at home, were not terrible. During her interview, Katarina mentioned, for instance that for her, 'the worst thing was seeing those children on TV in the refugee columns'; at this point she started crying. Awful things were happening at home too, and some of the things which were witnessed or heard about, such as a mother living in a corridor or a refugee family having to live in the barracks office, just added more layers to 'all that' horror. 'Horror and terror' as well metaphors of 'insanity' are used in place of talking about the real terror which took place. For instance, in the extract below, 'that' violence is never explicitly addressed because, there is a clear struggle literally to find the words to describe what happened:

> There was so much insanity there, I don't know if insanity is the right word. I don't know, really. You can't even say they are bestial crimes, because even beasts wouldn't do the kinds of things they did to each other, everyone. That's something that stays with you, and within all that you don't see a speck of reason, a speck of humanity. No. There is nothing human there, it wasn't, it was killing, but also torture, torturing someone until he really dies. I don't know. It is worse than the concentration camps in the Second World War. I don't know ... is it something that people learned to do, or is it something we all carry in us? And photographs. Like those mujahedeen who now live in Tuzla, who posed with the decapitated heads of Serbs.[4] Or like that Četnik Ivan from Sarajevo, who that neighbour told us about, who at least once a week had to carry a decapitated head of a Muslim man though Ilidža. I just don't have the words. There, that's what stays with me. And then in the end, [NATO air strikes]. Maybe one day I will be able to connect all that, and to describe it, maybe twenty years from now. (Rada)

Studies which consider the impact of terror and violence usually focus on their consequences for the victims (e.g. Taussig 1989;

Scheper-Hughes 2004; Das and Kleinman 2001; Daniel 1996; Daniel 1994), and it is from these considerations that seminal work on the effects of violence on language emerge. However, 'distant audiences' (Humphrey 2002:x), such as the group presented here, may also have found something so terrifying and horrifying that they 'don't have the words' to describe it. Thus, rather than viewing silences and evasions as absences – and they are anything *but*, according to Riaño-Alcalá and Baines (2011:429) – they could be read as spaces in which violence has 'annihilated language' (Das 1995:184). It is the very absence of words and phrases which allude to it directly that demonstrate a degree of discomfort, disbelief and revulsion (c.f. Daniel 1994). In a study of victims of torture, Daniel finds that even those who have been tortured deny that torture occurred against fellow victims (Daniel 1994). He notes that this is because the pain of torture has an element of 'unshareability ... and incommunicability', unlike the 'much more socialised pains: the headache, the toothache, the earache ... that have been given names of recognition in the folklore and diagnostic labels in medical lore' (Daniel 1994:238). Importantly, this is because in such cases 'the *unbelievable* is also the unexplainable, and the unexplainable the *inexpressible*.' (Daniel 1994:238, added emphasis). This 'unshareability', which in Daniel's case affects those directly suffering physical pain, can also be applied to individuals affected by violence in different and unusual ways, such as the respondents in this study.

Following on from the inability to speak and communicate, a particularly interesting dynamic emerges. Whereas the unspoken 'horror' and 'terror' are only hinted at by the older respondents, they are fully revealed in conversations with the younger respondents. If 'horror' and 'terror' are some kinds of 'hidden knowledge', then younger respondents act as its amplifiers, and in their accounts the 'horror' and 'terror' are to attached to meanings, images, words, ideas and names. The hints and hidden stories are revealed, and what they narrate is quite often disturbing: family histories which were directly affected by conscription, death and war, friends who died, witnessed war, were potentially involved in atrocities or committed suicide.

Younger generations and 'hidden knowledge'

There are interesting familial and generational dynamics which govern discussions (or their lack) about wars and atrocities. Above, for instance, Mara talks about the things her husband saw; he does not. Children speak about relatives losing their lives, or going to war; but their parents do not; Petar's sister talks about his conscription; he barely mentions it. Of these, the parent-child dynamic emerged as the most interesting. This is the main instance where the question of age appears to influence narrative; with all other issues (detailed in the following chapters) there is much less, if any, generational differentiation. One of the respondents reflected on this:

> I sometimes listened to the news. Though my daughter always corrects me and says, mum, you only listened to one side, not the other. Especially over Kosovo. We know what they did to Serbs over there, and they wrote only about that. But what did Serbs do to Albanians. She says that Albanians were attacked too, that people attacked them in their own homes, before the air strikes. And that it wasn't only Serbs who were attacked. By the KLA, their terrorists. But, still. I am really sad that honest people suffered like that, the most. Those political hotheads, they don't go to fight, they sit in armchairs, and innocent people die. (Mara)

Whereas the older respondents justified their silence about the wars by stating these are things they wished to forget, younger respondents – quite often the children of those adults avoiding the discussion – openly addressed these silences and attempted to find answers as to why such questions were not being addressed. In addition, once the topics of war and war crimes were addressed, the younger respondents, those now aged between twenty and thirty, almost always provided very clear details about the 1990s as well as their own ideas as to what happened. For example, I interviewed both Filip, and his mother, Branka. When we talked about the war, their responses were very different. Branka said the following:

Of course, those stories about the war were around at the time [in the 1990s]. My ex-husband had family in Bosnia, and so I heard from them, because they participated directly. Many other people came here during the war. Everyone understood that that was just lunacy. That was in fact one political fabrication, not just of our governments but of European and American ones too, but it is the ordinary people who suffered. Those stories [about the war] have not completely disappeared – there is a small percentage of people who still hold on to those stories, but I think mainly they have been forgotten. It is understood that it was all insane. Of course, no one can change that now. (Branka)

This was a very typical response in that it hinted at some hidden knowledge ('those stories' referred to repeatedly), but before any answers are supplied, the narrative switches to explanation – 'that was just lunacy' and 'a political fabrication'. Branka's narrative raises many questions – what stories? What was 'lunacy'? What does everyone understand? When further questions are posed, the answers which follow do not provide any more detail than the one presented above. But, when I spoke to Branka's son, the hidden knowledge was 'exposed':

I was born in 1984 ... I was here [in Belgrade during the war], but my dad's family is from Banja Luka, and all my uncles were fighting in the war. They were supposed to come here to escape, and it was all like, now they are coming, now they are not. The worst thing is they didn't come here in the end. They stayed there. But one uncle, I know he was saying that twice he escaped death, he just jumped into some bunker and saved himself. But they stayed there. He had young children. My grandma was really scared, all the time going, are they coming here or not? ... My best friend here in the building, his dad is a Muslim, and his Mum is something, maybe Croat. He lives with his mum only. In the war, his dad left, he just went there and never came back. (Filip)

In Filip's narrative, details emerged which his mother never mentioned – such as uncles having to take part in war as they were unable to leave

Bosnia. A similar contrast emerged between the stories from Gordana and her son Slavko. Gordana's ex-husband, incidentally, is also a Serb from Bosnia. Gordana did not tell me what happened to her husband or his family, nor did she mention any of the things that her son told me later:

I was eight ... But I remember that in '91 we were supposed to go to Croatia on holiday but then we didn't. But I don't really remember the people's mood, just things from the TV. But now, if it wasn't for some films [about the war] that came out recently, I probably wouldn't remember anything. But now, it's totally clear to me what kind of language was being used on the news, the language from the Tito's era. They were using words like fratricidal war and that. You know that film *Wounds*?[5] Like that guy Pedja Stojanović, who was the newscaster in the film, how he read out the news, that's exactly what I remember. I remember literally those kinds of people from the TV. I remember more about Croatia, that Maslenica bridge when they destroyed it and when they destroyed the bridge in Mostar [...] My dad because he was from Bosnia, he was going there all the time whilst there was a corridor to get through, he was all the time there, he had a weekend house and went there. And he told me, I would say it was pretty horrific. Those were first-hand stories. In those parts where he is from, for example, Serbs were selling bullets to the Muslims. Literally. He said, 'we've sold out'. But not much else. He said that it was all a swindle and that the politicians agreed it all between themselves ... He can't stand this Ratko Mladić who bombarded Sarajevo from a hill. He told me all kinds of things that happened there. He was like a reporter. My dad was kind of neutral in his stories. He said what Serbs did to the Muslims and what Muslims did to the Serbs. Then I ask myself, who was at war there? I guess if people have a neutral stance like my dad, and don't get excited about the war, then I guess it was all because of political reasons. What affected me was when he told me that these people that we knew, that they were slaughtered. But the rest, I don't know, my dad used to talk about it so often back then when we visited friends that I just got tired of it.

The story was not elaborated further, so what Slavko's father was doing in Bosnia during the war was never made clear. What is clear, however, is that his father had seen something 'horrific' which was then conveyed to family and friends in Belgrade at some point. But, a discussion of that 'something' is avoided. It is interesting that the younger respondents often provided missing details, despite having often been too young to understand fully what was being witnessed or overheard. Certainly some of their information came from the media and other sources, but quite a lot – for instance information about relatives – must have come from their parents or other adults. Yet their approach to this information was very different to that of their parents. Suddenly, the missing elements surfaced: soldiers, volunteers, the dead.

In these younger generation's accounts, another set stories of stories emerged: those of deeply traumatised drafted soldiers and war volunteers. Here, informal knowledge emerges as important yet again, since much of this was learned from the former conscripts, refugees, or overheard from families. For instance, in one conversation, Ivan, took a long time to retell the story of his older cousin who was drafted for the war in Croatia. This account is quite unique, even amongst the younger generation, who, whilst providing details, did not always narrate 'the whole story' but only the snippets of what they knew and had heard. Ivan's story on the other hand, is 'complete' in the sense that it introduces us to a person – 'Mihajlo', Ivan's cousin, to whom he is very close, his time at war and what happened to him afterwards:

> Mihajlo was around thirty. He went to Vukovar [he was drafted] and then came back, I can't remember how long he was gone for, but I remember when he came back, we were at home and it was night-time. There was a call for my aunt, his mother, and someone just said, Mihajlo is coming back, he's coming home. We waited for him at my aunt's place, he arrived around midnight. He was totally … like, his eyes were like … totally wide. I guess he realised he was home, he started to relax. I have very few memories of that period of my life, but I remember looking at him that night and I can see him now like it was yesterday. He arrived and started talking all over the place, unconnected … like how

someone was chasing them, snipers were firing at them, then they had to crawl and lie in the trenches for a few days, in water up to their chests. They were even betrayed by some villager. He told them it was safe but they saw tanks. They just picked up their stuff and ran. A minute after they left the whole thing went up in flames. The house was hit. All that had really big consequences for him. He is such a nice guy. I never met anyone who really cares about others more than he cares about himself. He was always like that, but now the one difference is that after that he now feels really insecure, so that he feels he has to carry a gun. In the place where he lives, they know him and they leave him alone, even though you are not allowed to carry a weapon. The law forbids it. They just leave him alone. So he's kind of a bit crazy to be honest – he volunteered later on to go to Kosovo. So maybe he was missing something. Unbelievable ... I mean he always liked weapons but he was never the kind of person to go to war and risk his life for I don't know what. But we talked about this and he said over there [in Kosovo, during the war] he feels needed. Quite simply his life evidently lost all meaning [...].But Kosovo, I have other friends, my generation, who went to Kosovo, who returned. I once ran into a friend at the bus station, we took the bus together. We were on the bus for two hours and that whole time he talked, same as my cousin, unconnected. He managed to say some unimportant stuff like where they slept, what kinds of things they saw in this house, what the house looked like. And then he starts describing what they had to do, how they had to make models of tanks so the planes would shoot those, and then the most horrific thing that he told me was – he said everything so easily as if everything was so straightforward. He had convinced himself. They had convinced them over there. He simply said, we were not in any danger, we always knew where they will hit and we always hid in a safe place. And that's what he got into his head, and that's great – great that he man-aged to see it out that way. Imagine, every second of every day you have to think about whether a bomb is going to drop on your head. After three minutes I'd go crazy. Really, listening to this friend, it was horrible for me to listen to because I had known him since we were kids. I don't know, he wasn't [stops]. My cousin had to literally save his own life but he, I don't know, nothing on that scale happened. On some scale of horrors. I don't know. But I still think my cousin [stops]. There are lots of cases like him.

This is quite a complicated narrative. It is detailed and revealing but also features reflection and reassessment and does not sentimentalise what happened. Yet it is quite a difficult thing to talk about – Ivan also clearly wanted to get the story out there. He did not stop talking for quite a long time. The language again relies on colloquial medicalised language – the cousin is referred to as a 'case', with its psychiatric under-tones, and he is deemed to be 'crazy'. Then there is also a lot that is left unsaid: 'I still think my cousin' – what? The content is also revelatory. The 'horrors' of the war receive an articulation: the war has damaged people, there are 'a lot of cases like him'. This is something Ivan is still coming to terms with – understanding, accepting, believing – that his cousin would become so damaged and 'crazy', so as to become the kind of person who volunteers for war and carries guns. Then there is also the realisation that loved ones had gone through terrible experiences and nearly died; as far as 'coming to terms with the past' is concerned, these are also elements which need to be confronted.

In terms of such confrontation, there is also an added element, a hint of what Humphrey (2002) suggests – that atrocities which 'hor-rify and terrify' also 'confront individuals with an existential crisis of the self and the need to make sense of the world' since 'it is an internal bodily experience of fear, horror and pain in which the very self is bru-tally confronted and threatened with the reality of its own extinction' (Humphrey 2002:1–2). Ivan is shaken up by his friend's story because it could have just as easily been him – except, as he says, if that happened to him, he would 'go crazy'. Placing the self, implicitly or explicitly in these narratives serves as a kind of yardstick: 'if that happened to me, how would I deal with it?' It also demonstrates the proximity of the war. Again, it is not something that happened 'over there', but it hap-pened 'to us' and 'our' families, and could have happened to 'me'.

Finally, there is also the knowledge that what happened to them had happened to others, on the 'other' side, and may have been caused by the friend or the cousin, who may have committed atrocities. It is always a distinct possibility, and that grain of ambiguity and uncertainty hovers over many narratives.

Younger people often obtained their ideas about the war in retrospect, once they became conscious of the events or informed themselves through reading. Documentaries on B92 were cited as a particularly useful source of information – for example their recent films on the Prijedor concentration camps and their documentaries on Srebrenica – the very same sources of information which their parents' generation actively rejected as 'foreign-funded propaganda' (Rada). Likewise, whilst the older respondents attempted to explain their lack of awareness of such events at the time of their occurrence by pointing out the lack of information in the Milošević controlled media, younger respondents did not:

> I remember, in 1991 I was seventeen. [...] It was all very sad. I remember some meeting from Sarajevo was broadcast, I can't remember the events but I remember the emotions. I felt it was all very repulsive because the commentator [on RTS] was just so one-sided. [...] I think they were showing some speech by Radovan Karadžić [...] was it because the first shots were fired or something? But back then I felt that they should have tried to find out what happened, to stop it. But what they were commenting from the studio, and what they were broadcasting, that was [...] like, 'look at what they are doing to us, come on Serbs let's go.' I know I was really furious at that back then. When the war in Bosnia started in 1992, and listening to RTS [...] that was insane, that was totally like Orwell's brainwashing. (Novak)

> Of course I remember! But I was a child and for me the most important thing was what was happening around me. But we didn't have any losses amongst my family or friends, my father had heart problems and was not mobilised. So what I experienced of that period was what it was like to live in Serbia as a

twelve-year-old, and the situation was that from a completely normal life we just fell to the standard where we had to queue for everything, there was nothing in shops, and inflation just eats up your salary in one day. [...] Even when I watched the news, I still couldn't understand what was actually going on, why that war was being fought. [...] Always though, when someone was killed from the neighbourhood, one of the young men, they always talked about that. (Biljana)

Funnily enough, I do remember, I started high school then in the 1990s. [...] [E]ven then, I liked to read newspapers and I was interested in what was going on during the war; I read as much as I could because there was a media blockade. The media blockade was awful with regard to the war in Croatia and Bosnia, [...] from what we were told by the men coming back from the fronts. There were forty-seven, forty-eight men in [my parents' town], all reservists, who threw their weapons down once they were called up and refused to go to war and came back home [...] because they had people coming back before them and bringing home bombs, guns, ammunition. I could have, if I wanted, as a fourteen-year-old boy, got 300 Deutschmarks and bought an automatic rifle, for instance. Back then you just could ... I did have one bad experience. One of my friends went to the army when he was eighteen and he was in Kosovo. When he returned, he committed suicide. There were a lot of bad things like that. (Bojan)

Even though there were differences and doubts amongst this younger group too (for example, Ivan later admitted that he still has doubts over Srebrenica, discussed below), on the whole they were much more explicitly critical of Serbia's involvement in the war, highlighting its futility. In their narratives, wars are not about 'this' and 'that' but are explicitly about death, loss and tragedy. In one of our conversations, Biljana told me that for her, the most fitting description of the Yugoslav wars was summarised in the words of a young JNA soldier, featured on the news just as the war in Slovenia was starting:

He was lying down in the grass, and the reporter asked him, why are we at war? And he said, 'Well, it's like, they want to secede, and we're like, not supposed to let them.' And this soldier had a gun and was prepared to die but even he didn't know for what.

The general difference between what the younger and older groups remembered and narrated can be considered in the context of each generation's war experience (cf. Connerton 1989:3). The younger generations, especially those now in their mid-twenties to early thirties, have spent most of their lives with some kind of conflict in the background: as Sanja, a thirty-two-year-old respondent described, as soon as one conflict ended, another started. It was perhaps those generations whose lives have been most impeded by the 1990s conflicts and the NATO air strikes. In addition to the economic crisis, Serbia's younger generations grew up in almost complete isolation from the world during the conflicts, only to find that afterwards things did not improve. The changes after the fall of Milošević caused more problems for the young, who now found it impossible to find jobs, afford apartments and live independently. They are, on the whole, very resentful that their parents' generation and 'Milošević voters' left them such a legacy, and their resentment often showed through their critical and often cynical view of present-day politics and the 1990s.

Above, I illustrated how silences can be created, and how such silences and rumours may perpetuate further silences, not because of what is *not* known, but because of what *is* known. This challenges the dominant view of what the process of 'coming to terms' with the past might entail.

In their assessment that the process of confronting the past has not yet begun in the Western Balkans, Petritsch and Džihić point out that that is so because the 'societies are still waiting for a fresh beginning, an impetus that Spain received when it was accepted into the European integration process' (Petritsch and Džihić 2010:20). But this may not work in such a linear fashion. Thinking, assessing and re-assessing the past does not wait, and is not always or only dependent on external stimuli. Serbia, at the time that this research was carried out, did not have what might be viewed as such a break or fresh beginning, since Mladić and Karadžić were still at large, and SAA talks with the EU had been suspended. However, some thinking about or assessing the past had been going on in these narratives. The respondents demonstrate that they think about it, they react, they look for appropriate language, they circulate some stories and do not circulate others. These private reflections, and the existence of some hidden knowledge about the wars, and more specifically atrocities, demonstrate that many are aware of the past, but have great difficulty discussing it, often because it is too painful or disturbing, or at times too close to home.

This places the aims of transitional justice at odds with the ways in which some individuals actually approach and deal with the past. If 'confrontation' is understood broadly, then the above accounts can also be understood as attempts to confront the past. Some accounts above are clear in that they regret what happened, and implicitly sympathise with the victims but there are other phenomena, such as attempts at finding the right language to speak about atrocities, or finding the right metaphors. In Chapter Two I outlined how the idea of confronting the past has taken on positive values – that there is a confrontation because we can see regret and apology being expressed, for instance – but that we could equally think of confrontation in a more 'negative' sense, in which strategies such as silence or evasion could indicate multiple confrontations, processes of negotiation and navigation through vast amounts of disturbing knowledge, information and images. As such, they give rise to other narrative tools and frameworks – such as denial, acknowledgement, victimhood and conspiracy – which are further attempts at negotiating meanings and crucially, making sense of what happened.

CHAPTER 6

'I TRY NOT TO THINK ABOUT IT BECAUSE IT IS FAR TOO HORRIFIC': DENIAL, ACKNOWLEDGEMENT AND DISTANCING

Introduction

In the previous chapter, I demonstrated that narratives about the conflicts, as well as respondents' relationships with formal and informal knowledge produced about that period, are not straightforward, nor static. This chapter picks up those narratives again and zooms in on the specific issues of war crimes. In particular, this chapter unpacks some of the issues related to *denial* of war crimes, especially since denial of these issues is seen as a persistent problem in Serbian society (Ramet 2007; Fridman 2011), and as a key indicator that Serbia has failed to confront the past.

Official denial of war crimes has long been a noted problem for both Serbia and Republika Srpska.[1] In addition to this, a number of independent thinkers, quasi-academics and public figures regularly engage in activities aimed at denying, relativising or minimising war crimes as well as raising questions about the facts relating to well established facts and known events such as the Srebrenica genocide. This occurred across the pages of mainstream daily *Politika* throughout 2006, for instance, as well as tabloids such as *Večernje Novosti* and *Glas Javnosti*.[2]

The presence of denial discourses in Serbian political culture has often been extrapolated to 'society'. For instance, a statement about such denial in Serbian political culture also claims that 'Serbia shows all the signs of a neurotic, even psychotic society' and that 'just as a neurotic individual may not be able to confront certain facts about his own past, so too with a society, its own misdeeds constitute a subject to be avoided' (Ramet 2007:53–54). Likewise, discussing the importance of anti-war activism in 'combating denial' and silence in Serbia, a note is made of 'a reality in which the entire society may *slip* into collective modes of denial' (Fridman 2011:509, added emphasis).

In another landmark study, a similar problem emerges. An often-cited work interviews a number of Serbian activists, journalists and intellectuals and discusses to what extent the work of the ICTY has 'shrunk the space' for denial (Orentlicher 2007). The work conveys the sentiments of Jadranka Jelinčić, Executive Director of The Fund for an Open Society – Serbia, that knowledge produced by the ICTY's work ' "doesn't necessarily make people regret" crimes they can no longer credibly deny' (Orentlicher 2007:22).

At an individual level, denial of atrocities does exist. But it does not exist in a consistent, easily recognisable or coherent way, which makes the entire society, or even half of it, uniformly in denial. The problem with the interpretation is this: when war crimes and atrocities are *not* addressed by audiences, societies or speakers, the assumed correlation is that they do not know about it or refuse to acknowledge it. Silence and denial are seen as part and parcel of each other, and are often seen evidence of a failure of confrontation. This correlation assumes only two binary options (where 'to speak' = 'to acknowledge, to regret' and 'not to speak' = 'to deny'). Looking for denial, in the absence of explicit acknowledgement as the *only* discursive possibility and the only way of confronting the past, is far too simplistic because narrative devices such as denial do not exist in isolation from other discourses. For instance, as will be discussed below, denial frequently coexists with acknowledgement of atrocities. Moreover, there is a range of themes which appear across narratives: some respondents deny that certain things happened (though this was a rare occurrence); whilst some deny that war criminals should face trial at the ICTY (but agree that they should face trial at home). Others deny nothing but do have a difficult time expressing their regret. Where denial is present, it masks a complex ethnographic reality.[3] In current approaches, however, the idea and concept of denial are used to oversimplify issues; people deny because they choose to, or because they support particular political narratives (see Orentlicher 2007). This, however, does not even begin to cover the kinds of issues that denial actually refracts – as this chapter will go on to explore, denial discourses are an intersection of a large number of problems, such as personal loss, trauma, inability to talk, a wish to distance oneself from atrocities and a general inability to comprehend the scale of the brutalities which occurred. Overall, expressions of denial form a relatively small part of narratives presented here.

This chapter aims to expand the 'denial debate' and to point out that denial is much more complex and slippery than is currently presented and that a more involved consideration of it can reveal opportunities for transitional justice projects.

Denial: a discourse, rather than a symptom

To understand denial in Serbia, authors often draw on literature from psychology and behavioural sciences, which is used in order to conceptualise denial as a social, cultural or political phenomenon (e.g. Ramet 2007). Psychology uses studies of moral disengagement and moral rationalisation and cognitive dissonance (see e.g., Tsang 2002, Bandura 1999, Bandura et al. 2001, Bersoff 1999, Simon et al. 1995) to explain how humans restructure inhuman behaviour to make it appear acceptable (Bandura 1999:193).

Cohen, on the other hand, goes a step further and discusses denial responses to atrocities committed by others. In the social sciences, van Dijk (1992) and Cohen (2001) conceptualise denial as anything that is not a direct acknowledgement. Elsewhere, Wittlinger (2006:66) has phrased this as anything but 'a clear and unambiguous acknowledgement.' Therefore, denial is extremely broad (Cohen 2001): it can include anything from blame attribution to minimising the number of victims or the 'turning of a blind eye' (see Cohen 2001). Frequently, denial is *interpretative* (Cohen 2001), where it is used as a form of *explanation* ('it took place, but with fewer victims'), rather than categorical ('no, that event never took place') (see Cohen 2001). Following van Dijk (1992), 'language users' who pursue denial strategies are well aware that the statement they are attempting to deny is outside of social norms (van Dijk 1992:89). Since what is actually unknown cannot be *interpretatively* denied at the same time (see Cohen 2001), denial seems to be employed mainly as a *mediation* strategy (van Dijk 1992:97).

Thus denial, can be employed for a number of different effects and strategies. This is another aspect not captured by attitude-measuring surveys discussed in Chapter 2. For instance, Cohen suggests that we should consider what is being denied (*knowledge* of a crime? The crime itself? Its significance?); how it is being denied; by whom, and to what purposes (Cohen 2001). He identifies denial strategies amongst perpetrators, victims and bystanders. All groups can use the same mechanisms of denial such as justification, minimisation and rationalisation. According to van Dijk (1992) denial theory claims to understand not the structural causes of the behaviour ('the reasons'), but the *accounts* typically given by deviants themselves ('*their reasons*', added emphasis). It is concerned less with literal denial than with interpretations or implications, especially attempted evasions of judgement (Cohen 2001:58).

Understanding denial in its narrative, *account* form is of significance, since moving away from the current medicalised and psychologised view of denial as a cognitive block can yield a much richer analysis of the *accounts* provided by respondents. Thus 'accounts of denial are not mysterious internal states, but typical vocabularies with clear functions in particular social situations' (Seu 2010:442).

'Victims' in a 'made up scenario': contradictions, denial and acknowledgement

In the narratives collected here, there is no such a thing as a purely or exclusively 'denialist' account of atrocities. In the same way, there is no respondent who could be labelled as being completely 'in denial'.

Denial as a discursive device is, first, not always clear nor explicit, and secondly is dispersed through narratives, existing in complicated forms. It is often contradictory, or used to make contradictory statements and moreover, often co-exists with expressions of acknowledgement and regret. Denial, as I outlined earlier, is not a sealed discourse, but is highly permeable. In this, it has something in common with other kinds of speech, which often contain a number of voices and perspectives on the same issue (Smith 2004).

This is also why it is difficult to single out denial and analyse it outside of the narrative context in which it forms, especially when it addresses the question of atrocities such as the Srebrenica genocide. On top of the complexity and 'muddiness' of accounts of the 1990s presented in the previous chapter, accounts dealing with war crimes have an added layer of complication in that questions about war crimes and atrocities such as Srebrenica would act as gateways. Questions about war crimes would prompt long and complicated responses, which were not just about war crimes but might include everything from the atrocity in question to soldiers, conscripts, personal feelings, and politics.

Many respondents attempted to distance themselves from some answers which they gave, by narrating opinions and events in the third person or through using euphemisms and 'discursive black holes' (Jansen 2002:85). Respondents often narrated their accounts as 'appointed spokesperson' for their imagined group (see Jansen 2002). Distancing oneself from such events also allows for a different kind of narration; depersonalising allows war crimes either to disappear from the narrative or to be replaced by euphemisms, or the gaps which occurred where references to war crimes should have been were filled with other ideas. Thus, curiously, the 'gateway' question gives way to a narrative that is reflexive, yet is at the same time filled with evasions. Similarly, in his consideration of post-war German narratives about the war, Hughes finds that 'simply ignoring vast stretches of the past leaves an unstable vacuum' where 'the war damaged instead passed silently over inconvenient facts' (Hughes 2000:193); a vacuum which can be filled with implied or assumed shared meanings. But ignoring 'inconvenient facts' such as deaths or talking about the dead gives rise to a different dynamic, in which rather a lot and not very much is said at the same time. The extract below, in which the respondent discusses what she knew about the Srebrenica massacre, illustrates this very well:

> About Srebrenica, only later the real truth came out. But, an ordinary person would say, it is war, it happens, murders happen on one and the other side. I don't know why it was necessary, to me, I mean, me personally, I wouldn't hurt a fly, so that to me was completely sick, that kind of reasoning – to commit those murders on purpose. Alright, it is war, killings are on one side and on the other, but for it to be so organised, that to me is just beyond sanity. But, apparently, that's now the truth, that's how it's presented to the public. I always accept things like that with some reserve, there is always something hiding behind it, I am reserved, I don't give it too much importance, I mean, it's important, but how true is it? ... There's something that's not logical in that story. The army, and who was in charge. I don't know. I think the politics are confusing people, you know. I remember well when they proposed a confederation, but Milošević refused. He should have accepted, there wouldn't have been a war. Why didn't he? I think that would have been the best solution, now we have lost so much time and in these wars, and for what, so that everyone would have their own state. I don't know. But ... alright. Even that is better than war. Everything is better than war, because that's really, you know ... (Nevena)

Acknowledgement ('the real truth came out') and doubt ('I don't know') about the same event are expressed in close proximity to each other. Likewise, 'it' and 'all those murders' were unnecessary but, 'apparently' now 'it is the truth'. Something is being denied; the 'completely sick' event is still not logical. Ultimately, no conclusion is reached. This kind of response to Srebrenica and other atrocities (although we discussed Srebrenica the most), is the norm, rather than the exception amongst the entire cohort of respondents. A lot was said, but in the end, there is very little that is concrete or definite about any of the responses, and if

I try to classify all the responses and observations on the topic, it is virtually impossible to reach any kind of taxonomic break down. There is no category for 'the group that explicitly acknowledged atrocities', or 'the group that explicitly denied them' because there was some aspect of all those possibilities in virtually all narratives, in a myriad of different combinations.

But, what all narratives had in common was that there were implicit acknowledgements of the atrocity itself, together with different degrees of distancing. As the narrative above flips between implicit acknowledgement and possible denial, it also distances the event from 'normal' behaviour, using the language of illness that I identified earlier in this book. 'To *me*, that is completely sick' signifies a moral distancing too – 'normal people like me' do not do 'those kinds of things'. This moral distancing underpins many of the narratives which shuttle back and forth between acknowledgement and denial.

This tension between the event – which is acknowledged – and the possibility of someone actually having done 'that' (and moreover the discomfort of having to identify that someone) is illustrated in a number of other interviews too. For instance, in the extract below, Mladić and Karadžić are 'evil', but Srebrenica is phrased tentatively towards the end. The contradictory statements are highlighted in bold.

As soon as Karadžić and Mladić turned up in the media, I thought **what they were doing was disgusting**. What they stood for. I never changed my mind. I think Mladić was the much more extreme of the two, I think **he was a lunatic** who did what he wanted, and that's that. And Karadžić was supposedly some kind of an intellectual but I never thought anything of him, from the start I saw he was doing something evil, so it's not like we're supposed to be taking his thoughts seriously. *{Later on, addressing the question of whether there is any discussion of the two figures at the moment amongst his friends}* We still talk about it, which annoys me. People are still re-examining things. Just recently we were talking about how many people died in Srebrenica, and what the reasons were. But I think it is less important to identify those reasons, it is more important just to resolve those questions. **If someone did something there, let's just establish the truth** and let's leave it all behind us as **something incredibly ugly,** and let's not talk about it anymore. But let everyone do that. Let everyone declare their responsibility, and let's be finished with it. (Ivan)

And Filip, one of the younger respondents who spoke very openly about the wars, said the following about Srebrenica, in relation to the YIHR billboard campaign:

Well, we spoke about it [Srebrenica] when those billboards were up, like, I don't know, truth this and that. I mean – all right. Most likely there was all that from all sides and the Croats and everyone. But to me personally it wasn't clear why those billboards – we know that story. They don't have to show us pictures of graves. Those pictures were a bit morbid. I think, quite simply they didn't need to show us that. They could do that in another way. I think in other countries it's not like that. In Croatia and Bosnia. I think so. That is never shown in the same way as it is here. We have to stand behind that, it's done. But still, they didn't have to show it so publicly. If I wanted to find out about that, I would go on the internet. Although I did read some things on the internet and they are mainly foreign materials. They are all very different. They view things very differently. They see all of us Serbs as criminals. So I guess I wouldn't go to those sites. I would go to the library. Our library has all the old newspapers saved. Or I would go to the archive. Foreign websites, I would still look at them. There are all sorts of things there. There are those who say we are a heavenly people and those who say we are criminals. (Filip)

Then, there is the particularly interesting case of Veljko. Throughout the whole interview, and outside of it, he was very critical of Milošević, whom he had always thought 'a fool'. Veljko always implicitly acknowledged that he knew about war crimes and atrocities which occurred in Bosnia (especially through his condemnations of Arkan and others), and he said that he even took part in an spontaneous campaign to publish the truth about war crimes sometime in the 1990s. Yet when I specifically asked him if he knew about Srebrenica and Sarajevo, he replied (contradictory statements are highlighted in bold):

> **I can't say now for sure.** We suspected it, and some people were repeating what some others were gloating about. I apologise but I will say it exactly the way they said it – we screwed them over for all that from the [Second World] war. I took that as something awful, something very dangerous and something which will cost us in the end. Back then you couldn't say in the newspapers what I thought, and then we wrote things and copied them on the copying machine and sent them to each other, **us traitors and foreign mercenaries** [...] and **we will pay. That's what all these trials are about, so that we'd pay.** And now, I ask myself if I could see what would happen to us, **not because of our behaviour**, not because of that, because others made that even worse, but **we were the most responsible** because we really did gloat that **we took part in something inhuman.** (Veljko)

Veljko distances himself from the atrocities by denying (or not admitting) that he campaigned against the regime which implicity or explicitly supports them. He distances 'us' and 'our behaviour' from 'something inhuman' by suggesting that 'those trials' are so that 'we would pay'. All of these narratives contain 'contrasting voice[s]' which offer 'a different perspective on the same past' (Smith 2004:254). First, the multiple perspectives demonstrate that not knowing is not the problem. Rather, it is knowing. It is *because* they know and *what* they know, that there is a problem for respondents – in their view it is just too awful. Inhuman, sick, disgusting are all words that were used. In this way, polyvocality (Smith 2004) can be understood as a way of negotiating sort of a moral maze (c.f. Seu 2010). Atrocities are acknowledged but expressions of doubt at the same time act to distance respondents from the truth – is there really someone who could do something like that?

As outlined at the start of this book, violent events are usually not received uncritically by persons who experience, perpetuate or witness them, but undergo different degrees of mediation or justification in order to be incorporated into an individual's or group's existing beliefs about wars, violence and themselves (Sorabji 1995, Bar-Tal 2003, Daniel 1996, Cohen 2001). Events which lie outside their daily experience, such as wars, act as a 'counterpoint to culture' and require certain strategies of explanation in order to be understood within the parameters of existing cultural beliefs or in order to be incorporated into existing beliefs (Daniel 1994:208, Taussig 1984). These narratives are so contradictory and confused in part because the respondents do not really have any adequate tools for understanding the violations that took place during the wars in Croatia, Bosnia and Kosovo. How does one, after all, make sense of mass murder? How is this reconciled with the 'profound human need for normality' (Matić 2001:79)? This question seems to underscore many of the narratives presented here.

There are also narratives where denial is more explicit – but equally contradictory. For instance Mladen's response is quite confusing. He never supported the wars, but he followed the news closely during the 1990s. When I asked him if he knew about Srebrenica, he replied with contradictory statements, which are highlighted below:

> No, all of that only came out after the Dayton Agreement ... we listened to the news then, but unfortunately, Srebrenica was missed, with **so many victims**. But, all those **revelations** were **probably tailored** after the Dayton Agreement, when most of the blame was apportioned to the Serbs. Up until Dayton it was all somehow in order and that somehow lasted – and then, that sentence was passed on the Serbs, and then **Srebrenicas and whatever camps were being discovered**. Even today I think **that's just a big made-up scenario**. It's impossible that Serbs are so wrong, that they were simply declared as war aggressors ...

> [*Later; in the same interview*]
> **I remember a lot of what I read** in the papers back then. I had the opportunity to hear both sides. Back then, a large proportion

of the news was true even though they were regime newspapers. But **there were a lot of Serb perpetrators**. There always have been. (Mladen)

It would be easy to analyse this as straightforward, textbook categorical denial 'even today I think that's just a big made-up scenario', if it was not for the contradiction: 'Srebrenica was missed, with so many victims.' A similar detail is noted by Scheper-Hughes in an interview with a former apartheid-era South African defence minister, whose narrative is marked with the co-existence of denial and acknowledgement of apartheid era violence (2004b:426). The contradictory nature of denial is also observed by Cohen, who points out that 'denial is neither a matter of telling the truth nor intentionally telling a lie' since 'there seem to be states of mind, or even whole cultures, in which we know and don't know at the same time' (Cohen 2001: 4–5). This feature is not unique to denial. Smith suggests that the presence of contradictory voices demonstrates that memory is a process, an 'on-going and actively constructed set of views on the past, each view engaged by, and reflected back on, the other' (Smith 2004:263). Following Strauss (1990), Smith concludes that contradictory voices are a regular part of 'naturally occurring speech' and that 'multiple representations of the past circulate in the same community [...] because individuals learn and process memories differently and independently and because societies are heterogeneous' (Smith 2004:263). This is crucial – if contradictions form a part of 'naturally occurring speech' then how do we capture this in 'coming to terms with the past', which appears to be looking for singular or homogenous discourses? In normative terms, this is perhaps desirable, but is it actually possible? Given the contradictory discourses on the past, where neither denial nor acceptance/remorse are clearly articulated nor separated, it may be more productive to broaden transitional justice projects in Serbia to take this complexity into account.

Serbs as perpetrators

Going back to the previous contradictory statement about Srebrenica there is an odd addition of 'Serb perpetrator'. In this extract, it appears that denial is focused on perpetrators, specifically Serb perpetrators, rather than the event itself. This motif of denying or distancing perpetrators from the crimes is a common theme across a number of interviews, all which grapple with the idea of possible perpetrators; someone had to have 'done it' (the Serbs? the conscripts? the generals? the volunteers?). And, where 'we' did do something 'inhuman', there is also the question of how it is represented. For instance, this extract connects the question of perpetrators to the broader theme of how 'Serbs' as a group are represented as a result of the crimes committed. As the extract demonstrates, the grievance over what is perceived as overwhelmingly negative representations of Serbs as a group, quickly replaces the discussion of Srebrenica. The extract comes from an interview with Vlado, one of Petar's friends. As a teenager, Vlado was sent away from Belgrade in the 1990s, to live with relatives in France. His extract draws on this experience and highlights how interwoven the themes of denial and representation can be:

> I don't doubt that it is all correct, and I don't doubt that Serbs committed many crimes and everything else. I think that that is just one instance of crime, amongst a whole set of crimes that happened during that war. Of course, that video [Scorpions] was shocking, but the fact that those things actually happened, that didn't surprise me. But what really bothered me was these representations of Serbs that were going around in the West. I do think that it is for certain that members of the Serb nation committed a lot of crime, but it's that one-sided representation that really bothered me … For some time it made me really angry that some facts, which I don't think were completely true, had become the truth in the Croatian and Bosnian media and the Western media too, but in some Serbian [media], had become official truths which can't be disputed. But to me it is not certain that some of those things are completely true yet they had become official … The worst thing is that those stories in the West about the war were really anti-Serbian. It was very obvious. For example, when there was some incident in Bosnia during the war they would

always say in the beginning that Serbs did it, even though it wasn't certain. Or if Croats or Muslims did, but it wasn't certain, they would say the Serbs did. And then days later they'd print a tiny article with a correction to say it was the Muslims. I was not indifferent to that. I lived in a place where I had friends and teachers in school coming up all the time to me and saying, how do you feel? Do you support that? How do you feel that you are a Serb, and Serbs are doing all those things? It was really unpleasant. Many times I was made to feel really uncomfortable by normal, ordinary people just because of my nationality.

The following response came from Ivan, when I asked him about whether he had heard about Srebrenica and Sarajevo. They are presented both as 'crimes' and as something not believed:

I heard about that. Srebrenica a bit more recently. I don't know, you know ... When I heard about those crimes, I have to admit, I didn't believe them. It's somehow, you know, it was somehow, some kind of an instinct that I just could not believe that, that some member of some nation would do something like that. I really don't know why. All the people of a similar group will defend in the most brutal way those things which they believe in. When I think about it a bit more, that first impression that I had, I think that still persists, I still look at it all with disbelief, even though there is a lot of evidence for it, and most likely, it is the truth, most likely, but I try not to think about it, because it is far too horrific, even though we did it. I mean, we and all other nations ... But it's interesting. You always feel some kind of doubt. This strange history of our people has taught me that I have no idea what to believe. Was it all propaganda or – ? But my own personal feeling is that, my personal feeling is that I am horrified. Not horrified that someone from my nation did something like that, but horrified that a man did something like that. But where doubt is concerned, there is doubt but then again those facts, where do they come from. I don't know. Everything that we've listened to all these years, and there was a lot of covering up of information. I don't know if the situation is better today – is probably is – but media. Back in those days we had only one television [channel]. But my view [*stops*]. (Ivan)

Then, there is also Ana's response, to the question on Srebrenica:

In the beginning I believed that they were telling the truth. However, now the story is completely different. It is said that those TV stations had a conspiratorial role against the Serbs and Serbia, especially when the world's opinion was against Serbs as a genocidal people. That was the one thing I could not accept, that Serbs are a genocidal people and I will never accept that. I ask myself, when I watch the news, they say Serbs killed 8,000 [in Srebrenica] and sometimes they say 7,000 ... and I can't believe, deep down in my heart I can't believe that they killed 8,000 Muslims. I can't believe that. Serb people are not a genocidal people. (Ana)

Later:

[...] I would really like to know the truth about Srebrenica, because even today one TV station from Mostar, TV Most, had a programme which said something else, but today you just don't know whom to believe. But I just can't believe that any of the Serbian commanders was a criminal, a mass criminal. These things which I keep hearing today, that Markale in Sarajevo was a set up by the Muslims and the Americans, secret supplies of weapons by Americans, and that for example Operation Storm was commanded by the Americans, that they cleared the terrain and then behind them followed the Croats. All this you heard in Belgrade at parties, in bars, in offices. But it was after 5 October that the media really started, that they really started saying Serbs killed everyone, that Serbian people committed that crime. Crimes around Bosnia, that Serb commanders committed them ... At one time I trusted the foreign media like CNN, I believed in the beginning that they were telling the truth. However, now they are saying a completely different thing, it is being said that those same TV stations actually had a conspiratorial role against the Serbs and Serbia, especially when there was a huge shift in global public opinion against Serbs, the Serbs as a genocidal people. I couldn't accept that, that Serbs are a genocidal people, I couldn't accept that, and I don't accept that now, I will never accept that the Serbs are a genocidal people. (Ana)

These extracts are examples of narratives in which acknowledgement of atrocities and doubt coexist. Ivan at first did not believe it, but it appears that now he does ('even though we did it'). Then revulsion: 'my own personal feeling is that I am horrified.' Ana on the other hand believed it at first, but then she doubts something – it is not clear whether she believes it did not happen but rather that the Serbs are not a 'genocidal people'. But, if acknowledgement is implied, or buried under layers of questions, what is it that allows doubt (or denial) to exist?

Here, ethnicity plays an interesting role. In many of the extracts presented so far, victims and those who suffered, are often unnamed, or are 'those poor people' or 'ordinary people' who got caught up in the wars. Everyone is a victim, and victims are rarely ethnically framed, despite such a strong polarisation of the conflicts of the 1990s along ethnic lines.

As Ana and Ivan illustrate, the most difficult things to believe about Srebrenica were those aspects which challenged the fundamental beliefs about the war and about the group to which they see themselves as belonging. Ana not only says 'Serb people are not a genocidal people' but also adds that 'I just can't believe that any of the Serbian commanders was a criminal, a mass criminal.' Rada pointed out something similar: that various criminals and wartime 'degenerates' claimed to have acted in the name of 'Serbianness', but 'without knowing what this word really means'. Thus ethnicity is closely related to particular moral values and acceptable forms of behaviour. This can also be observed in the frequent absence of 'ethnicisation' of any of the indicted or convicted war criminals, and the explicit and determined separation of the war volunteers from 'Serbianness' and their subsequent compartamentalisation as 'the lunatics' and 'the sick'.[4] This illustrates that, in denial, there is an element of 'moral accounting' (Seu 2010:442), where 'a denial account does not simply give a plausible, acceptable story about an action (e.g. "this is what I do"), but also crucially provides moral accountability for the speaker ("this is why what I do is alright")' (Seu 2010:442). Here is another account which attempted a rationalisation, a broad denial, of Serb-committed atrocities:

> Q: *What did you know or hear about war crimes from '91 to '95, Srebrenica, for example, or Sarajevo?*
>
> A: Well, look, it's really difficult to be objective in those situations, especially if you are aware of the background, and then you know that you, watching all of that, then listening to those people who were over there fighting then coming here, whether that was Croatia or Bosnia, when you listen to all that, when you listen to the ways in which the Serbs were fighting the war, the ways in which the Bosniaks fought the war, then you see that some things aren't all that, they [the Muslims] are fighting the way they are fighting. Serbs, regardless of how they fought before then you hear from one side that the Muslims with their attacks are going for Ozren, then for Sarajevo, and all that time they first let the children go, then women, then old Muslims, then the unarmed, and then, only after them come the armed Muslims, and all this happened as they went into frontline attacks. However, it happened, for the first time, I have to say, that Serb soldiers killed children (Rada).

The answer is from the start an attempt to negotiate and rationalise, because Rada never actually answered my question about what she knew or heard. The response is defensive and justifying ('it's really difficult to be objective in those situations') for something which is implied but never articulated. The first seven lines do not actually state anything; we do not know what she is trying to say until halfway through the response. This shocking concession suddenly makes clear why the build-up was so defensive and pre-empted with a justification that 'it is really difficult to be objective in those situations'. Objectivity, in this case, does not only apply to the person hearing this kind of information in 1990s Serbia, but also to the Serb soldiers on the front.

This extract also addresses another important point, which lies in the subtext of this rationalisation – more often than not, individuals do not want to be associated with people who might have committed horrific crimes, and certainly nobody wants to be seen as the perpetrator. Evidence of war crimes undermined what most people believed about their groups – Serbs, but also neighbours, friends, people who went to fight. This also challenged their ideas about morality, especially when contrasted with their own belief ('I wouldn't do that, so what kind of person would?') they unmade worlds, 'both real and conceptual' (Nordstrom 1995: 131). In a way, distancing 'the Serbs' from the atrocities is also a way of distancing oneself, as seen in the frequent reiterations of morality and moral boundaries, throughout the narratives.

Denial in this case can be understood as a strategy of defence (van Dijk 1992; Seu 2010) which may be pre-emptive or which may presuppose 'implicit or explicit accusations' (van Dijk 1992: 91; Seu 2010:441). For instance, in research on denial in responses to humanitarian campaigns by Amnesty International, Seu, drawing on van Dijk (1992), suggests that respondents display an 'awareness of a normative moral imperative – they *ought* to be responding ... thus confirming that denial statements are part of a defence strategy, presupposing implicit or explicit accusations.'

Here, denial as a defensive strategy works as a distancing factor; an attempt to distance the speaker and their ethnic group from the perpetrators who could have committed such atrocities. Monroe (2008:722) argues that individuals do not 'consciously' define themselves as 'evil-doers'; and this is the undercurrent of using denial to attempt a positive self/group-representation. After all, if the event itself is not denied, someone must have 'pulled the trigger', and nobody wishes to think it could have been them – or someone just like them, a Serb or a family member.

Denying and acknowledging responsibility of 'the generals', the conscripts and 'the lunatics'

The question of perpetrators hangs over all knowledge of atrocities. ('I am horrified that a man did that'; 'I can't believe a Serb would do that') Atrocities, horrors and murder are all implicit in many of the narratives presented thus far. But atrocities have perpetrators, and, as the previous section highlighted, the Serb perpetrator is distanced, and often, the respondent's own moral boundaries are emphasised. Thus responsibility for atrocities was denied, in reference to certain individuals but less so for others.

This was especially evident for a group which came to be known amongst the responents, as 'the Generals', and included figures such as Ratko Mladić and Radovan Karadžić (the latter, of course, was not a general but was frequently placed in the same category as Mladić). The position towards them is ambivalent; they are neither heroes nor villains. The failure of Serbia to hand over Ratko Mladić and Radovan Karadžić to the war crimes tribunal in The Hague (until 2011 and 2008, respectively) can be seen as a spectacular failure of Serbia's judicial and political systems in its efforts to address the past by cooperating with the ICTY. Following on from this, Anastasijević notes that an interpretation of this problem – the failure to hand over Mladić in a timely manner, is frequently seen in the following light:

> [The] Serbs have failed to face the demons of their recent past, and are now doomed to repeat it. By failing to arrest and prosecute war crimes suspects such as General Ratko Mladić and by refusing to show proper respect for the victims of the Srebrenica genocide, so the argument goes, Serbs have sacrificed their future for the sake of nationalistic myths of the past. (Anastasijević 2008)

Similarly, writing in *The Guardian* following the arrest of Ratko Mladić in 2011, Misha Glenny writes that this may finally lead to 'Serbia's moral rehabilitation' (Glenny 2011). There is often an assumption that the absence of Mladić and Karadžić from the ICTY had also led to some kind of valorisation of these men, by the Serbian society.

But perceptions of indicted and convicted war criminals are rather more ambiguous in the interviews presented here. Most of the time there is much indifference towards people like Mladić and Karadžić, and certainly not much sympathy. As the extracts below illustrate, phrases which indicate uncertainty ('I guess', 'I am undecided') are used frequently. Moreover, they are frequently understood in the context of what is perceived to be unfair treatment of Serbs:

> I don't think they are heroes. I think differently about Mladić than Karadžić. Karadžić was a political leader and so he deserves much harsher punishment. Let's remember Sarajevo, those films that CNN made and that Karadžić used for his own political promotion. I remember those films went around the world, and I think they did a great disservice to our people. That was all political promotion and I strongly condemn him ... But for Mladić, I don't know what he did. Here we have the least information. I still think he was a soldier, and a soldier acts according to political orders. Only in that context can I find some explanation. On the other hand, I think if that tribunal has been set up, if there are already sanctions against this country and our people here, then if he is a hero, he should turn up over there. And he should tell us – why? Tell us, this is what I did. The question is, did he do everything he is accused of? I don't even know the indictment. Just genocide, genocide, genocide. Is it really genocide or a different story? ... I don't know. They always mention Srebrenica. But they don't say exactly what Mladić did, or what others did. (Branka)

I don't think they are heroes, but I don't think they are criminals either. I mean, what was done was done. That one, what's his name, Karadžić, he's probably more guilty than Mladić because he was a statesman. I think he – Karadžić. Much more guilty than Mladić because he was a politician and the other one was a soldier who carried out those political orders. But still, I am sure that they probably did commit all those crimes against the Muslims and Croats, and if they really did and if there is evidence then they have to be prosecuted. But also, I think that just like they have to answer for what they did, then so do the Muslims and the Croats – everyone has to answer for what they did and there is no excuse there. But what really bugs me is spite,[5] like that spite that they have because they have taken more Serbs to The Hague than Croats and Muslims put together. We are not the only ones guilty. Everyone is guilty in equal measure. Everyone was killing. And Muslims, they even had the mujahedeen. They quite simply are not heroes. Mladić and Karadžić can't be heroes but on the other hand I don't see them as huge criminals either. (Filip)

This is really complicated, about those two and what we did. War criminals or national heroes, that's how they are presented. Now, from which view to look at it? The winner writes history. And then, what are exactly their misdeeds, as opposed to their good deeds? To be honest, I am undecided. They as generals, I guess, they had a duty, Mladić I mean. Karadžić is a different story. But I think this huge hunt for him, and now they are affecting the prosperity of our country without actually doing anything. That's a bit – I can't stand that kind of blackmail. That means, give us Mladić and we will give you 100 million dollars. That's just funny. I think every Serb feels that they personally are being judged. (Ivan)

I think, I am convinced that they [Mladić and Karadžić] should not go to The Hague. First because Mladić was an officer and listened to orders, he was in charge of an army and his orders had to come from somewhere ... They keep saying that when NATO bombarded us, they were just following orders, so in the same way Mladić must have been following orders ... Pavković and Lazarević[6] were officers. (Katarina)

Much more explicit and straightforward condemnations, such as the one below, were not as frequent; and, even this extract skirts around the issue of war crimes.

They had their supporters. But, according to command responsibility, Mladić must answer [at the court]. And that neuropsy-
chiatrist – he is mad man. During the whole war, he was often in
Belgrade, and he was even drinking champagne and gambling.
In the casino. That was during the war – he was getting drunk
in the most expensive places in Belgrade. They need to be punished. (Nikola)

What emerges most frequently is an undecided position regarding the
roles of indicted war criminals in the atrocities committed. There is a
sense of confusion as to whether 'the generals' did 'it' – commit atrocities; and, a feeling that if they are punished that 'others' – non-Serbs
– ought to be too. They are not glorified and they are not labelled as
heroes, contrary to popular representations of such figures in the 1990s
(see e.g. Čolović 2000). The only exception was when Miroslav found
his son wearing a Mladić T-shirt, but in this case it seems that his son
had no idea who Mladić was.

What might explain such ambiguous views, and especially such
intersections of denial and acknowledgement? First, they are viewed
from the vantage point that no one really understands, what exactly
happened in the wars. Secondly, other dynamics confuse the moral
positioning of respondents towards these figures: the perception that
not enough other groups' soldiers and leaders are on trial.

But why are they distanced from the crimes which are implicitly
acknowledged? What sheds light on this dynamic is the relationship
that many respondents had or still have, with the army as an institution and an idea. For instance, Gordana calls Pavković an officer who
'they say was like a father to our soldiers'. Mladić in particular is frequently cited as a military man, a general. Many of the respondents
have had or still have direct or indirect involvement with the military. All the older male respondents had served in the Yugoslav army
as conscripts. A number even have fond memories of this time. Then
there are the respondents who narrowly escaped conscription (Mladen,
Miroslav, Nevena's husband, Mirjana's son, Mara's son-in-law), those
who did not (Petar, Ivan's cousin and friend, Rada's close friend), those
who had worked close to the military (Jovan; Gordana's grandfather

was an army officer). Thus the army was close to many, and certainly reflecting on one's draft, or the sheer luck of escaping it, must have sat uncomfortably next to the indictments of other 'military men' such as Mladić. Miroslav illustrated this convergence well – he was horrified by the war (it was a 'cataclysm') and by the knowledge that he may have had to go and fight 'for someone else's ideas'. And, as Mladen stated once, 'What if I had gone [to war]? Maybe I would also have to face trial.' Similarly, in a study of German post-war family memory, Welzer et al. (2002) find that 'German victimhood by far outweighs German culpability in family memory' (Wittlinger 2006:74). Furthermore, the authors conclude that 'whoever committed the crimes in the war of extermination ... one thing seems to be clear ... Granddad was no Nazi!' (Welzer et al. 2002:284 in Wittlinger 2006:74). Criminals are thus distanced from one's own immediate surroundings, as the truth sits too closely to home, with its close relations to the military.

The military trope is complicated further through frequent invocations of young people, children and specifically 'damaged youth', all often cited as a main source of worry for the older generations. This was both specific and conceptual – respondents worry about their own children and their schooling, upbringing and so on, as well as projecting this onto a more general anxiety about young people damaged by war. This appears to have been exacerbated after the experience of the 1990s and the NATO air strikes in particular, as older respondents frequently mention physical scars of wars (mutilations, disability, psychological stresses) as embodied by the young. But 'the young' were also conscripts and played a military role. This is the intersection at which the tropes of 'unwilling' and reluctant conscripts and 'damaged youth' converge. This is illustrated by Mirjana's story. Mirjana, whose son was conscripted into the army in the late 1990s as a 19-year old, related the following episode. We had just been discussing the indictments of Mladić and Karadžić when Mirjana's narrative suddenly turned to her son and his swearing-in ceremony, an incident I referred to in Chapter Four, and which Mirjana found to be one of her most formative experiences of the 1990s:

> When my son went to the army, there were parties for three days, you know how it is, and on the fifth day he's off to the army. I was

deeply unhappy, when we turned up at the swearing in ceremony
and when I actually listened to the words, where my son, swears,
together with all the other young men, that he is giving his life over
to his homeland. That he is at their disposal. I just froze. I was in
shock, and didn't know how to go home after that. You know, you
look after someone for nineteen years, for what? So that he would
become cannon fodder in some senseless war? The military is a serious matter, and those people defended me, you and other people on
these territories. If they did something wrong then the Serb people
have to put them on trial ... You know, there are too many ugly
things for one life, and that makes me very unhappy [...]

Can you believe, that for the first time in my life I broke the law,
when my son's friend turned up here one night, he'd been conscripted [to go to Kosovo] and [since he refused to go] the police
were after him day and night, and he was always staying at different
places. He turned up here beside himself. I was confused by my own
behaviour, because I said to him – run away. Youth does not need
to lose its life. Because that was madness. That was not defending
your homeland, that was not, I don't know, what that was, I did not
even know how to call it, what was happening, how to determine
what that was. Young people died. We still don't know how many
of them died. We still do not know how many invalids we have.
I once went to the orthopaedic [ward in the] hospital. And in the
waiting room I saw a few young men, about eighteen-nineteen, and
none of them had a right leg. I thought to myself, why don't they
have legs? Then I realised it was because of the land mines[7] – they
had stepped forward, with the right leg. We don't know how many
people like that we have. Not just like them, but many many young
people who are invalids. We still don't know and I will never live to
know that. The truth will one day be available, but it will be a tragic
revelation for those who live to see it. Everything that is happening
here on our territories and with our people is shameful.

Mirjana's view is that Mladić and Karadžić are – predictably – not
heroes, but neither are they criminals, even though she is 'horrified'

by what happened in Bosnia, so much so that she broke the law by hiding a runaway 'draft-dodger' later. Denying the responsibility of Mladić in particular, in this way acts to further distance oneself and loved ones from the 'horrors' of the battlefield and atrocities. If 'the Serbs' could not have done it, then 'my son' and 'people like my son' (i.e. the military and the conscripts) definitely could not have. An added element of tension is present when those who were drafted and returned traumatised – such as Ivan's cousin – because the possibility of their involvement in an atrocity, a massacre or someone's death, will always be there. These ambiguities about military personnel, familial and close, are often thus reflected through ambiguous discussions about indicted criminals such as Mladić, who, through his role as an officer, is close to the relatives of those who took active part in the wars.

The 'lunatics' and 'losers' who went to war and acknowledgement of atrocities

In attempts to negotiate, deny and distance 'the generals' and the conscripts from atrocities, another dynamic emerges: responsibility is not denied altogether because there is an almost universal agreement that various war volunteers and paramilitaries, not only 'did it' but were crazy and on a murderous rampage. Clear distinctions are made between those who were forced to go to war or try and escape it (the conscripts) and those who chose to go (the volunteers), with 'the generals' suspended ambiguously somewhere in between. When discussions about the volunteers emerge, atrocities are not only acknowledged – both implicitly and explicitly – but are assigned to perpetrators, with names, and without any redeeming features or morals.

In Chapter Two, I discussed how metaphors of illness and disease are used to describe the 1990s. Similar language is often used to describe certain 'deviants'; war volunteers and paramilitaries, to whom atrocities are attributed in instances that they are acknowledged. As with most themes raised by the respondents, the question of the 'lunatics' who went to war is also contradictory. It acknowledges that atrocities occurred, but also denies that anyone 'normal' could have committed them; it had to be someone who was 'insane'. This is yet another case of what everyone 'knows', pitted against what no one wants to have ever heard or known. The case of the volunteers is possibly one of the aspects of the 1990s that is kept quiet the most.

In the previous chapter, I discussed how people such as former soldiers conveyed certain kinds of knowledge, mostly disturbing, and directly related to atrocities, or what later became known as such. But, often, all discussion of those men is avoided. Why does no one want to talk about the volunteers who went to war, given that for a few respondents they are quite proximate and are in some cases relatives and neighbours? Stories of those who transgressed the moral codes, for example, Branka's acquaintances whom she reluctantly admitted had volunteered for the war, were excluded. Branka's story never went beyond that singular admittance, and Ana's was similar: '[a friend]'s husband, he just went one day, and then he came back' (though she elaborated on this much later). Nevena, for example, could not bring herself to tell me the stories and rumours of murders she heard during the war, and asked her husband to tell me instead. Ilija, her husband, resumed the story one day. The bar which he managed in the 1990s was, in his account, a place where dubious characters spent much time. He recalled that after drinking heavily, they would 'show off':

> What they did in this and that village, how they knew Arkan. In the clubs where I worked [Belgrade nightclubs] everyone knew everyone else and people were always talking. Stories always going around, men talking about Knin, Bosnia, to show that they were important. No one really paid much attention to them.

He recalled stories of murders that had allegedly been admitted, before adding that no one ever thought of this as a war crime, because 'war crimes did not exist then'. Existence of war volunteers and their activities was frequently hinted at, if not always explicitly articulated. For instance, Jovan broached the subject by mentioning the following:

> I didn't take part in war. That's not just me defending myself, but I really did not. No one from my close friends took part

either. There were some stories – also not from my building, and we have fifty people living here. For other apartment blocks, I can't say, because over there there were some different things.

Jovan does not mention what 'some stories' were about nor what 'some different things' were in other apartment blocks. Even though almost all of the older respondents wished to downplay their acquaintances with war volunteers or conscripts, or stories heard from the front, it turned out that this group was a key source of (often compromising) news and crimes. For example Bojan, who was seventeen in 1991, said:

I knew some reservists who went to war [voluntarily]. When they came back they were talking about everything. And I took the effort to find out as much as I could, to learn what was going on because I didn't believe there could only be one side in that war [one side as represented by Serbian media] where Serbs were only the victims. That was such a fairytale. (Bojan)

Biljana also added to this in relation to the Kosovo conflict. A number of her older friends and friends of friends had been drafted for duty in Kosovo. She mentioned that 'guys who went there, they came back and said what was happening, and there was no doubt what was happening to Šiptars. It was literally [ethnic] cleansing'. The subtext, of course is: how did they know? What did they see? Did they take part? Ana's daughter mentioned at the time of the interview one of the volunteers her mother had known.

I was seven so I don't really remember much. But my friend's dad went to war, and then he went to war also in Kosovo. My dad was there [in Bosnia] but he wasn't fighting he was filming something for the army. One of our cousins also went to war, he was killed. But I don't know by whom. Was it the Croats or the Serbs, or in Bosnia, I don't know, but it was right at the end, and he went as a volunteer. Yeah, most people that I heard of who went, went as volunteers. One day, another friend, her dad volunteered the first day of the war [in Croatia] and then the same also

for Bosnia because he was [a Serb] from there ... You know, those
who returned they hardly talk about war. Like this friend of mine,
when I am at her house, if someone opens the door suddenly her
dad jumps. I guess they don't talk in front of him about the war
because it might stress him out. There is another friend, he says,
one day out of the blue, his dad got up and left for the war, and
they didn't know anything until he came back. He went to fight.
He and his friend who lives nearby just left. All these people are
from Belgrade. (Iva)

Ana, who confirmed some of the stories later, spoke with less ambi-
giuity about murder carried out by one such volunteer than she did
elsewhere about atrocities:

[*When I asked about the Scorpions video*] That was horrifying. I'm
sure it is, that is horrific and it's always on the TV, the murder of
those seven young Muslim men. But seven is not eight or seven
thousand. But I heard from a man who took part in fighting as a
volunteer on the Serb side, he said they found a dead child inside
an oven. He said when he saw that it all went dark in front of his
eyes and after that, he did not care whom he killed. If you see a
dead child, how else would you react? So that means there were
horrifying things on one and the other side. That man lives in
Novi Sad now, and before in Tito's time he was in jail for nationalism ... As a student he was saying how Muslim nationalism,
faith-based, existed. I don't know if it existed, I never felt that.
Just before the war he went to Bosnia and then he volunteered.
When he talked about what kinds of horrors he saw, and he said,
I didn't know whom I killed or how, when that happens you just
go, you see that and you go and destroy, you have that feeling.
(Ana)

Other respondents, in speaking about the volunteers and parami-li-
taries, were equally as explicit and unequivocal in stating that what
they had done was wrong:

A: Most people went there to kill and steal, not to fight a war. From all sides.

Q. Who did, the army?

No, not the army. Not the JNA either. No, not them. Those other ones, the political parties who had a private army. It was mainly them who did. (Danica)

I don't understand when they say someone is guilty because of their command responsibility. Command responsibility. How is someone going to stand up in court and be judged on that? He would have had to answer to the command of his officer or he would be killed. It's a different thing when you are rounding up civilians and killing them and in great numbers. But a soldier killing a soldier that's different. But this, those paramiltaries that went all over Bosnia. Arkan's group, all they did was murder and rape. (Gordana)

Why, if all of these issues seemed to be well known, is there such a reluctance to discuss them? In a discussion of the Sri Lankan conflict, Perera points out that 'one of the fundamental features of post-terror societies is the reality of having to live with torturers and murderers' (Perera 2001:190). Furthermore, in such societies 'many people may be destined to live ambivalently with their tormentors for the rest of their lives' (Perera 2001:191). Some of the respondents in this study had to cope with similar knowledge; clearly, some acquaintances, co-workers, friends and relatives had been transformed from the ordinary and into combatants. This had to be understood together with the possibility that they may have, in the course of that transformation, become murderers, rapists or looters. Living with ambivalence which Perera describes, often meant not knowing for certain whether a particular acquaintance had engaged in such activities, and living, at the same time with a general knowledge and almost certainty that those who went to the conflicts in Bosnia, Croatia and Kosovo voluntarily, *had* somehow transgressed social norms and moral values. This is reinforced by the large numbers of men attempting to escape conscription (see Miličević 2006) to avoid such transgressions, and later, trials and confessions for various paramilitary units which confirmed those suspicions.

Thus, given the circumstances of the conflicts, many respondents here had come to the conclusion that those who fought voluntarily had to be 'mad' or 'sick' in order to do so; in fact, they did not just fight, but *killed* and *murdered*, as Ana said above. This kind of labelling is often used to reinforce the distance of such 'types' from 'the normal people' who would not do such a thing. For instance, Branka had informed me that she had known several men who had volunteered for the war in Bosnia. When I asked if they were her friends or family, she said, 'Friends. Well, not really. Acquaintances. Not even that, business contacts,' before going on to suggest that they had always been 'the suspect types' anyway. Miroslav and Slavko too were particularly aggrieved that the war, and war crimes, occurred 'in that way', because they knew 'the kinds of people' who volunteered for paramilitary services:

> I knew what kind of people went to war. I could have never taken a gun to kill a man for someone else's ideas, even if I had received a mobilisation notice. Look, my daughter is called Ana, and my friend in Croatia had a daughter Ana. So I am supposed to stand in the trenches and point the gun at him? We are the same, what would be the point? My daughter would have been scared if I went to war, and my friend's daughter would have also been scared for her dad and I am supposed to shoot him? To me that is just inconceivable ... Most men that I know, who went, went because they were forced to. A few went voluntarily. That was not a surprise because they were on the margins of this society. These men who went to war ... they are all basically bloodthirsty degenerates. I knew them, from certain circles in Belgrade – all losers. The kind that never did well at school, never did well at work, failed relationships. So, he thinks, now I'll take a gun to prove myself! ... When I hear that someone threw a bomb over there in Kosovo, I stop and think, what kind of frame of mind is

that man in? That he can take a bomb and throw it at a house? That's just totally unnecessary. (Miroslav)

The dark shadow over all those wars, starting with Slovenia right up to Kosovo, were people who even in peacetime sit in cafés and occupy themselves with crime and stealing. This was an exceptional opportunity for them, and they jumped right in. I am speaking above all about Arkan, but not just him, but the whole gang of criminals. Those who would just decide by themselves to go to some village, which was protected, let's say. It was a well-known fact that during the whole of those wars, people tried to protect their villages and even protect people of other ethnicities, but then you'd get five fools with guns, who'd enter the village in some military vehicle and just kill everyone. And then, they'd say, who did that? Serbs. Then the other side seeks revenge. Then Serbs seek revenge. And then all over again. And it was the same in Kosovo. Because most of the crimes committed there were exactly because of those kinds of people. There is the testimony of this one Albanian, who managed to get through to the end of the war. He used to be an officer in the Yugoslav army ... He said, there was a massive crime carried out in Djakovica,[9] over eighty people were killed. He said the people who did that just sat around all day drinking. At night they go to an Albanian neighbourhood, kill everyone, steal everything, put it in a truck and carry on to the next place. (Slavko)

In addition to the distancing already described, in Miroslav's extract there are also added elements, and so the deviants are distanced through education, failed relationships and generally the kinds of things that are deemed to make one successful; all bound up with discourses of masculinity (where the 'real' and successful men from his circle went to war because they were forced to). The rumours, stories and existence of paramilitary volunteers negated most of the ideas that were commonly held about the war, and especially contrary to how these actors were presented in the Serbian media and politics. During the early 1990s, even political parties sponsored paramilitary units (for instance Vuk

Drašković's SPO and Vojislav Šešelj's SRS). They were often framed as the modern-day successors of brave and 'holy' warriors like Obilić from the Kosovo epics (see e.g. Čolović 2000, Prodanović 2004). From my respondents' stories and their evasive answers, I gathered that this did not seem to be the case, however, as the volunteers were so over-whelmingly rejected as functioning members of the society, much less seen as 'heroes'. When this perception developed is difficult to say but it would appear that some of the volunteers were 'not a surprise' from the beginning.

This type of criticism was especially directed at Željko Ražnatović Arkan, whom many thought of as vulgar, tacky and hypocritical. Svetozar was the most bitter, saying, 'Arkan goes there and steals things and kills people, then he comes back here and gives thousands and thousands of dinars to build a church!' There were also some very unequivocal condemnations of those who participated:

> Everyone who participated in that war is a criminal. Like this Arkan. I think he was just mixed up in some political game. He didn't go there to liberate Serbia, no, he went there because someone probably offered him some money. I personally wouldn't go there from some kind of desire to just kill people. I wouldn't do it for money. But he was probably someone who could do that. I wouldn't. I feel sorry for a cat if I hit it with the car, I couldn't possibly kill a man. (Filip)

The contradictory stories of paramilitaries, as well as the avoidance of the subject and the negation of their existence, indicate that paramili-taries and other 'unsavoury' characters were also heavily bound up in ideas about morality. Veljko, for instance, had found such boasting distasteful, and both he and Svetozar indicated that 'real' warriors did not behave like that. Stories like this spread quickly amongst circles of friends, and they became the first real 'evidence' that something con-trary to the 'just' and right war of self-defence claimed by the regime.

Given that most respondents had come to know about what later turned out to be criminal behaviour from former volunteers as well as rumours about the same, it is no coincidence that when war crimes *are* acknowledged by respondents, they are attributed to 'a few lunatics, like Arkan' (Biljana) or 'some sick people who went there for money, or were bought by the West' (Rada's daughter, Mina). Feldman refers to this tactic as a process of 'individualising excuses for violence', where it is deemed that immoral behaviour in times of upheaval and conflict is not part of a broader trend or actions of a group, but is rather carried out by a few 'bad apples' (Feldman 2003:69; also Subotić 2011:162). According to Feldman, who cites the example of a South African former general blaming apartheid racism on a few individuals, 'this individualizing perspective obscure(s) any clear understanding of institutionalised racism or its inflection of the state's counterinsurgency campaign's terror' (Feldman 2003:69). Above all, it also illustrated an implicit acknowledgement that criminal acts, atrocities and brutalities did happen, and were committed by someone on 'our side' (except such deviants are pushed as far away as possible from 'us').

On the other hand, the paramilitaries, volunteers and other 'bad apples' personalised the war. They *participated* and their direct involvement must have exposed 'the hidden' or 'the unspeakable' of war. However, with paramilitaries and rogue soldiers actually 'boasting' about what they did, according to some respondents, the distance between the respondents here and the war (together with its horrors) 'over there' suddenly collapsed. The paramilitaries and volunteers spoke about murder, death and rape – all the horrifying and distasteful elements of war, things that most had suspected but preferred not to think about, suddenly had a label, and moreover, a perpetrator with a name, face and family who often lived close by. It may have made some question their own complicity or true distance from the conflicts.

The conceptual leap required to think of a conscript son or a drafted cousin as a potential war criminal is quite a large one. Thus, borders are drawn, and 'we, the normal' condemn 'all this, the sick and the crazy'. And here is that language of pathology again; if the people who committed the atrocities are sick, they can also possibly be cured, (De Leonardis 2008). Is this projection of madness and disease onto volunteers a denial of war crimes? On the one hand, it denies that 'normal' people, conscripts, sons, friends, committed the same, but on the other hand, it is also because of what *is* known, that these borders of normality/disease need to be drawn. Drawing on Plato's conceptualisations of medicine, De Leonardis suggests that in a

> 'medicalised conception of society', such as one where 'deviant citizens' are seen as 'diseased', for the deviants 'there are only two possible perspectives: the return to virtue by means of punishment or of forceful reeducation on the one hand, and the actual or civil death (i.e. the exile) on the other. They are a scapegoat ... whose real or metaphorical elimination purifies the body of society.' (De Leonardis 2008:37)

Overall, if denial in its broadest sense – drawing on Cohen (2001) and van Dijk (1992) – is understood as something that masks a much more complex reality, then there are implications for transitional justice. First the strategy of distancing oneself from crimes and atrocities suggests that there is something unpleasant to be distanced *from*. This is an implicit acknowledgement that atrocities did take place, but not expressed in the kinds of language sought out by transitional justice projects. Moreover, it appears as though such projects seek discourses which exist unified and visible at some societal level. They appear to be seeking out confrontation as expressed in speech (and social action) without taking into account that 'naturally occurring' speech (Smith 2004) does not function in a uniform, clear or quantifiable way.

There is not a great deal of coherence in any of the above extracts, and no real expression of clear-cut denial or acknowledgement. Instead, much of this is veiled, suggested and implied. The narratives do not use the language of transitional justice; 'I condemn these crimes', 'I want to talk about Srebrenica', but nevertheless regret and revulsion *are* expressed, or suggested. Denial is a defence mechanism (e.g. Zimmermann and Rodin 2004; van Dijk 1992), a way of both shielding oneself and understanding the incomprehensible and the gruesome.

This would suggest that transitional justice and related projects may need to clarify exactly what kind of acknowledgement of past atrocities is 'good enough' to be considered a confrontation with the past. It raises the question of how regret is to be expressed. Is it enough for such projects that acknowledgement be nested somewhere together with a denial of something else? Is an expression of revulsion enough? Or does it need to be followed by an apology? In addition, such projects need to recognise the complexities masked by denial narratives: a lot of people, asked to confront these, are personally bound up in these violent histories. This raises the question of possible guilt and responsibility (what are the respondents distancing themselves *from?*) and denial is one way of negotiating not just one's own possible complicity or proximity, but revulsion, horror and morality. To what extent do they feel personally involved? To what extent could they be said to have contributed to what happened? This is an immensely complicated area, and I do not think that a conclusive answer is possible, given that for the respondents themselves this is something which they do not yet understand.

CHAPTER 7

'HAVEN'T SERBS ALSO BEEN KILLED?': VICTIMHOOD, RESENTMENT AND MARGINALITY

Introduction

One of the most interesting themes emerging from the research material collected here is that a number of respondents emphasise notions of victimhood. 'Us', 'others', the 'poor people' who died, the displaced, the young people, the children: are all identified as the victims of many perpetrators (the 'lunatics', the criminals, Milošević, NATO, the 'political hotheads') and of many different kinds of crime (the unspoken horrors, murders, wars, propaganda, NATO air strikes). 'Victimhood' is a broad category, and in the collected material a sense of different levels of victimisation is invoked, and sometimes traced back to a much more distant past. It is also here, in discussions of victimhood, that 'Serbs' become identified as an ethnic category, unlike in any other aspect of war narratives. These are also the rare occasions in which ethnicity is used at all in these narratives.

What can be made of this dynamic? At times, 'the Serbs' have been criticised for interpreting recent history from the position of a victim. For instance:

There is no major victim community in Serbia whose political violence and experience offset the rhetoric of nationalist leaders. As [Antonela Riha, journalist] emphasized, 'What is important for understanding, we don't have victims [in Serbia], only refugees. Serbians don't know what it's like to be victims.' (Orentlicher 2007:91)

This gives way to two discussions. As this chapter demonstrates, the presence of own-group victimhood narratives does not mean that regret and horror over 'other victims' is absent. Secondly, victimhood can be based on both experience and perception. Therefore, it is perhaps useful to examine what kinds of experiences and understandings of the recent history may lead to victimhood discourse. This is where ethnography is extremely useful for exploring and understanding the deeper issues that surround these discourses. One of the main aims of ethnography is to describe and understand experiences as they are lived by 'subjects' (e.g. Hammersley and Atkinson 2004; Gray 2003; Davis 2005).

In this chapter, I propose that presence of victimhood motifs in narratives about the past may be considered as the result of the difficult personal experiences of the 1990s, which include issues previously discussed (death, physical illness, existential problems, broken relationships and friendships) and the experience of NATO air strikes. In turn, I will also consider how this experience which helps shape own-group victimhood narratives, might further complicate transitional justice mechanisms and projects which identify singular victims and perpetrators.

In these narratives, there is a perceived disconnect between the acknowledgement that others *were* killed, and that 'the Serbs' were too. This difficulty is then compounded by a deep inability to articulate much about the atrocities and speak of them. These violent incidents have no precedent (c.f. Kusno 2003) and no framework; they are horrifying and terrifying. Serb victimhood, on the other hand, has a pre-existing narrative – an articulation of the experience in history, literature, culture and politics. Still, the importance of such motifs in history, culture and politics must not be overstated as a reason for the presence of victimhood narratives in discussions of the recent past and atrocities. Perhaps more importantly, the reason for this could be located in the experience of the 1990s (equally 'horrifying' and 'terrifying'); and the perception that this has not been acknowledged or recognised in some way.[1]

In preceding chapters, I highlighted that current frameworks of transitional justice or initiatives dealing with the past in Serbia do not take into account that Serbian audiences may have multiple subject positions towards the conflicts. Transitional justice works primarily with clear-cut categories of victim and perpetrator (Sriram 2007; also Borer 2003:1088). At times, as Sriram notes, the 'heinous, invasive and quite personal' atrocities which occur during mass violence, 'tend to create and reify categories of people in a society – victim and victimiser, collaborator – and yet there is unlikely to be a true consensus as to who belongs in which category' (Sriram 2007:586–587).

Thus, because transitional justice as a concept is divided along victim-perpetrator lines, it appears not to have created frameworks through which we can approach populations that do not fit any of those categories explicitly, or may fit in overlapping roles or, to use Humphrey's phrase, may be labelled 'distant audiences' (Humphrey 2002:x). In the study presented here, the respondents form the very audiences at which transitional justice projects are aimed, and are often asked to confront the past, 'just like in Nazi Germany' (Vulliamy 2011), and so seem to end up being viewed through frameworks designed for perpetrators, who must confront their guilt and wrongdoings of the past. Whilst this certainly rings true for the Serbian leadership during the Milošević era and those participating in the wars, it is much more difficult to apply to 'society' as a whole, since many individuals occupied very ambiguous roles during the conflict. The 1990s were a difficult period to make sense of and it was unclear, furthermore, where one 'fitted' vis-à-vis political developments. Did voting for Milošević make one a perpetrator? And what of those who supported Milošević and then changed their minds? What about those who resisted the Milošević regime and protested against it throughout the 1990s, but did not succeed in preventing the war and atrocities? Are they more or less perpetrators? Are they bystanders? And what about those individuals who knew friends and family who volunteered for war but did nothing (or could do nothing) to prevent them from going? And what about those, presented here, who see themselves as victims of Milošević (see also Clarke 2008), but also as victims of the 1990s and of the NATO air strikes?

The lack of clarity and possible subjectivities emerging from these questions, greatly complicate how respondents position themselves towards the conflicts of the 1990s. They do not fit clearly into any category. No one in this study actually took up arms to engage in warfare but some do admit supporting Milošević. To what extent do they view themselves as complicit, and to what extent should we view them as such? Whilst many others can be thought of as 'bystanders' (a questionable category at best), many have at the same time occupied various kinds of victim positions too: some had lost family and friends in the conflicts, or suffered in other ways at hands of a repressive regime.

At the heart of the victimhood trope, as it appears in these accounts, is the question of acknowledgement of silent victimhood. Being a victim, especially in transitional justice, means that one can seek redress, justice or acknowledgement. Currently transitional justice projects emphasise and prioritise victims and ask that the Serbian public should acknowledge these, the victims of 'others'. Quite rightly so. However, this focus first of all assumes that the Serbian public does not already acknowledge these, and furthermore, inadvertently excludes and marginalises other kinds of possible victims. There are victims of crimes and war crimes, but there are also those who understand themselves as victims based on their understanding of their own experience (see Ferguson et al. 2010). In other words, in transitioning societies, there is a 'complexity of victimhood' (Ferguson et al. 2010:861).

This chapter, therefore, considers some of the victimhood narratives present in these reflections on war crimes and considers to what extent they may constitute a response to perceived marginalisation, injustice and exclusion from the victimhood narratives of transitional justice. The aim is to highlight that narratives which victimise the self, or one's community, are not always attempts to obliterate the victimhood of others and deny their suffering but may be attempts to position oneself in a more favourable way towards recent developments, or attempts to make sense of one's own, often deeply unhappy and difficult, experience of the 1990s.

All the 'normal people' are victims of the 1990s

Wars produce victims. Just as the spectre of potential perpetrators hovers over the horrors of the past, so do victims. Humphrey, following Foucault, writes that atrocities have a 'triadic structure', involving the presence of ruler (or perpetrator), victim and people 'for an effective performance' (Humphrey 2003:173; Humphrey 2002). Thus:

> The people had to know and see the excess of violence on the body of the victim and hear his confession if the spectacle was going to be pedagogic and politically legitimising. (Humphrey 2003:173)

In the respondents' narratives, the victims, named or implied, include a large and diverse group. Primarily, that group consists of 'all those people', or 'poor people', 'those poor women and children' (there was often a special emphasis on children, both respondents' own and children of others), 'all normal people'. In opposition to this, stood the 'sick' and 'insane' perpetrators, and the 'political hotheads' who started the war, which 'normal people' would have never initiated. There were victims of war, of disease, of politics and of NATO air strikes, as well as victims of 'the West' (this is discussed at length in the following chapter).

If metaphors of mental and physical illness are used to distance the 'sick' perpetrators from 'us', then in the same way the emphasis on 'normal people' who suffered at the hands of the 'insane' ones, brings *all* the victims of war closer together. There is often no ethnic distance between the victims; indeed, ethnic labelling of victims is rare, and this fits with the general and sweeping conclusions usually drawn about the war and 'all that horror':

> It was a civil war. A typical civil war. People against people, one people destroying another. Serbs destroying Muslims, Muslims destroying Serbs. A civil war. I always remember those four [leaders]. If it wasn't for those four there would have never been a war. I would have never gone to fight against a Muslim, why

would I when I worked with them in Zvornik, like we were brothers? No one asked you what you are. We worked together in the daytime and in the evening we all went out drinking and partying, dinner, music. We were not bothered. (Nikola)

With this, helplesness was often felt too:

I always say I am trying to forget all that, if is possible to forget something like that. Recently, no, it isn't possible. If there was something I could have done to stop it, I would have done. To prevent it, I would have done. But we are totally helpless, someone else is always calling the shots. (Svetlana)

The idea often present is that 'we all' suffered in the 1990s. Demonisation, dehumanisation and intolerance of 'ethnic other' groups – the kind which occurred in the political and media discourse of the 1990s – never became a feature of the narratives. Drakulić (2004:66), for instance, writes that Croats, Muslims and Albanians had been subject to demonisation in Serbia for ten years before the Srebrenica massacre, a step-by-step 'psychological preparation' which made the 'fall of Srebrenica' possible. Although hate speech was present in the Serbian media and Serbian politics the 1990s, it certainly did not occur in the interviews, especially if one follows Bugarski (2002:93) in defining it as a 'vicious form of public defamation [...] with the aim of satanising an ethnic, racial, confessional, social or political group.'

Rather, the 'others' are more often presented as close, and familial. Proximity to these groups is often emphasised, and so the wars are labelled, for instance, 'fratricidal wars' (Svetlana); or as Mara laments; 'it made me really sad that a brother could turn on his brother.' There is a general sense in which they are all 'us'.

Thus, some of the most shocking aspects of the facts surrounding war crimes of the 1990s was the 'impact of terror and violence applied in familiar settings and on familiar people' (Sorabji 1995:82). In her analysis of the Bosnian war, Sorabji points out the importance of *komšiluk*, the immediate neighbourhood, which in the former Yugoslavia was often seen as close as one's own family (Sorabji 1995:90–91). Likewise, respondents in this study often emphasised this conceptual closeness to the rest of the former Yugoslavia, with the older generations often suggesting that the borders of 'their country' were from the Vardar River in Macedonia to the Triglav Mountain in Slovenia. Whilst Feldman, theorises the absence of 'others' in narratives of war as 'cultural anaesthesia', suggesting that 'erasure' of others' bodies gives wars and violence a sanitised character (Feldman 1994:407), it could also be argued that the absence of 'others' in accounts of violence stems from a desire to mediate the effects of violence against those persons. Ethnic others are thus absent, because there is at once difficulty in understanding them as *others* and difficulty in facing the fact that violent and horrific things happened to people to whom they were physically and conceptually close (Sorabji 1995:91).[2] As Susan Sontag notes, 'People are often unable to take in the sufferings of those close to them' (Sontag 2003:88). In an interesting anecdote, Sontag also describes how a citizen of Sarajevo (of unspecified ethnicity, but 'of impeccable adherence to the Yugoslav ideal') switched off the news upon seeing the war in Croatia, stating, 'Oh, how horrible,' noting that switching off is '... normal. It's human' (Sontag 2003:89). Sontag adds that 'her unwillingness to engage with these premonitory images of nearby war was an expression of helplessness and fear' (Sontag 2003:89).

I wish to illustrate similar points with the inclusion of a very lengthy interview extract. One of the older respondents, Danica, did not believe that the Srebrenica and Markale atrocities happened 'in that way'. Her response to these is perhaps a textbook illustration of what can be conceptualised as denial (Cohen 2001). But upon further discussion a number of revealing dynamics emerged. Danica is one of the respondents who constantly kept repeating that the war of the 1990s was 'a dirty war, the dirtiest'. The extract begins with Danica's understanding of two atrocities; the interview later shifts to her reflections on her time as a school teacher in Germany, sometime in the 1970s, teaching Yugoslav diaspora children:

When Markale happened. Then they bombarded Serb territory. That was a war, no one knew who was fighting against whom. Muslims against Croats, and against Serbs, and Serbs against them. No one knew. That was the dirtiest war of all time. The dirtiest! But, Serbs are not to blame all by themselves. No, no, no. These others, they are to blame too. I don't know how it was, I wasn't in Bosnia at the time. But I do know that there are villages which have been completely flattened and no one remained. Everyone killed. Muslims killed the Serb population. There, in Milići, in Bratunac. There in Kravica. In Kravica they flattened everything. And now they tell us, this Srebrenica. It's not true. They are just against Karadžić and Mladić, who were protecting their people. What they did was to take all the Muslims who died somewhere else, to bury them there. [...]

[...] I had, in Germany, great friends. I mainly taught Muslim children, most of the class was Muslim children and then when the war started, I was also in Bosnia [she retired just at the start of the conflicts]. I loved those people so much, and they loved me too. There was no Muslim house where I didn't go. The children used to wait for me in the street, and say, 'Teacher, my Dad told me not to go to school without you.' I never went hungry there. I really loved all of them. I could not imagine that someone would want to harm my children, or someone would harm theirs. I have no words to explain how much I loved that community [in the village in Bosnia]. And in Germany there were kids from all over, from Slovenia, from Croatia. All over. It was all, it was like one soul. I didn't see them as different and they didn't see me as different. I came to Bosnia, and they asked, what faith are you. I said, who cares. You don't need to know. But they didn't like people from Serbia to teach their children because they didn't like their accent ... But no, I tell you, back then it was really, harmony. In Nuremberg we had really great friends from Sarajevo, he was from an old Sarajevo family. We were really close, their son was in my class. And once they went to Sarajevo for seven days, and they left the child Admir with us. When he was a baby he nearly died, he had some infection because he had an operation and the doctor didn't do it properly and they were always scared for him. But they left Admir with me, and the mother, she was really dear to us, she said, Danica, I am leaving Admir with you because I don't trust anyone else. [...]

[...] But here in Serbia, I don't know so many Muslims. There aren't that many here in Belgrade, not anymore. It's over ... But during the war. This war. This most rotten war. I am walking the park. And sitting there, one woman, with two little daughters, and the woman is pregnant. Third child on the way. We talk, I say where are you from. Over there I see some other women whispering, like they want to say something bad. And she says, I am from Bosnia, I don't know some village by the Drina. And the war is on. She says my sister is a midwife here in a hospital, I ran away with the children. I say, where is your husband, your sister's husband, do you have anyone? She says no, they all stayed over there to fight against the Serbs. I say, so you came here to save the children and give birth, and they are over there fighting. I said, listen. Listen really carefully. I have never hated anyone. Not Muslims. Because my mother was from Herzegovina and I grew up with Muslims and we were like brothers. But please, I said, don't come to this park anymore. Those women over there would rip her apart. And I never saw her again in the park. But that's Serbia for you. I don't know what would happen if a Serb woman went over there to give birth during the war. They say that only Serbs were raping and killing. But everyone was doing that, everyone. And the other war [the Second World War] what's that like in comparison to this one? In comparison that other one looked respectful. My father-in-law told me. He says they ended up in some trench and over there they could see the other army but, he says, I was shooting into the air [to miss on purpose], and I could see the soldier on the other side shooting into the air too. Back then a Serb soldier didn't have to think about if he was going to kill a woman or a child. A Serb soldier will never be like that again.

[*Later*]

Mladić should not go to The Hague. If they need to put him on trial they should do it here in this country. Srebrenica. Is it true? Was it investigated? Over there they brought, they say, there is no one there buried, that they just shot them. They say now seven eight thousand, but how many Serbs were killed in Bosnia, and how many women and children? Oh it was all rotten. War never brings anything good, to anyone.

I present this lengthy extract here as it illustrates several themes. First, denial, which gives way to reflection, and within which sentiments about the war are buried – it is 'rotten' and 'dirty'. Everyone was killing and Serb soldiers were to blame as well as the others. But the story of Muslim friends, which is almost a lament, told in the past tense ('It's all over'), might provide some insight into the rest of the account ('I couldn't imagine that something would happen to their children'; the subtext at the very end is that this 'something' was done by Serb soldiers who did not behave honourably). Thus in this context the sentence about what the other women might do is odd – is it a displacement of some kind of feeling that the respondent may have been feeling herself?[3] It is unclear, and this story was not told again. The extracts contain very explicit denial in places. However, what it signifies and what it is all about – distancing, possible guilt, confusion, anxiety, lament for lost friends and how things were – is buried quite deeply in this narrative where denial, acknowledgement, victimhood and anxiety for others are all intertwined. Captured in a survey, the gist of these extracts may just appear as denial of an event, but what that hides would never come out in such a methodology.

Of course, there were those who identified Serbs as victims of the conflicts too, and instances where Serb victims were highlighted. As Chapter Five already described, in understanding the conflicts, the respondents drew on what they observed around them, and so refugees in Belgrade featured in some of the accounts about victims:

Listening and hearing about those wartime actions, those were really horrific things for all of us, and they had an awful effect on the psyche. Especially the beginning of the war, the massive convoys of refugees from Bosnia and Croatia. People who were coming to Serbia were running away, Serbs running away from the *ustaše* invasion. According to their stories, awful things were happening. We took [...] a family of eleven refugees into our house, and everything we saw, that simply had to leave awful impressions on us [...] obviously we are going to help them, they are my people [...] They told me at the beginning of the war, in the village in Bosnia where my parents used to work, that was a Serb-only village and [...] there nothing happened during the wars in Slovenia and Croatia until the party of Alija Izetbegović came to power in Bosnia. A teacher in the primary school [...] the first thing he did was to put up a green flag, which was the flag of the Muslim SDA party, and, obviously, the local Serbs organised themselves and took the flag down. (Ana)

With this extract I will return briefly to my earlier point, that respondents had difficulty verbalising things which they found horrific; this was not the case only in instances where they spoke about the victims of others. Here, displaced Serbs from Bosnia and Croatia are being discussed, and what happened to them is not verbalised as atrocity, but through euphemisms of 'wartime actions' and '*ustaše* invasion'. It is notable also that the perpetrators are '*ustaše*' not Croats; in earlier extracts, Rada refereed to the 'mujahedeen', not Bosnian Muslims. In the same way that the Serbian perpetrators are seen in extremes (the deviants of society, not ordinary people) so the perpetrators of other ethnicities are presented in their extreme political formations that do not represent the majority. Implied in this is that it was not the 'normal' Croats or Bosnian Muslims who did the killing; they are the 'conceptually close' others (Sorabji 1995). In this narrative, the Serb victims are those who were observed directly and indirectly, the realities converging as the columns of refugees that Ana sees on television end with refugees in her own home. Her narrative contains victims because she has seen them; it is not merely the case that they are imagined Serb victims which monopolise accounts of war.

Being a victim: the NATO air strikes

As well as witnessing the victimhood of others, there is also the experience of being a victim. Even in the strictest sense of that word, where the victim suffers at the hands of someone else, all the respondents here are victims of the NATO air strikes. As Serbian author David Albahari noted, '[a]fter the [NATO] bombing in the spring of 1999, I noticed a lot of changes in people, perhaps because at that point they had truly experienced the burden of war' (in Vujičić 2005). Furthermore, Bock-Luna (2008) writes that the NATO air strikes against Serbia were a crucial turning point for a number of Serbs.

Debates on 'facing the past' often overlook this significance of the NATO air strikes. In current approaches towards transitional justice, the project of facing the past directed at the Serbian public requires an addressing and acknowledgement of the horrific crimes against Muslims, Croats and Albanians carried out in the 1990s. In so doing, the approach ignores that other events deemed to be troubling, difficult or traumatic – such as the air strikes – may influence the relationship to the violent past one seeks to acknowledge and under-stand. This is especially evident in discussions about the NATO air strikes: the perception of injustice, and the perception that Serb vic-tims of the 1990s and 1999 have not been acknowledged or dealt with, ensures that the NATO air strikes remain an unresolved issue, which complicates the broader debates about the past in complex and unexp-ected ways.

The significance of this event is made very clear in respondents' nar-ratives. Given that they are also narratives of war, suffering and often terror, they are extremely different to those of the 1990s conflicts. Whereas there is a reluctance to talk about the 1990s and these events are presented in vague, opaque language, the most common response to the NATO air strikes is the opposite: there is an eagerness to talk, and the language is precise, detailed and names violence, deaths, and feelings of terror. These stories can also be located more commonly in the everyday, and are discussed openly.

This is despite the fact that almost all the respondents in this study experienced the air strikes directly, and some had an extremely trau-matic and difficult time. One respondent's is wife, for instance, suffered a heart attack during the first day of the air strikes. Another respond-ent, Ana, watched one of the targeted buildings from her window as it burned. As a result of the air strikes, Rada experienced panic attacks, and after the bombing she went back to work, but signed off on long-term sick leave soon after that. Others hid in basements or shelters or sent their children away to stay with relatives in the countryside. It was a conflict experienced directly, and one which left a number of bad memories for many — stories are still told about the smells of the basements, or the fear of not knowing whether one's building will survive if hit. For instance, Mara narrated the following:

> All the windows in our flat were broken when they bombed the Chinese Embassy [near the flat]. My daughter was so scared she couldn't get out of bed. And when those [air raid] sirens went off, I had to go and sleep, I had to go to work the next day. But my husband and his cousin, they sat here all night in silence staring at a candle — they were scared. And my daughter. I had to go to her room with a torch and give her some slippers. All that just because someone spread a rumour that Mira Marković [Milošević's wife] was in the embassy building, and they killed those Chinese people, several of them, and some were wounded. We just heard screams, it sounded like cats. Then I remember the fire fighters arriving. And just before that, I had said to my [other] daughter — she was pregnant with her third child — I said, give me the other two kids and I'll look after them at home, I have this hotel here, and a Chinese Embassy here, and they won't aim at that, we are in a safe location. But they hit the hotel, they hit the embassy, and over there five hundred meters away, they hit that other building, it was a military building.
>
> We were all here, and then a bomb fell nearby. They say a bomb of 2240 kilograms. We had this shelter but everyone was sitting near the door. When the bomb fell there was a wave. And that wave shut the door! I had for over a month some kind of sand stuck in my skin, large grains. (Svetozar)
>
> You see consequences of war in terms of illness, people are much more sick that they used to be, especially after the [NATO] bombing, because all that was a huge stress. And for young

people, OK, economic problems, yes, but this, they [young peo-
ple] are in some kind of spasm. They are all really nervous, they
live in some kind of strange time, not like we did. I remember
my childhood. It was a childhood, carefree. Now, these kids, I
don't know, I look at them and I just see stress, non-stop some
kind of stress. And I really think that's a consequence of the
air strikes. You know, a lot of young people are dying. A lot of
young people are committing suicide. (Katarina)

The narratives about the period of the air strikes are forthcoming, with
clearly fixed meanings and linear story lines. They gave the impression
of events which had a definite start, middle and end. For instance:

Yes, that was in '99, I was exactly twenty years old. Well I
remember it, of course, I remember exactly, because a few
months before that, we heard that there would be air strikes,
but no one believed it. But there, on the 24th it happened and
the sirens went off [...] I and my parents were having dinner
and watching the news. And then the presenter on the news was
totally surprised just like all of us and he told us we all needed
to go to the air-raid shelters [...] and really just then, everything
started to shake. (Biljana)

One day, soldiers had to drive me to work, and the next day
drive me back, there were no buses [...] There, by my mother's
house ... that's where the soldiers were stationed. Sometimes when
the sirens went off, we'd go outside and guess who shot whose
plane down [...] Where the bomb fell, we'd guess whether it hit
Obrenovac or somewhere else, then one day we were watching
Sremčica burning when they hit something there. (Nevena)

Well, my place is here and the Chinese embassy is 150 metres
away. That it was bombed by mistake, no-one can convince me
that it was bombed by mistake. The building that was supposed to be targeted was 500 metres away from the embassy,
but the embassy was not targeted that night but a few days later.

But if they targeted the Chinese embassy, why did they also target Hotel Jugoslavija? (Jovan)

That was in 1999, I was sixteen and that was the year I went from eighth grade to high school. They targeted the power station which is across the street from us. For the first month, everyone was panicky and went to the shelters but after that no, nobody cared. I remember once the sirens were on, and we went outside to play basketball. The kids didn't pay any attention to it, and suddenly they started to bomb and then all the mothers came out of the building and started screaming at their kids to go inside. One of the little kids who is a real brat, he was so scared that he lay down on the floor and and couldn't move. The sky was red. That [power station] was probably 300 meters from here. But luckily the wave went to the other side, not our side, but in some buildings, their staircases collapsed and windows broke but not in our building. But us, we were just happy that we didn't have to go to school. Back then we were against the West, we hated them and today when I am older I am still against that. They did not have any right. My mum says that because of one man, they attacked a whole people. If they wanted him they should just find him, but not bombard a whole country. (Ana's daughter Iva)

How did I feel back then? Totally lost. I felt awful, because it was my twentieth birthday during the air strikes. That day was horrible. I felt like I did not exist, horrific. I couldn't go anywhere, but also I had no idea what was happening. I was here in Belgrade but my mum went to work, even though the factory where she works was actually hit once. Their factory made something that was connected to weapons, so they always knew there was a risk that they would be hit, they were always tense because they knew something could happen. But they still went to work. So that was such a strange situation, I had really mixed emotions. I was really angry at everything, but I also felt that I should still make the most of things, enjoy what I do have. So my friends and I had fun as much as we could, having parties at home mainly. We just ignored the sirens, but not for a second did I think about that. I don't know, I guess I felt that we could avoid being hit. They wouldn't aim at us [in Belgrade], there were no army barracks or anything near us. But where my parents lived yes, that worried me. And just the thought that one country was being bombed by the whole world. That was just horrifying. (Ivan)

We were watching the news day and night before it happened. We were not afraid of the danger. The immediate danger was huge. Civilians died. But at the moment that it is happening to you, you are not conscious of it. Only when it's all over, you real-ise what happened. We were in Belgrade, we didn't go anywhere, although we had a cottage in the countryside [in an area that was not targeted] and could have gone there. I don't know why we didn't go there to hide. We mainly sat around at home, and watched the BBC [...] that night when the bombing started ... we just watched the news and started phoning friends. People just couldn't believe it. We went to the shelter once then we realised, this is pointless. The bombs are so powerful they'll just bury us down there. I'd rather die in my own bed. (Gordana)

Although these narratives, like the war narratives, contain explana-tion, opinions and blame, they were also illustrated with phrases of certainty and precision (e.g. 'exactly', 'just then', '300 metres') which is missing in the stories of other conflicts. Precision or 'generalised, technical, subjectless, and detached accounts' appear to be 'a part of a process of precise documentation and historical recording for pres-ervation where 'each detail was reflectively presented as essential and significant' (Malkki 2002:132). Similarly, Daniel (1996) suggests that severely traumatised victims of violence are able to narrate such inci-dents in precise detail, often without showing emotion, and that it is the level of detail which actually points to a deep traumatisation. This clearly traumatic issue has not been dealt with in any public forum other than by the governments of Milošević and Koštunica and extreme nationalist grassroots organisations such as Dveri Srpske and Pokret 1389 (the '1389 Movement') who engage in emotional and reactionary anti-NATO and anti-Western arguments. Unlike the war crimes of the 1990s, the NATO air strikes do not appear to have been picked up by NGOs or other transitional justice projects, which is of particular concern to the respondents here.

The NATO air strikes are significant in that they are often used as a prism through which other problems of the 1990s are understood and explained, and quite frequently, this happens through either narratives of victimisation or conspiracy. At times, in respondents' accounts of the conflicts, the NATO air strikes were frequently confused and conflated with the conflicts in Croatia and Bosnia, and yet at other times, this was referred to as '*the* war', and at others narratives moved seamlessly between all the different conflicts. In that sense at least, the past cannot be compartmentalised. That NGOs and transitional justice projects did not engage with the NATO air strikes as something which had to be addressed in 'facing the past' projects is significant – majority of the respondents interviewed here felt that it should have been. The impunity with which NATO is perceived to have acted resulted in increased resentment, a belief that at least someone ought to be on trial for the air strikes, or that at the very least, they should be asked to talk publicly about their experiences. At present, many feel that a rather traumatic event that they had personally gone through had been metaphorically swept under the carpet, whilst they are being asked to confront the suffering of others. As I demonstrated in the previous chapters, to an extent that confrontation is happening already: at the very least, regret and acknowledgement are felt, even if they are not always articulated very well, or are at times overshadowed by the sense of resentment over one's own suffering. Many narratives presented in Chapters Five and Six seem unable to move on from that. This repetition and constant insistence on Serb victimhood is heavily influenced by the NATO air strikes, which arrived at the tail-end of a very difficult decade. Together with the ICTY proceedings, they seem to have contributed retrospectively to a cumulative sense of victimisation – the 'first all that, and now this!' effect (Jansen 2000:404).

That sense of victimisation, which has no real outlet or space of engagement, is difficult for many respondents to comprehend. They see that punishment of Milošević, Mladić and others is pursued, and whilst they feel that the same should be done to NATO, they see no action being taken. It is this perceived injustice, combined with the marginalisation of their voices from the 'coming to terms with the past' debate, which leads to the creation of conspiracy theories as ways of understanding significant aspects of the violent past. This dynamic is explored at length in the following chapter.

Physical manifestations of victimhood:
death, injury and illness

Victimhood, in these narratives, also has a physical manifestation. As well as the frequent appearance of metaphors of disease, such as suggestions that the wars were 'sick', a number of respondents also discussed physical manifestations of disease, amputation and death. The context of these is interesting, as most such stories of physical ailments narratives emerged when I asked the respondents what they thought the consequences of the 1990s were. My intention was to discuss the political consequences, possibly the social ones too (and so I left 'consequences' as very broad) but the number of answers which discussed the physical consequences was surprising. Clearly, as Scheper-Hughes writes, the wounded or amputated 'out-of-place bodies' haunt imaginations of the survivors (2004a:175). Moreover, this illustrates that the body, or rather bodies, of the ill, the dead and the injured (such as former soldiers) became physical manifestations of the perceived, witnessed or imagined collective victimhood, and one which often incorporates all victims of all wars. This became particularly acute after the NATO air strikes, when rumours of uranium bombs and radiation began to circulate, and the narratives again conflated all conflicts and their injured into one. For instance:

> [*About the consequences of war*] Oh, there are so many. When I see that. [*Pause*] Once when I went to the spa,[4] I saw young men in wheelchairs, one had no feet. I cried! And then, once it was raining and I saw a man on crutches, he couldn't hold an umbrella. Oh, I think so many mutilated and invalid people all from this war! The number of cancer victims is also increasing, more and

more young people have cancer ... I feel so sorry for all of them, there are so many people who are really gravely ill, who knows how long they have to live? And over there, they [NATO] were throwing uranium bombs, to me that's a crime. The West is deaf and blind, they are doing what they want in the world, and we have to pay the price. We really paid the price. But someone has to be responsible. (Mara)

{In an earlier part of the interview this respondent also talked about her shock on seeing young men with no legs at the orthopaedic ward} I think there are so many consequences. The hospitals are full of cancer patients. My friend is a doctor ... and she said that there are more and more people ill with cancer and tuberculosis. An epidemic. They say it's a cancer epidemic. Our hospitals are full, but no one talks about that. At one time, there was a period when people had to wait for seven days to bury the dead, that's how many people were dying. And I'll tell you what, when I was in Canada I read the newspapers over there, and they said, quite openly, the USA is testing out the latest weapons on Serbia, and that the consequences will lead to the death of the population, within three to five years. Death of the population. And when I said this to my friends, they said, come on, don't panic. And today, they tell me, this man and that woman, died of cancer, I say, I am not at all surprised. The Canadian papers wrote about it openly. That radiation is expected from the bombs. And we are eating food from Serbia, all of it comes from Pančevo, which was bombed, so the Pančevo soil is soaked in radioactive material. (Mirjana)

We are a sick people. Psychologically and physically destroyed people. We are the sickest nation in Europe, the highest consumption of sedatives, antibiotics. The highest percentage of people dying from cancer ... Now comes the quiet death. One had to survive all those stresses, everyone their own way, and one day you just have to break. And then this uranium, it's all over, so that we now have the quiet dying out of a people. Look at the obituaries in the papers. Not just old people anymore, everyone from children to the old dying [of cancer]. Is it like that in Europe? I don't think so. (Rada)

In this dynamic, the victims from Serbia suffer physical consequences. Victimhood is directly observed, sometimes physically felt. These illustrate Humphrey's point that 'even if the atrocity of war remains invisible during the course of the war, it inevitably surfaces once war is over as a legacy of bodily memories, and scars in veterans and victims alike' (Humphrey 2002: 45). Victimhood thus becomes tangible, rather than 'just' imagined. In understanding the wars, the atrocities, these physical wounds offer a focal point for the experiences felt, and things which were suspected or assumed ('we were victims, too'). The bodily wounds of the disabled and the sick are, in a sense, projections and physical expressions for the suffering many felt during the 1990s.[5]

There are also other tangible manifestations of victimhood which may lead us to questioning what the scope of 'victimhood' is in transitional justice. I have already written about the difficult experiences of the 1990s that most, if not all, respondents here had gone through. In addition to that there were instances and tragedies – often direct consequences of the war – in close proximity to some respondents, which gave a further physicality to victimhood. Many of these stories exist hidden from view of both the gaze of transitional justice projects and public discussion, yet have a deep impact on how the past is conceptualised. For instance, Bojan's friend committed suicide after returning from the draft which took him Kosovo. Ivan's cousin was clearly traumatised after returning from Croatia. One of Nikola's nephews developed diabetes in the early 1990s upon being drafted into the army, which the family attributed to the extreme stress he suffered whilst there. Then, there are the extreme anxieties which do not perhaps manifest themselves as physically: Vanja's family worried about her brother when he was drafted into the army and not heard from; Mirjana's worry about what might happen to her son if the war goes on. The list of other illnesses, physical and mental, reported by the respondents as having been suffered and witnessed within their immediate circle of friends and family in the 1990s is long: a nervous breakdown, a prolonged hospitalisation in a psychiatric ward, cancer, alcoholism, treatment for depression and anxiety, domestic violence and an attempted murder. The insistence on illness and disease demonstrates yet another point at which the wars 'over there' converge with the personal, lived experience. Whether they were caused by the conflicts or not, the illnesses and tragedies become understood as a part of that experience. Pain, whether physical or mental, argues Morris, 'takes us outside of our normal modes of dealing with the world' (Morris 1993:25). It 'introduces us to a landscape where nothing looks entirely familiar and where even the familiar takes on an uncanny strangeness' (Morris 1993: 25). In attempting to understand the linkages between physical pain, experienced or witnessed, it is useful to draw on Morris' suggestion that 'we experience pain only and entirely as we interpret it' (Morris 1993:29).

The experience and interpretation of pain, physical suffering and witnessing of physical defects in others makes the concept of victimhood much less clear-cut. If we understand a victim as someone who suffers, then we can also understand – as these respondents do – these kinds of experiences as a victimhood, together with the victims who suffered much more explicitly (through death and injury or loss of family). It was an altogether different experience of victimhood. As Feldman notes, both the role of victim and perpetrator are 'self-ascribed and shifting' categories since, in 'political terror' the 'pathogenesis of violence' is such that anyone 'can be called victim and any victim can be marked as perpetrator' (Feldman 2003:69–70).

As a constantly repeated theme, self-ascribed victimhood and suffering also indicate a process of cultural traumatisation, as repetitive themes in a society or in individual narratives are seen as a need to reassert basic, undermined beliefs (Sztompka 2000:456). Moreover, victimhood has moral appeal. Identifying oneself as a victim carries with it a certain amount of passivity and fatalism (Schöpflin 1997:29; Monroe 2008); a world where things happen, rather than being caused by the person presenting themselves as a victim. There is also a parallel here with the use of medical language and viewing the 1990s as 'diseased'. In this, it is interesting that cancer crops up so frequently. Cancer, as something malignant and virtually impossible to control, is an apt motif and trope in the respondents' discussions of victimhood, since it is a situation where the patient is virtually helpless. This kind of subjective self-victimising is not something which can be 'combatted' with facts about the past. As Monroe argues, 'people do not consciously arrange themselves along a moral continuum with the goal of defining themselves as evil-doers or people who ignore the needs of others' since most people want to feel that they are doing good, not evil' (Monroe 2008:722).

This passivity also suggests a lack of responsibility, a distancing from the events and horrors of the 1990s, especially if we recall Parson's view of those in the 'Sick Role' as passive (Parsons 1975). This again raises the question of possible feelings of guilt. Is victimhood, together with positive self representation (victimhood, distancing of war crimes from selves, families and 'the Serbs' but not from 'the lunatics'), an attempt to negotiate or evade a feeling of guilt, or thoughts that one's actions (perhaps, voting for Milošević, or indirectly supporting him), may have led to the suffering of others? Of course, this question is further complicated by one's own experience of suffering and pain in the 1990s at the hands of others (Milošević, NATO and so on). However, an interesting point to raise here is that the accounts of war and atrocity are often saturated with resentment over the perception that 'only the Serbs are presented as the guilty ones'. As discussed in Chapter Six, guilt and responsibility are not clear to the respondents either, and hence these narratives could be understood as attempts to negotiate those meanings and positions. Living with that ambiguity is uncomfortable, and so clearer, less morally dubious positions (such as that of victim) are sought out.

Marginalisation and resentment

The need to represent oneself and one's group in a positive light is contrasted sharply with what is perceived to be their negative representation by others. There is an overwhelming feeling amongst all age groups that, as they have acknowledged the suffering of others, and given that 'all normal people' suffered in the war, their own suffering should be acknowledged too, or at least, the picture of 'Serbs as the only guilty party' should be redressed. In this sense, the respondents see themselves – and the Serbs in general – as victims of what they deem to be misrepresentation.

This covers several things. First, it is aimed predominantly at the Western media (there is a general perception that much of it is anti-Serb); as Branka complained once: 'according to them, there were no Serb victims and what I went through, that didn't matter, nobody cared that we had no milk to buy, nobody showed that we also suffered because of Milošević.' This was also aimed at various NGO campaigns, which are also seen as anti-Serb, and the perception is that they are only concerned with condemning Serb atrocities. This, furthermore, is related to the perception that the ICTY cannot be a just and fair court, since it prosecutes more Serbs than members of other national groups. The inability to control such representations, leads to further resentment and marginalisation:

> They keep mentioning the Serbs, but I think other people of other nationalities must have done something too. But no one is talking about that. They are just not showing all the sides. Because you can't have just one side taking part in atrocities. It must be that, just as there were many Serbs, there were others too. But in public, they are not even mentioned. In any case, I think of all of it as sick. But still, I don't understand politics, the military, and all the rest of it, and how it all happened, so I don't really have the need to think about something so ugly. (Nevena)

> You know, they showed the war in Sarajevo and they'd say, Serbs did this and that. I remember that market in Sarajevo, there was I don't know how many people dead there, they were showing the pictures, like Serb criminals, you know. But then when we heard people who came from there, that was a whole different story. We knew people whose whole families had been slaughtered by Muslims, completely, a whole family. They are saying, Serbs killed this and that. But who's killing the Serbs? Refugees everywhere. From Knin, Serbs are running away. From Bosnia, Serbs running away … and who's bombed? Serbs are … It turns out we are a nation that's really – that we're killing, slaughtering,

all that, but in fact...haven't Serbs also been killed, how many murdered and slaughtered, and how many children?...[when Milošević died in The Hague] And at that time I said, you know, maybe he wanted to prove something, to prove for the people, even though for us as a people, it was really not great during his time. No, it was not good, but he wanted to prove something, to remove some kind of guilt from the Serbian people [...] That responsibility, to free us here of that. Of that – that we are a genocidal people. (Katarina)

It is evident that a crime happened in Srebrenica, of which these people [in Serbia] did not know...But, the information that Muslims, on that same territory in the space of three years killed 8,000 Serbs – that supposedly doesn't matter...Those were two men [Karadžić and Mladić] who led specific operations on the territory of Bosnia and Herzegovina. The aim of those operations was to protect the Serb population, Serb inhabitants and to create one state in which Serbs in Bosnia and Herzegovina would live. And you can't say that's a bad thing. If Tudjman can create a Croatia by expelling all the non-Catholics from there, and over here you have Karadžić and Mladić who are creating Republika Srpska where they can take in, in one geographic area, all the people expelled from Croatia and from Bosnia, then I don't see anything bad in that. They are looking for Karadžić and Mladić, great. What did the Croats do with Ante Gotovina? They let him go. He was in jail for two years, the biggest criminal who killed I don't know how many people. Around two years. If that's OK then they can't look for Karadžić and Mladić. (Petar)

[About the NATO air strikes] It is talked about all the time, on TV. NATO air strikes but also about Serb atrocities in Croatia and Bosnia, but about Croatian atrocities towards the Serbs, no. About Muslim atrocities towards the Serbs, no. About Albanian atrocities, no. That's not talked about. They are creating an atmosphere where every Serb is supposed to feel guilty. (Petar)

[Discussing Srebrenica] Now they are saying 8,000. The West made it up. And here [in Serbia] they are saying 2–3,000, certainly not more. But also, in the same way, 3,000 Serbs were killed in Sarajevo and around Srebrenica, certainly one and a half thousand Serbs, houses burned to the ground, several villages burned. And now [Naser Orić] is not responsible for anything. So that means there are different criteria in the judgements [at The Hague]. Only Serbs are supposed to be punished. Everyone did the same things, only Serbs have to pay the price. I think, personally, that all these great powers, in order to justify air strikes against the Serbs, that's why they gave them that epithet of demonisation. (Mara)

It's unpleasant, to know about it [atrocities] especially when you know others did it too but no one is talking about it. It's somehow, I don't know. Everyone should go to trial. Everyone who has committed a crime has to go to court. So it's painful. Either we should all say we did something wrong, or not. But this, it's painful ... It turns out only Serbs did it and no one else ... (Nenad)

The question of victimhood is not an easy one to untangle for the respondents, as they are attempting to process several conflicting problems. The first is that they have directly observed Serb victims – refugees, the disabled, the sick and themselves – in their view, something clearly must have happened to all those people; they must have suffered at the hands of someone. But who? That 'who' and the 'why' does not, in their view, make much of an appearance in public discussion, and so it skews the rest of their view on the conflicts. For them, it does not add up that one set of victims is publicised but another is not. Hence, the accounts provided above attempt to work through that, and in the process distort the narrative towards Serb victims. Most of the time, as in the first extract, a discussion of Serb victims does not deny outright the existence of other victims.

But, these answers are also a response to questions about atrocities where it is explicit who has been killed – in Srebrenica, for instance. However, the answers proceed to discuss Serb victims. This narrative strategy can be read in two ways – first, as a case of role reversal (see e.g Bandura et al. 2001), where the roles of perpetrators and victims are reversed, to the effect that the victim's suffering is denied. This tactic is also highlighted in family memory and narratives of German victimhood (Wittlinger 2006; Welzer et al. 2003). In the German case, this is compared to a case of 'Chinese whispers when a story is continuously passed on to the next person until its content and message are hardly recognisable' (Wittlinger 2006:74). The concept of Chinese whispers might be a possible interpretation – the respondents above clearly hold some misconceptions about Srebrenica and other key events – but not a wholly satisfactory one.

One of the possible explanations for a lack of separation between 'their victims' and 'our victims' in accounts of atrocities committed by the Serbs is that it is due to the question asked, or rather not asked. On reflection, in my interviews (and indeed in less formal conversations) I did not ask about Serb victims, nor did I raise any questions that would allow an answer which would lead to those discussions. My questions, which concerned themselves with the conflicts, were about Mladić, Karadžić, Srebrenica, the siege of Sarajevo, the atrocities in Kosovo, and so on. In their content they resembled the kinds of questions sought out by NGOs and their projects (Did they know? How much did they know? What did they think of it?) albeit phrased in a much more open-ended way.

In other words, the entire interview (or conversation) did not provide an opportunity to discuss the question of Serb victims. That opportunity had to be created by the respondents, and it cropped up in their responses to questions about crimes such as Srebrenica because these were the instances in which the question of victims was discussed explicitly. The agenda is not to deny that Srebrenica happened at all, but to voice resentment that 'our' victims seem to have disappeared. This is clearly something that they feel the *need* to talk about, an unresolved issue, and something that they need to consider in *their* confrontation with the past. In turn, they feel that this part of the story of the violent past is not only excluded, but made not to matter. Amongst the respondents, there is often the perception that it is somehow taboo or shameful to talk about Serb victims, especially publicly. They are, in effect, creating 'alternative discursive spaces'

(Chuengsatiansup 2001:63), in opposition to what is deemed to be a hegemonic narrative of confrontation with the past.

The respondents here are thus located at the margins of debates about the past, as they believe their stories of Serb victimhood and their experience of the 1990s to be excluded and unwelcomed. Margins, or the idea of marginality, can be understood as 'the afflicting experience of those whose social existence has been excluded, discounted, dehumanised and displaced by dominant political discourse' (Chuengsatiansup 2001:32). Marginalising such experiences, then, or allowing important parts of the violent past to be understood as marginalised, or not engaging with them, deepens resentment further. For instance, in a study of German expellees between the 1960s and 1990s, Wittlinger notes that expellee organisations such as the Homeland Societies 'fostered and institutionalised the collective regional identity of the expellees, 'thereby ensuring that their past suffering did not fall into oblivion' (Wittlinger 2006:73). In contrast, in Serbia there is no organisation that engages with suffering and victimhood as it is perceived by the groups of the majority; those who did not fight nor were displaced or hurt (there are groups for refugees or the displaced). This lack of engagement leaves 'the ordinary' without an outlet for their accounts, and without a 'sponsor' (Humphreys, n.d.) to articulate their victimhood and acknowledge their cause. Of course, Serbian political and commemoration culture is saturated with references to Serb victims of all wars, past and recent (see e.g. Gödl 2007), but following Humphreys' important point, the 'sponsor', or audience which is needed to acknowledge Serb victimhood has to be an outsider, not someone who already occupies the same viewpoint as the speaker (Humphreys n.d.) – and certainly not someone from the political community within Serbia, from which most respondents claim to be disengaged from, or have little respect for.

This lack of outlets and acknowledgement also deepens resentment towards transitional justice projects in general, and resentment is often externalised through the perception that, not only are Serb victims made not to matter, but they also receive unfair trials at the ICTY:

> There you go, Orić got a two-year sentence. He was already in jail for two [or] three years, and now he's even going to get a

prize. And what are we going to do with all those in Kravice, Skelani, those he killed himself? It's a mockery. They are looking for Mladić, but without him, all those in Kupreš Polje would have been killed. And Orić two years, ridiculous. There's just no reasoning behind that. You can't say, I'll punish you symbolically for killing a thousand or two thousand Serbs [...] but I'll hang the Serbs because they killed eight hundred. So that's that, it means you're the victim again, and why, I really don't know. (Rada)

Even young people, much more informed and ready to criticise Serbia and its institutions, had a very ambivalent – and at times negative – view of the ICTY:

I don't know. The Hague ... it's not that I don't think it should exist, it should, but you can't convince me, and this is not like someone who says The Hague is totally stupid, but the fact remains that there are a lot of Serbs there, and I don't know, maybe two Croats and Muslims, and the rest are Serbs. No one can convince me that that is justice. But also because I was young all these years [during the war] no one can convince me to feel guilty for what happened. But generally speaking, people here don't really have that sense of guilt. But maybe some should. Maybe the people who could vote at the time that Yugoslavia was falling apart, and when they chose Milošević. Yes, the people who chose Milošević should feel guilty, but not me, to me it all just happened [...]

[...] I still have this wish for the image of us to be a bit more positive. Not go to the other extreme and say we're not responsible for anything. Because it is obvious that people from this nation exist, people who did those things that were not right. But it's a different question now, why some people here feel no responsibility, but maybe to some extent they should. I don't agree really with that idea that we are victims, and everyone should feel sorry for us, I am not one of those people who says we are all misunderstood. But definitely there is an element of truth there, that we are victims a bit. The picture of us that the world had is a bit skewed, and not always correct. But I still won't stand at the opposite end and say we did nothing wrong [...] (Ivan)

I don't get that attraction to Karadžić and Mladić. If you are throwing bombs at people in Sarajevo, from a hill, they can't do anything to you all the way from down there. I think that Mladić is just a sick man. But Karadžić, he seems a bit crazy, he's a psychiartrist and supposedly some poet as well. For some time, I figured, he's OK. But recently I started to understand what kind of person that Karadžić is, because I watched something on B92, and I heard how that man speaks – like, 'Balije,[6] let's go get rid of them'. But Mladić is my neighbour – his house is twenty metres from here. But, there is something. A tiny amount of my sympathy. It is because other people have not faced a trial. Alija got through, Tudjman died, I don't know, apart from that one general, I don't know a single Muslim general [on trial]. I think justice won't ever be served. They died or got lucky. (Filip)

[...] There are some odd things. For example Šešelj, they treat him really badly, apparently he lives in a really damp cell but he is an asthmatic. Then some prisoners they maltreat. I think that court is not fair. It is political, and it is hypocritical. I find that revolting, but, how can I explain this. But still, they are doing a really good job. That is to say, a really good job where Serbs are concerned. Sometime ago, there was a hundred prisoners, about 60 were Serbs, maybe one or two Albanians or Macedonians, the rest were Muslims. If it is real justice, and if someone has to put them on trial then fine. But I don't think that court is totally objective or unbiased. (Slavko)

Resentment over perceptions of unfair treatment are strongly defined, but are also often conflated with a number of other resentments: not just unacknowledged victims, but also unfair representations, economic war losses, unfair judicial procedures but also a resentment directed at personal losses during the 1990s. Rada highlighted this point when she said that, 'we lost everything and gained nothing.' In one of our conversations, she mentioned that she was particularly aggrieved that:

> We won nothing in that war. Even the things we had have been taken away ... Nothing remains after all that bloodshed. In Croatia and Bosnia, and in Kosovo, the war happened and the war is over. And we still live, even though we didn't have a war here, since 1990 we have always lived with some kind of threat, aggression and uncertainty. When I was in Bosnia [in 2006] people over there are much more relaxed than people here [...] even though there was a war there [...] We are non-stop, you always feel that you are someone who has to pay the price for war, and that's why that agony still continues. Sixteen years we've lived in that agony [...] There is no end, they've been blackmailing us since 1990. [...] (Rada)

That 'there is no end' is illustrative of the idea that the past is very much thought of as being in the present (c.f. Dawson 2007) but also points to one additional issue: there is no 'cut-off' point which delineates a 'now and then' (Kent 2011:4), at which point the past 'stops' and has to be confronted. For the respondents in this study, there is nothing that can provoke such a cut-off point; for instance, nothing to wait for that might provide closure – no bodies to find and no one's return to await. Their perceived victims, the mutilated, the disabled, themselves, carry on living in the present (observed in a lot of use of the present tense), unacknowledged and feeding the cycle of resentment.

Furthermore, middle-aged respondents, even if they had not been personally involved in the war, nor had lost any family members, still lost a great deal of their former lives. Some pointed out that they had lost friends in other republics, and as well as losing the economic wellbeing they once had, they also lost a sense of place – the country they had been born into had shrunk rapidly in the 1990s and their movement outside of the country became suddenly limited: they are in fact the so-called 'transition losers' (Bićanić and Franičević 2006:188). Resentment 'stems from the perception that one's group is located in an unwarranted subordinate position' (Petersen 2002:40), and must also 'be understood as an emotion distinguished by its concern and involvement in power' (McCarthy et al. 1997:278). This sense of disenfranchisement in war narratives is acute. Furthermore, McCarthy et al. argue that resentment operates through its own logic and through 'processes of simulation that usurp contemporary experiences of the real' (McCarthy et al. 1997:278). In this way, victimhood as an interpretative framework is based on perceptions ('simulations') and not necessarily 'the real' ('facts'). Both resentment and victimhood are therefore strategies of 'holding down a moral centre' (McCarthy et al. 1997:278).

The creation of 'alternative discursive spaces' (Chuengsatiansup 2001:63), in which the experience of one's own suffering and perceptions of injustice are articulated in a context in which there is no external engagement with the same also creates an ' "agentative moment", a shift in the sense of oneself from an object being acted upon by the world, to a subject acting upon the world' (Chuengsatiansup 2001:63, citing Daniel 1996:198–92). This fits with the notion of this particular 'ordinary' audience of Serbian citizens as a group often written *about* (Clark 2008) rather than one which speaks for itself. This dynamic is often explicitly expressed in complaints about certain representations and a lack of power to change them, together with frequently expressed sentiments such as 'the winner writes history' or references to the ICTY as 'victor's justice'. Victimhood narratives, which emphasise one's own victims, turn the audience into 'subjects acting upon the world' (Chuengsatiansup 2001:63), by being able to subvert the dominant narratives and insert the history deemed to be repressed.

Most of the time, this subversion of the dominant narrative of confrontation with the past, one which is understood to exclude Serb victims, importantly does not re-write history for the purpose of obliterating other victims. The ways in which these histories are re-narrated, focus on 'the big powers' such as 'the West' (in retrospect, following NATO air strikes) and its tools of justice, and so the reason for the exclusion of Serb victims is often found outside the former Yugoslav space. In other words, 'our' victims are not suppressed because 'Croats/ Muslims/Albanians' are pretending they did not do it, but because 'outsiders' are suppressing these stories. This dynamic is discussed at length in the following chapter.

In conclusion, ideas about victimhood thus work on two levels: first, in acknowledging, implicitly or explicitly, that there were victims on all sides ('those poor people'), but second, in that context, in wondering what has happened to 'our' victims, and expressing resentment at their marginalisaiton. This mixed view of victims poses a challenge to transitional justice, both in terms of practice and conceptual literature. Given that transitional justice requires a clear categorisation of victims and perpetrators (Sriram 2007), this might put it in conflict with the ways in which the past, and different actors roles within it are actually understood. Furthermore, since positions of victimhood are much more appealing than those of perpetrators, it is difficult to imagine that any one group, such as 'Serbian society' that does not fit so easily into any one transitional justice role, would willingly identify itself as a perpetrator. Equally, attempting to argue against the impulse of self-victimisation will not yield the desired results, since respondents clearly *have* felt under physical attack at times in recent history. It should be taken into consideration that the levels of victimisation are multiple, both visible and invisible, and that this has bearing on how transitional justice projects are interpreted by those subjected to them.

Ultimately, this raises the question as to how we are to understand and conceptualise victims and victimhood? On the one hand, this should be pretty clear – victims suffer at the hands of perpetrators who, often, have broken the law – and most of those victims would have suffered directly, physically, and bear the scars. But, when one's belonging to a victim category is not so clear-cut, yet one perceives oneself as such, where are lines to be drawn, and who has the moral authority to include and exclude self-subscribing victims? Is there a criterion by which we can include victims who have suffered physically or mentally at the hands of perpetrators, but exclude victims who have suffered indirectly, or differently? Can, for example, Serbian conscripts and their families be seen as victims? Can people who have undergone severe stresses as a direct consequence of the wars, such as losing friends through suicide or losing family members to psychological instability, also be seen as victims of those conflicts? And if not, why not? And how might these people then be labelled?

Finally, this raises the question of what should be included in ideas about confronting the past. As discussed previously, the current transitional justice projects in Serbia are interpreted by the respondents as singular; they do not align with the experience of the past held by some of their target audience. As Schwandner-Sievers notes in relation to Kosovo, 'the quest for justice and peace needs to take into account social emotion and its socio-cultural location. If it does not, it will be doomed to encourage processes of subversion, and ultimately, failure' (Schwandner-Sievers 2007:104). The final chapter of this book takes up the theme of subversion within war narratives, with specific reference to the conspiracy theories that surround the ICTY amongst the respondents.

CHAPTER 8

'WAS IT ALL A PART OF A SECRET PLAN?': SUBVERSION, RESISTANCE AND 'THEORISING FEARS' THROUGH CONSPIRACY

Introduction

In Serbia, one is never far away from a conspiracy theory. More often than not, these conspiracy theories involve deep political problems or inexplicable events. In this study, many of these conspiracy theories addressed the breakup of Yugoslavia, the death of Milošević, the NATO air strikes and war crimes. For example, it is frequently claimed that the Otpor resistance movement was funded by the CIA in order to overthrow the Milošević regime and for the purpose of gaining access to Serbia. During my research, the Open Society foundation also came under attack for funding international scholarships for students from the Balkans: it was seen as a 'secret plan' to ensure all the best and brightest young people from Serbia were taken to the West. The NGO sector faced similar accusations. It was staffed by 'traitors' and 'foreign mercenaries' (also in Kostovicova 2006:28), with secret designs to destroy Serbia from within. Then, many new stories and developments became incorporated into existing perceptions. For instance, commenting on a news item about the growing sales of coastal properties in Montenegro to wealthy Russians, Rada and Katarina interpreted this event as follows: the properties were being sold by the Russians to Albanians, who were buying land to encroach onto territory close to Serbia and Kosovo. In the story, Albanians used Russians as proxies because Montenegrins would, apparently, not want to do business with them. But this hinted at a much broader issue that many Serbs attempted to understand at the time – the prospect of Kosovo independence. The particular conspiracy implied is the Albanian 'takeover' of Kosovo. This story formed a part of set of similar stories, or variations on the same theme. Another respondent suggested that the border between Kosovo and Albania was kept porous on purpose during Tito's rule of Yugoslavia to encourage Albanian migration into Kosovo. These stories, in turn, were often linked to the 'international community' and their attempt to somehow gain control of Kosovo and so obtain access to the Western Balkans.

Serbian political culture is also rich in conspiracy theorising (see Byford 2006). Since much of this theorising is the product of the Milošević or Koštunica regimes, as well as parties such as the Serbian Radical Party, and scholars such as Smilja Avramov, it is fairly easy to dismiss them as nationalist or ill-informed and ignorant opinions when they appear in the narratives of the ordinary public. The conspiracies which appear here are much more complicated than that, however. Above all, as Parish (2001) and Skinner (2001), following Gluckman (1966) and Evans-Pritchard (1987) suggest, such theorising tends to 'absorb' the 'rational' as well as the 'irrational'. Therefore, 'perhaps it is possible to look at the processes which are used to substantiate beliefs and conspiracies rather than dismissing them… as illogical' (Parish 2001:12; Skinner 2001).

The conspiracies regarding Kosovo are only a prism through which much broader issues (and conspiracies) are refracted. Typically, a rather small cast of characters appears in most of these, and so 'the West', the EU, the Vatican, NATO and 'the international community' are blamed for breaking up Yugoslavia, the conflicts and war crimes. Sometimes, these conspiracy theories are located in the distant past; sometimes the distant past is invoked as a conspiracy taking place in the present (interestingly, Bock-Luna 2008 identifies a similar dynamic amongst émigré Serbs in California). Whereas it is difficult to get to a point at which individuals are discussing 'the past' as a site of war crimes, massacres and murders, it is much easier to hear individuals and groups discussing those same issues through a conspiracy theory. To an extent, this is also true of victimhood, and it is furthermore interesting to note that both victimhood and conspiracy theory became dominant political narratives in 1990s Serbia. As ways of discussing atrocities and horrific events of the past, conspiracy theories offer two things: a depersonalised narrative and an alternative history, in which '"the evil comes from the outside" and not from within' (Bock-Luna 2008:197).

But what do they suggest about confrontations with the past? What role do they play in the process of reflecting and thinking about war crimes? Scholarly literature tends to ignore these kinds of narratives and they are often viewed as 'the poor man's cognitive mapping' (Jameson 1995 in Parish 2001:6). As Hellinger suggests, conspiracy theory is often dismissed as 'pathology' (Hellinger 2003:204 in Bock-Luna 2008:186). In this chapter, I will illustrate how conspiracy theories about the past can be viewed as alternative and rewritten histories, ways of negotiating meaning, reclaiming narratives and reacting to exclusion.

To the analyst, conspiracy theories have much to offer. Instead of existing simply as amusing stories of how the 'uninformed' might see history, they shed a rather revealing light onto a number of dynamics, including the way in which the 'international community' and its role in the Balkans is viewed and recent history understood. In turn, this leads on to much insight regarding how the respondents in this study saw themselves and their society vis-à-vis the conflicts, and how they understood and perceived (in)justice.

In her work on migrant Serbs in the San Francisco Bay Area, Bock-Luna comes across conspiracy theories quite frequently, but proposes to view these as both 'a rational and emotional response to political circumstances, e.g. to the feeling of being 'under attack' (Bock-Luna 2008:186). Similarly, this book does not view the presence of conspiracy theory as delusion, irrationality or the product of misinformation, but rather as subversion of dominant discourses on the past, as well as an attempt to find an alternative history to the conflicts, spoken from a position of marginality and based on 'real perceptions of injustice and misrepresentations' (Bock-Luna 2008:186). These strategies are often used as explanatory mechanisms and the speakers here seem to be looking for answers to histories and problems for which they find currently available answers unsatisfactory. They are ways of exploring and negotiating meanings and constructing alternative histories for 'the world around them' which is 'no longer as it should be' (Grohl 1987:1). As this chapter argues, it is precisely this added level of complication which makes denial of war crimes difficult to separate from broader feelings of disenfranchisement and resentment, and which complicates current approaches to 'coming to terms with the past'.

A convenient way to define a conspiracy theory would be by using David Aaronovitch's example, where it is 'the attribution of a deliberate agency to something that is more likely to be accidental or unintended' or 'the attribution of secret action to one party that might far more reasonably be explained as the less covert and less complicated action of another' (Aaronovitch 2009:5). Conspiracy theories attempt to establish relationships, but almost always include a 'relatively small group of persons – the conspirators – acting in secret' (Keeley 1999:116, in Clarke 2002:134). They 'form the constant process of interpretation wherein even the most minute fact or coincidence related to a host of other facts becomes evidence of a wide-scale or global plot (Beatty 1999:4). Things which are not necessarily linked – the ethnic conflicts, NATO, the US – can be constructed as such in order to create what appear to be credible stories. The narratives use 'personal attribution, leap[s] of the imagination, specific construction of the enemy, Manichean moral dualism, an apocalyptic tone and an idea of mass manipulation' (Byford 2006:36). Importantly, as Fenster suggests, conspiracy theories operate as cultural practices of interpretation and 'as *narrative* forms that circulate throughout political campaigns and movements, journalism, and popular culture' (Fenster 2008:13, added emphasis).

Conspiracy theories are global. Fenster suggests that the appearance of conspiracy theories is an integral part of democratic politics (Fenster 2008) and, as Aaronovich points out, there is also a degree of 'fashionable conspiracisim' in the West, especially pertaining to September

11 terrorist attacks (Aaronovich 2009:5). Likewise, as Smith (2001) suggests, certain aspects of our present political and economic divisions, such as the ways in which we engage with capitalist institutions 'is, and has always been, a prime site for conspiracy theory' (2001:153) As examples, Smith cites 'shadowy cabals like The Illuminati, the Masons, the Bilderbergers... the Trilateralists' amongst those who have often been identified as working behind capital (Smith 2001:153). 'Conspiracism' is evident in Serbia, and interestingly, Byford identifies some of those same actors as key figures in the Serbian political culture of the Milošević era (Byford 2006 and Byford and Billig 2001). According to Byford (2006) and Moore (2002) conspiracy theories are usually the explanatory tools of the marginalised and disenfranchised. Serbia, in many ways, has been and still is on the margins of Europe and 'the West', and, as Byford points out, Milošević presented this position as something laudable, suggesting that Serbia was the 'last bastion' of resistance against Western imperialism (Byford 2006).

Various conspiracy narratives originating from the Milošević era did not disappear from the Serbian political sphere. Throughout the 2000s, politicians such as Vojislav Šešelj often accused the ICTY of various conspiracies, an accusation which gained a popular following after the death of Milošević. It is evident that, at least for the Milošević regime, they offered a way out – blaming others and blaming history. For instance, Bugarski notes that during the conflicts an Orthodox Serb priest was quoted on Radio Novi Sad as saying: 'We pray to God that God will reason with our enemies for that war to stop.' Bugarski (1996: 289–291) remarks that this was for it to be 'known who is the only party who can stop the war, and in no combination can that be us [the Serbs] – the only thing we can do is to wait for it to eventually happen.' The idea that the conflicts were a part of an anti-Serb conspiracy was also propagated by Milošević and close associates such as intellectual Smilja Avramov, who is on record as late as 2000 claiming that the USA and the Vatican were behind the war in Bosnia (Byford 2006:231). Furthermore, history and historical sequences of events are often called upon to give an explanatory hand to a conspiracy theory. According to Fenster (2008), past and present often merge in conspiracy theories, which are placed in single interpretative frameworks

(Fenster 2008). Certainly, amongst the responses collected there, history and conspiracy often converge.

The specific recurring motifs and themes in the narratives here can be categorised along the following lines: (1) NATO implemented the airstrikes in order to gain control over Kosovo for various military and political reasons (similar ideas are also recorded in (Byford 2006) and Byford and Billig 2001); (2) 'the international community' did not get involved in the 1990s conflicts because it always wanted to see Yugoslavia broken up; (3) the ICTY is a 'political court' whose aim is to make the Serbs accept blame for war; (4) the wars started because there was always an anti-Serb conspiracy on behalf of the Muslims and Croats (but this theme was almost marginal compared to how frequently the international community was identified as the key actor in inciting the conflict); (5) Milošević and Milan Babić were murdered at/by the ICTY and (6) the war crimes of the 1990s can be attributed to injustices against the Serbs in the 1940s. The stories were connected and often became each other's constitutive elements.

But, why are the conspiracy theories of Serbian political culture so often found amongst individuals – particularly those included in this research? As this book has already illustrated, such subscriptions to alternative versions of events are not likely to be the result of a lack of information about the 1990s, since they often incorporate well known facts about the era, but re-told in vastly different interpretations. The question could be formulated in a different way – why are these narratives of conspiracy and denial, which circulated during the Milošević era – not strongly opposed and resisted by individuals, given that they do express regret and horror at the actual events themselves? Moreover, why are they presented and circulated as more plausible than the truth behind these events?

A closer look at such motifs in narratives of respondents here might offer some answers. The first feature of conspiracy theories is that they do not always replicate exactly the conspiracy theorising propagated during the Milošević regime. Conspiracy theories are constantly being invented and reinvented, using different actors and relationships. As this chapter discusses, this is perhaps one of the main functions of conspiracy theorising amongst this group of respondents: it is an active search for an alternative reading of history that is more appealing and believable than the one(s) currently offered. Why this should be the case at all has a lot to do with the content of violent histories, which are, in many ways, difficult to believe, as the respondents frequently highlighted. In this, it is no coincidence that 'ethnic others' featured in these stories less often than 'outsiders' who are often deemed to have played a much bigger role in the wars. This resonates with the frequent sentiment that 'ordinary' and 'normal' people could not have caused these wars.

Although not all respondents subscribed to these views which relied on conspiracy theory to make sense of the past, those who did were not viewed as 'deluded' by their peers. Above all, no one identified those particular accounts as conspiracy, but rather a legitimate and reasonable interpretations of events. Understanding the accounts presented here as conspiracy theories is my own interpretation, based on the elements which appear in the narratives presented here, and in which I identify the presence of the most significant discursive elements of conspiracy theorising: the rejection of existing accounts, and attribution of responsibility to actors with 'secret plans' (Aaronovitch 2009 Fenster 2008; Spark 2001).

'They planned it before': blaming the wars on outsiders

To understand the context in which most of the accounts containing conspiracy theory are formed, it is important to consider the significance of NATO air strikes discussed in the previous chapter. The constant presence of NATO and other international actors in conspiracy theories told here owes a large debt to the presence of the same during the late 1990s (see Byford 2006; Byford and Billig 2001), as well as to the importance of the NATO air strikes themselves. The NATO air strikes in general are, as Bock Luna (2008) suggests, a significant event but also an *unexplained* one. The reasons offered for the air strikes not appear plausible to this group of respondents. Because the air strikes are inexplicable and unresolved, so too are the rest of the conflicts, and frequently conspiracies involving the NATO airstrikes are used to make sense of the earlier wars.

Previous chapters discussed that most of the respondents' narratives about the war are in fact analyses of what they thought had gone wrong. The persistence with which ideas about the causes of the war appeared indicated that is one of the most unresolved aspects of the past, especially since just about all of my respondents mentioned at some point that they still do not understand 'why it all happened' and why the wars were necessary. However, they frequently attempted to find answers in the NATO airstrikes themselves, 'borrowing' some of the key actors from this event, to try and understand the earlier conflicts of this (as discussed below).

Thus, the causes of the wars were predominantly attributed to a range of parties, particularly, the loosely-defined 'West' and 'international community' and sometimes to Croats and Bosniaks. The wartime Croatian president Franjo Tudjman and Bosnian president Alija Izetbegović were sometimes singled out, but there was less critique of Milošević. When these accounts did criticise Milošević, they sometimes presented him as a puppet of the West, acting on foreign orders. Some respondents also suggested that the war and the break-up of Yugoslavia were all part of a larger 'plan'. For instance:

America. They planned it before. Serbia needs to be destroyed, brought to its knees. America and England are the biggest enemies. America, Germany and Austria. They were helping [Operation] Storm in Croatia when everything was cleansed. [The refugees] told me. And you know who was the head of Storm. The one who is now the president, Agim Çeku. [...] In Storm, Americans, that was planned by Americans and by Germans, and those were American weapons and the American army went ahead first and Croatia was cleansed of Serbs. (Danica)

Absolutely, for sure, there existed a plan, because stories were being told as soon as Tito died, at least in Belgrade. That there exists a plan for the break-up of Yugoslavia, and that there exists a plan for the Green Transversal which is the creation of a great Islamic state from Doboj to Iran. That was being said in Belgrade, in Belgrade, publicly after Tito died, for the break-up of Yugoslavia and that scenario probably existed, I think that scenario is a part of globalisation, which means American occupation of the whole world. We will be an American colony. (Ana)

These politicians did what they wanted, and what their foreign mentors imposed on them [...] Politicians made the people fight, the leaders of the former republics. In the secession of the former republics, certain politicians had the support of the West and some did not. To me, that was an artificially incited conflict, with help from the West. (Mladen)

That war was basically a political fabrication, not only by our governments but by European and American ones. (Branka)

I think that was something where someone manipulated us, our memories and our intolerance from the previous events. Someone drew us into a horrible and dirty game. And that someone does not live on these territories. (Mirjana)

The idea that external powers conspired to break up Yugoslavia is, of course, dismissed by most scholars of the region (see e.g. Ramet 2004a and 2004b). Yet, for the respondents in this study, this explanation is presented as not only a plausible idea, but also the most convincing one. One particularly interesting aspect of the 'war conspiracies' is the ways in which they crop up at times when disbelief over other causes of the wars are expressed. In particular, the idea that people in Croatia and Bosnia turned against each other was rejected almost universally by the respondents. Partly due to such categorical rejections of these explanations for war, some respondents were inclined to think that something else must be at play. Notably, that something else is often some greater or more mysterious power. As demonstrated above, those mysterious, powerful actors are a pick-and-mix of the usual suspects of conspiracy theories: the US, Germany, Europe, the West, as well as a hint of Islamic fundamentalism represented by the 'Green Transversal'. In an interesting parallel, Bock-Luna also identifies the Green Transversal as a feature in conspiracy theories amongst the Serbs in California (Bock Luna 2007). But, rather than just taking aim at the powerful, these conspiracies assign *active* roles to outsiders, whilst most 'insiders' of the Yugoslav conflict appear passive. This is often presented in the context of disbelief that 'the insiders' could take part in war. The two extracts below represent a popular sentiment amongst my group of respondents.

> [About the Kosovo war] *Was it* the Albanians? Or the Americans? There was that idea that there is a map of the world, how it's supposed to look at certain periods. So, Serbia, and everything. Someone thought it up, someone likes to play God, so they decided that. I really don't believe that people of whatever nationality had that much hate towards each other. Especially not towards someone who was their neighbour for the last thirty years, that I really can't understand. I simply can't accept that we, as people, as humans, are so evil! I find that really hard to accept. And so, I am inclined to think that someone was mixed up, that someone wanted to play God. (Svetlana)

> I don't really know why the wars started. Some people say that it was a set up on the part of the US. I think that's possible. You see, in Iraq they attacked a country, just because it annoyed them. Maybe they need it [Iraq] to access something else. From what I've heard, they save, I don't know, billions and billions of dollars if they build a road across Europe and not Africa, to get to oil. So maybe we were in the way for that. But the war, what happened there, believe me, I have no idea. Although, maybe people didn't get on so well. Maybe there were some tensions in the whole of former Yugoslavia. But maybe it was something else. (Ana's daughter, Iva)

Whilst conspiracy theories are often judged as misguided rants of the ill-informed, we should also consider how such stories fit with the wider experience of people who narrate and believe them. For instance, in this study most of the older respondents expressed frequent *disbelief* over the recent events, starting with the breakup of Yugoslavia, and on to wars, war crimes and NATO air strikes. Put simply, many had never believed that such developments would ever actually occur in their lifetime, and especially not in the violent way in which they did. Yet, they occurred, and in a relatively short space of time, arriving one after the other in quick succession. Events that were once thought to be implausible actually took place. Viewed from that position then, conspiracy theories presented here do not seem so implausible to those who had to live through such events.

Moreover, living through all of these events over the last two decades also meant being subjected to competing and contradictory accounts of the truth: the Milošević-era version, the versions produced by nationalists, the radicals, the 'internationals', the activists. What happens when so many competing accounts exist? In a different context, reporter David Grann captures this very well. Writing about the death of Guatemalan lawyer Rodrigo Rosenberg, in what looked like a political conspiracy, Grann, noticing layers upon layers of secrets and hidden truths surrounding the case, notes that 'the proliferation of counterfeit realities underscored the difficulty of ascertaining the truth in a country where there are so few arbiters of it' (Grann 2011). Similarly, Živković suggests that during the 1990s in Serbia the level of misinformation and opacity was such that the ability of anyone to ascertain 'what was really going on' was 'severely impaired' (Živković 2001:176). In other words, the events of the 1990s were so extraordinary and incomprehensible to these respondents, and explanations offered were all as incredible as each other.

Above all, conspiracy theories blaming NATO et al. for any number of events form a search for a culprit. If the war did not start because people turned on each other, then who started it?[1] The air strikes appear to have offered new possibilities of understanding. They helped with retrospective reasoning: the shady, powerful 'someone else' who possibly caused the breakup of Yugoslavia suddenly came into focus and the reasoning went thus: if NATO and the West were inclined to bomb Serbia, then clearly, *'they'* must have also been behind the breakup of Yugoslavia. This 'war as a self-fulfilling prophecy' is also identified by Bock-Luna, who also adds that:

With nineteen NATO countries undertaking military action against Serbia, the 'unjust' persecution of Serbs manifested itself blatantly, being widely read as a punishment and revenge, instead of a 'just', 'humanitarian' intervention as NATO named its operations. The NATO war against Yugoslavia reasserted all conspiracies, characterising the realisation of long held speculations and nationalist fears, namely that 'the whole world' conspired against 'them'... This time, the enemy so clearly attacked from outside, exemplifying that Serbs were singled out unequivocally out of the complex muddle of warring parties in the Yugoslav conflict. (Bock-Luna 2007:197)

Perhaps it is also a need to rationalise and simplify the 'complex muddle' that led some respondents to weave conspiracy theories around other phenomena, too. The 'West' is also seen at times as responsible for Milošević and his access to power:

That man just turned up out of the blue. And he turned up when he was returning from America. He spent six years in America as a director of Jugobanka. He was a banker. He finished law school but was involved with banking and spent six years in America as a director of one of our banks, and after those six years, he returns to Serbia and then becomes a politician and everyone treats him like God. Then you notice that something is not quite right. Then Tudjman turns up [...] And then you realise that there are three or four individuals who were easily corrupted, who would be obedient and who would do what they were told to do. But, I think they were surprised by Milošević, I think they are probably still surprised today that Milošević did so much that benefited the West more than it benefited his people. And that's why they kept him [in power] for as long as they've kept him. (Petar)

I say, that Milošević did not come to power just like that, and I think that in all of that there were much bigger players involved.

We can't even imagine what was going on there! He didn't turn up just by chance. (Biljana)

I think he had to be in jail here, not there in The Hague. And not just to go to the tribunal, go through and say what he wanted to say. He had to be sentenced, with a maximum sentence for what he did to this country, because he ruined it. He helped the West ruin this country, he and his collaborators. He was not acting alone, no. (Jovan)

These ideas about Milošević's rise to power highlight one of the main points of conspiracy theories: the identification that 'something is not quite right'. As Byford (personal communication, August 2007) points out, in conspiracy theories it is enough to hint at the existence of 'something else' for the discourse to be a 'good enough' explanation. Conspiracy theories sometimes do not offer evidence nor feel a need to name actors or plans, because 'their' existence is simply taken for granted.

In this sense, one aim of conspiracy theories can be said to be the displacement of responsibility, or what scholars such as Cohen (2001) might connect to or label as interpretative denial. It is also a 'displacement of a desire for political significance and a reification of interaction which fetishises individual signs' and which 'places them into interpretative structures which seek to fix their meanings once and for all' (Beatty 1999:4; Fenster 2008). But why the need to fix meanings in this way or to blame 'outsiders'? Finding blame elsewhere is more than an attempt to evade responsibility. For instance, van Dijk suggests that such 'attribution processes' can be understood as strategies of 'making sense' (van Dijk 1990:175). They are invoked in order to establish relations between cause and effect, necessary for the establishment of coherence (van Dijk 1990:175). They act to 'explain our own negative actions and failures' through an explanation of their context and so they have a strong 'self-serving' aspect (van Dijk 1990:175). Conspiracy theories depersonalise history, especially with the inclusion of outsiders. This allows the speakers to remove themselves from any sequence of events that may have caused the wars, atrocities and the suffering of others.

More specifically, it is often 'in the absence of a credible narrative' that 'alternative explanations arise', especially during societal/group insecurity (Moore 2002:202, 204). Thus, conspiracy theories here can be seen as attempts to make sense of the 'senseless' (Moore 2002:202), or to create 'another reality' (Renard 2007:54). Viewed from the 'grass-roots level', the sheer number of narratives about Serbia's still do not offer a 'good enough' explanation for what happened; giving rise to conspiracy theories that try to address this.

NATO, Europe and Kosovo: 'theorising fears'

Perhaps no other agency is as frequently invoked in conspiracy theories in Serbia as NATO. Various conspiracy theories surrounded the NATO airstrikes and the idea of (at the time rumoured and anticipated) Kosovo independence, particularly due to the incomprehension that a superpower like NATO would be interested in intervention in a small state such as Kosovo. In 1999, as airstrikes were taking place, Byford (2006:11) was struck by many people's readiness to talk about the event largely in narratives with many elements of conspiracy theory. The idea that NATO wished to destroy Serbia was disseminated widely in the mainstream media and by mainstream political parties' press releases during the air strikes (Byford 2006:227–228). The DSS's press releases were published in *Politika*, with sentences such as 'the real aim of these air strikes is to cripple Serbia economically for a longer period of time, and thereby reduce it to a status of an American quasi-colony, incapable of any kind of active role in international life' (In Byford 2006:227). Similarly, Vojislav Koštunica, who soon after the airstrikes became the president of the remaining Yugoslav Federation and subsequently Prime Minister of Serbia, claimed in a statement to the weekly *Nedeljni Telegraf* that the 'real motive for the air strikes [...] was the 'campaign into the East and getting closer to something which represents an important polygon for future wars and conflicts, and that is Caspian oil' (Byford 2006:228). According to Byford (2006:241) isolationism was one reason why conspiracy theory became a dominant discourse for interpretation, since Milošević's '"no" to the new world order' meant that 'conspiracy theorists found themselves in the mainstream', pursuing their 'obsessions with an "external enemy"'. Although Byford (2006:14) states that conspiracy theorists have become marginalised since the fall of Milošević and are now confined to conservative politics, this kind of discourse on NATO and Kosovo in particular remains dominant in private narratives. Whilst Byford found that in 1999 the most significant conspiracies were anti-Semitic, there was no indication of this amongst my respondents, and it became clear that their theories were generally anti-Western:

> They [the West] have a different aim. And here, they said air strikes were over Račak and the repression of *Šiptars*. That has nothing to do with it [...] not an end to aggression. They had their own aim, to let the NATO army enter and take over Serbia. (Stevan)

> If the Americans wanted to bring democracy to Serbia [with the air strikes] because of one man thanks to whom we don't have a democratic society, they could have just arrested him. But it is obvious that there was another aim, to bomb a country, to bomb a people. They could have arrested him but the aim was something else. Bomb us, take Kosovo away, a part of our territory. [...] (Ana)

> Why is Kosovo interesting to the Americans? Well because they built their Aviano air base there,[2] the biggest in the Balkans, and they are now closer to the Russians. They made a centre for narcotics mafia and for dealing, everyone knows that the CIA deals with drugs and weapons. Everyone knows that the biggest American earnings come from weapons. America just collapses if it's not at war. They always have to create wars. (Petar)

> They did it because they couldn't break the regime by any other means, just like in Iraq. So they tried, by any means, by infiltrating their people into the opposition party in Serbia and so on, they kept trying. But one man, who was their perfect ally

because of the Dayton agreement [...] they changed their minds about him and it turns out that because of him, the whole nation has to suffer. (Mladen)

All the different strands of conspiracy theorising concerning war crimes and the breakup of Yugoslavia come together in ideas about Kosovo, and it is really here that such conceptualisation emerges as a tool for coping with uncertainty, fears and lack of control (Parish 2001:4). In writing about conspiracy theories, Parish draws on the work of Anthony Giddens and Michael Taussig, to suggest that 'the lack of control many of us have over our everyday lives means that we must all learn to ride what Giddens calls the "juggernaut of modernity"' whilst the 'complexities of the social-economic-political world' can be described as 'in a state of perpetual nervousness in which shock and normality are related, and rupture destructive of normality' (Parish 2001:4). Drawing on a diverse set of examples, such as the 'outbreak of accusations of Satanic abuse' in 1980s 'sink' estates in Britain (La Fontaine 1998) or the conspiracy theories over organ theft in South America (Comaroff and Comaroff 1999), Parish suggests that such approaches may be attempts at 'theorising fears' in an age of widening inequality gaps and 'the desire to find closure amidst the uncertainties of late capitalism' (Parish 2001:4–6).

This is especially visible here, with references to NATO and its attempts to 'take over' Kosovo. Taken together with narratives of conflict and war crimes, much anxiety is expressed and the 1990s themselves were filled with insecurity and fear. Furthermore, as Humphrey points out, 'becoming a spectator of death and surviving in a postmodern world is anxiety ridden' (Humphrey 2002:103). The uncertainties and lack of coherence, as well as fear over one's future, existential circumstances and other problems, easily feed in to conspiracy theories as a way of explaining 'the whole thing', since these attempts to 'theorise fears' reveal attempts to create 'neat explanations in an untidy big world where there is no great centre anymore' (Parish 2001:6) and where individuals (in this study) may feel they have lost control over events. In 2006, the question of Kosovo independence had just begun to heat up as Serbia and Kosovo commenced negotiations (see e.g. Weller 2009 and Ker-Lindsay 2011). Independence already looked to be most likely outcome, and the opening of the negotiations marked yet another monumental historical change for people in Serbia, producing further anxiety.

Kosovo is of immense cultural, historical and religious significance for Serbia (see e.g. Duijzings 2000). Yet anxieties surrounding independence went much deeper than that. In the same way that respondents felt that most of the events of the 1990s took place outside of their control, so they felt about the (then upcoming and clearly foreseeable) independence of Kosovo. Once again the visible chaos, and events that spiralled seemingly out of control, mirrored their personal fears. In addition, given that much of the 1990s was explained in the context of horror and terror, 'theorising' one's own fear through various conspiracies is an almost logical progression of this frame of reference. Thus, conspiracy theories implicating NATO and the West in Kosovo's independence became a way of externalising fears regarding political uncertainty and general incomprehension of the sequence of events starting in 1990.

The ICTY conspiracies

NATO's involvement in Serbia also provided a retrospective 'secret plan' in yet another situation: the war crimes trials at the ICTY. As many respondents had difficulty in comprehending the conflicts of the 1990s, so they also had trouble comprehending war crimes and the magnitude of atrocities which they signify. But, as the previous chapters demonstrate, the question of denial, where it appears, is much more complex than obstinacy or refusal to accept responsibility. In addition to the dynamics already elaborated, this section introduces another element: that denial can also be embedded in narrative contexts of perceived injustice, which plays very neatly into the hands of conspiracy theory.

Whilst conspiracy theories concerning the ICTY or war crimes in general were fairly common in Serbia's political sphere throughout time that the fieldwork was conducted for this research, they were used somewhat differently in the private sphere. For instance, the SRS in particular offered rather a lot of examples of this kind of theorising. However, it is important to note that at the time its leader Vojislav Šešelj was awaiting trial at ICTY. Conspiracy theorising in that sense allowed the party to relocate the problem – from Šešelj and his alleged involvement in war crimes to the court itself. In the private sphere, the 'Hague Conspiracies', as I label them, straddle a somewhat more ambiguous ground: they are not always explicit attempts to deny the existence of war crimes, but are often attempts to raise questions about ICTY itself. This is clearer when a particular pattern is taken into account: war crimes themselves rarely feature in this particular set of narratives, whilst 'The Hague' is mentioned frequently, and quite a lot more after Milošević's death in 2006. The death of Milošević whilst on trial at the ICTY, consisted of precisely the kind of detail (or lack of) which conspiracy theorising is drawn to, and makes use of. The death was seemingly sudden; the case against Milošević apparently looked shaky. After his death, his lawyer produced a letter Milošević allegedly wrote about his worsening health problems, the supposed refusal of the Tribunal to allow him to travel to Russia for medical treatment and his supposed claim to his lawyer that 'they are poisoning me' (e.g. *Večernje Novosti* 2006a, 2006b, 2006c).

This played right into the hands of a number of ICTY conspiracies which existed already. Broadly, this included a belief that the ICTY is 'a court for Serbs' and that several people including Milan Babić (who committed suicide) had been murdered there. In the first few days following Milošević's death there was a profound sense of shock and the respondents to whom I spoke at this time, in particular Emilija and her pensioner friends, as well as Rada, Mladen and Gordana, seemed to take it for granted that he had died due to health complications. However, in the week between his death and his burial, the media created a panic and reported the news predominantly within the frame of various conspiracy theories. By the end of the week, the same respondents had changed their mind, and started to think that Milošević really had been poisoned. The interviews below were conducted several months after the death of Milošević, and feature frequent references to an unspecified 'they', who seemingly hold much power over the recent events:

> Oh he was murdered! I think so. That was a diplomatic move, from what they were saying. Not just our people but foreign channels, because there weren't that many actual concrete things that he was indicted for. They had no real argument against him, nothing objective. On the other hand, life over there is degrading because you are in a cell for twenty four hours. That is quite simply a horrific burden. That's a particular type of torture. So now I think, I mean, look, it's symptomatic that our people are dying over there. I don't think there's anyone else that has died at The Hague. This other one [Milan Babić], why did he commit suicide? But, suicide, that was a better story, and so, they did a great favour for the Serb nationalists. He will stay a hero. And, Slobo has gone, but what about this regime they implemented? It was all on the BBC. This regime [of Vojislav Koštunica], they installed it here. What now? They are also not good enough? (Rada)

> They can do that because they are a shameful court. They don't work objectively, they are biased. It is too biased.[3] The court works on someone's directive, and it is a shameful court! Shameful. Babić supposedly committed suicide. You know, if you bring someone to that level of degradation… But when they murdered Milošević. Milošević was murdered. If they don't give you adequate medical help, they can kill you, they don't have to hold a gun to your head. He was murdered, and Babić was murdered. (Mirjana)

The conviction with which the death of Milošević was conceptualised as a conspiracy may owe much to media representations of the event, but it has also a lot to do with the plausibility of the idea, viewed from the vantage point of my respondents, in which the war itself was highly suspicious and incomprehensible.

Conspiracies surrounding Milošević's death were a part of the wider view of the ICTY and Europe, which were very often – by all generations alike – portrayed as powerful entities that do not listen to the needs of the people they try to 'sentence'. As Mladen pointed out, 'I don't think the ICTY is concerned with justice. What kind of justice is that? Everyone knows that justice is on the side of those who wrote this whole scenario.' Large and powerful actors such as the ICTY or the EU, with complex organisational structures and politics not easily comprehended by some outsiders, are easy targets for conspiratorial narratives, and it is no coincidence that in and outside of Serbia a significant number of major conspiracy theories, such as those surrounding the assassination of John F Kennedy, involve large organisations, for instance the CIA or the FBI (see e.g. Aaronovitch 2009).

In terms of the ICTY and war crimes, the conspiracy framework plays a useful function for those who find it difficult to accept that what they thought about the wars may be wrong and that crimes were committed supposedly in their name – particularly as my respondents were keen to emphasise that they were against the wars. In that case, they will look for ways to undermine that judicial process, which they interpret as 'judging the whole nation'. They are likely to react against a media representation that speaks in terms of collective responsibility, whilst also trying to understand the possibility of Serb responsibility for warcrimes. The elements which are available for people to work with – the deaths of Milošević and Milan Babić, the perceived disproportionate indictments of Serbs, NATO airstrikes, catastrophic wars – will inevitably be linked together in a way which most suits the interpreter speaking from a 'losing' position and who reads Serb history as a long list of similar injustices. The 'losing position' here refers to the respondents' feelings of having 'lost everything' in the wars, whilst not having their votes or opinions respected. These feelings also come after the NATO airstrikes, where many realised their own ideas and actions are often not enough to prevent such external attacks, just as with the wars of the 1990s.

Once the credibility of the ICTY is undermined, then it is easier to understand and dismiss indictments or evidence for war crimes. Similarly, its judgements and sentences are rendered implausible and false. For example, Biljana Plavšić confessed during her trial that she was aware of organised violence against the Muslim population of RS.

When Danica and I spoke about this, she said, 'It's not true. They made it up. It was a forced confession.' Similarly, when Emilija one day read a news article to me about the suicide of Ana Mladić (Ratko Mladić's daughter), she complained that, 'Now they are trying to make it look like suicide! But they killed her, because of her father, because they wanted him to confess, to go to The Hague.' Similarly, in one of our conversations, Branka told me the follwing:

> Do you know that no one here knew who Mladić was, until we heard there was an indictment. He was just some general, like all other generals, and suddenly, when there was that indictment he became a star. The Hague made him a star.

When asked why, Branka pointed out that 'nobody likes The Hague'. The 'popularity' of Mladić is hence not exclusively due to his persona or character but rather due to the perception of the ICTY. This idea is resonant amongst respodents. Respondents who defended Mladić and Milošević almost always did so in the context of the ICTY, rather than out of a particular respect for them. Mladić, who was simultaneously a hero and a coward, was 'not a real Serb' because he remained in hiding. Milošević who was usually described as a 'fool', in the context of the ICTY became a 'defender of the Serbs' because he 'defended Serbia on trial, not just himself' (Mladen). As Dyer notes 'star images are always the product of a set of institutions rather than the individual star' (Dyer 1998:152–3).

This also highlights the question of power relationships. In this book, I understand power not as a top-down projection of influence, but in the Foucauldian sense, where 'something called Power, with or without a capital letter, which is assumed to exist universally in a concentrated or diffused form, does not exist' but rather, 'exists only when it is put into action' and produces reactions (Foucault 1982: 219) In this conceptualisation,

> a power relationship can only be articulated on the basis of two elements which are each indispensable if it is really to be a power relationship: that "the other" (the one over whom power is

exercised) be thoroughly recognised and maintained to the very end as a person who acts; and that, faced with a relationship of power, a whole field of responses, reactions, results, and possible inventions may open up. (Foucault 1982:220)

Foucault thus argued that power can be exercised only over subjects who have the ability to respond to power, producing reactions (Foucault 1982:219–220).

Throughout this book, I have discussed the instances in which the respondents feel disenfranchised from a number of processes, especially in transitional justice projects. And ICTY can be added to that list. Above, one of the respondents pointed out that Milošević should have been tried in Serbia. Another respondent mentioned something similar: that Serbia is seen as a country not 'good enough' to prosecute its own people. In the wider context of the international state system, where a monopoly on legal proceedings is seen as an important feature of state sovereignty, the holding of war crimes trials outside Serbia is seen as deeply problematic by the respondents presented here. Or to put it in the way that the respondents saw this, because the ICTY is seen as a 'prison for Serbs' the outcomes are clear: Serbs will always be sentenced. In other words there is a feeling that there is nothing else that can be done; the outcome of that particular history is predetermined because there is always a powerful actor with a 'secret plan'. Although power as conceptualised by the respondents in these narratives is quite absolutist – the secret actor with the power to determine our fate and history, regardless of what 'we' do – their narratives of conspiracy themselves constitute responses to that rigidly perceived power and influence of secret actors. In a Foucaudian sense, they are engaged in a power relationship with actors they find oppressive, and are responding to the perceived oppressions through counter-narratives about the past.

In that sense, the ICTY is an institution with perceived power, and the only way to subvert that power is by theorising the court in such a way that its legitimacy is undermined. Clearly, the ICTY is just one institution subjected to this kind of theorising, and this happens in the wider context of the suspicions of the 'international community' following the NATO air strikes. However, this has a very strong relevance for transitional justice. In the Serbian context, the ICTY is a landmark project of transitional justice, and is seen as a crucial tool in bringing about reconciliation in the region through the establishment of truths which cannot be denied (ICTY, n.d.). But this approach overlooks the hidden power relationships, perceptions of injustice and disenfranchisement inherent in such mechanisms and how these can give rise to doubt, rumour, hearsay and conspiracy. Furthermore, as Skinner argues, conspiracy theorists cannot be dissuaded from their world view as conspiracy theories 'can only be reiterated' and since 'to a certain extent, it is not possible to dissemble a conspiracy' (Skinner 2001:108). In this sense, transitional justice projects come up against another hurdle: many NGOs continue in their attempts to alter views such as those presented here, without regard for their complexity or the context in which they are created, or feelings of marginalisation they may embody.

Conspiracy as subversion and resistance

Conspiracy theories should be treated as a 'tradition of explanation', and 'historically-contextualized discourses' rather than as the results of a 'special cognitive process' (Byford 2006:79). The focus should be on the processes which lead up to the creation of conspiracy theories as well as their content (Goertzel 1994:740). Therefore, the conspiratorial ideas presented here offer a rounding-off for most of the ideas and difficulties of a problematic past presented thus far. Conspiracy theories, taken together with the other dynamics this book considers, such as the difficulty of talking or verbalising past events, denying atrocities and self-victimisation, tell us a great deal about the position of marginality of the 'silent majority', rather more than they tell us about what that group thinks about the past, specifically.

This is an important dynamic to consider. When asking a group, or society, to 'come to terms with their past', it must not be forgotten that, whatever views they hold, and whatever we wish to convert them to (if that is desirable at all), their views are not formed in a vacuum, nor are they independent of their experience or their position towards the past and present, a relationship frequently highlighted by memory scholars (Olick et al. 2011).

Individuals who speak from a position of perceived or actual marginality are likely to engage in forms of resistance (c.f. Scott 1989). Here, 'the past' has become a site of resistance; that resistance does not come from opposing the facts about the past, but rather from resisting power relations and dominant narratives, which are not seen to align with one's own experience. Resistance, in this book, is viewed in terms of Scott's 'everyday resistance' which includes any number of insidious activities that embody protest but may not necessarily translate into visible political activity (Scott 1989:34).

The respondents here often have no means of taking action which may make them visible to the gaze of transitional justice, since they are disconnected and disengaged from the initiatives aimed at them. The NGOs that work to help them to 'come to terms with the past' have failed to engage this group since they have misunderstood their concerns, problems, anxieties and perceptions of justice and injustice. Their view, that NGOs, the ICTY and 'the West' have monopolised discussions of the past, can be seen in the ways in which attempts to redress that imbalance often focus on the *actors*, and not just the *content* of the past. As I have demonstrated repeatedly throughout this book, dispute about the facts of the past is relatively rare. But power relations which lead up to the discovery of those facts (as embodied by the war crimes trials, or publicisation of atrocities through various NGO initiatives), or the actors engaged in their representation, are problematised, as well as the discourse surrounding the 'coming to terms with the past' initiatives. The institutions and actors which are seen as dominant in transitional justice are viewed with much suspicion, and the extracts below illustrate this interplay of dynamics:

> The wars were about breaking up our national being – absolutely from the outside. Personally, I have neither respect nor understanding for all these international organisations that are here, not just in our country but in all countries that are in transition. I think they are all here with a specific task, but one which is not in our interest. I would thank them and ask them to please

leave. I think they are doing a lot against these people, and these regions... And this, what is happening in these regions and with our people is shameful. You know, I have the impression that fascism dominated in the end. Because all those who were on the side of Hitler in WWII, they are now in the European Union, or will be very soon. They don't want us and the Russians, because we were against Hitler. That means that fascism won. Because Hitler had the idea to split up Serbia and divide Yugoslavia, and it turned out that's what happened in the end. (Mirjana)

All this that's happening now, it's not called Hitler anymore but the European Union. I have nothing against the European Union, but they realised after WWII what they should do, the same thing that Japan did. Japan, all the countries it held imprisoned during the war, it now holds them imprisoned economically. And, the European Union was made in that same model, and in the European Union you have all the countries that were occupied by Nazi Germany. And we all know who started the whole union story – Germany! (Petar)

What does such a fixation on 'Europe' and indeed, NATO and other 'internationals' suggest? Most of these agencies here are conflated and seen to be part of each other, but a quick look at Europe in particular sheds interesting light on the issue. Just as some of these interviews were being carried out, the EU suspended Serbia's Stabilisation and Accession Agreement (SAA) negotiations, which highlighted European power even more. 'Europe' decides if Serbia is 'in' or 'out'. 'Europe', and its constant stream of visiting dignitaries, decides Serbia's fate. 'Europe' funds NGOs. 'Europe' is supporting Kosovo's independence. 'Europe's' historians write 'our' history, and 'Europe's media' represents 'us'. Above all, 'Europe' supported the NATO air strikes, which given the popular interpretation of Serbia as a defender of 'Europe' during the Ottoman era, makes 'Europe' ungrateful (Čolović 2000:39–43). It is 'Europe's' historians and media who have, according to the respondents here, decided that 'Serbs are guilty' and have to 'pay the price of war', whilst at the same time 'Europe' (together with the US) does not step forward to claim responsibility and 'confront' *its* past over the air strikes. 'Europe' is thus powerful, 'a region of most sublime values of justice, freedom and equality, but at the same time a place where those values are perverted' (Čolović 2002:42). 'Europe' is also conflated with other actors such as NATO and the ICTY, to the point at which comes to represent 'the international community' itself.

There is no other way to 'fight' such a powerful adversary other than through narrative, and hence such narration may be viewed as a 'weapon of the weak' (Scott 1987). Scott (1989:33–34) draws our attention to the 'everyday forms of resistance' of the 'lower classes' which are often overlooked in favour of explicit political action. In 'everyday forms of resistance', Scott includes 'such acts as foot-dragging, dissimulations, false compliance, feigned ignorance, desertion, pilfering, smuggling, poaching, arson, slander, sabotage, surreptitious assault and murder, anonymous threats and so on' (Scott 1989:34) and can be extended to include counter-narrative. For the respondents presented here, not only is 'the past' complicated, difficult, 'horrific' and 'insane', but it is also dominated by powerful institutions: the ICTY writes a record of the past, the NGOs and 'Europe' are seen as endorsing that view. The narrators feel they had no control over those versions of the past becoming dominant whilst their own experience is written out. Many of those interviewed here have difficultly in believing the conventional interpretations of the conflicts. This often leaves them at a loss as to how to account for it, but also strongly opposed to the idea of 'the West' and 'foreign' NGOs writing the history which they have not quite figured out yet. It is in this context that we can view attempts to explain the past through conspiracy theories about NATO and the West, together with discursive manifestations such as victimhood and denial, as a subversion of ideas of perceived Western power. Thus, the conspiracy theories presented here can be viewed as narratives of resistance (c.f. Scott 1989). As Abu-Lughod argues we can use resistance 'as a chemical catalyst so as to bring to light power relations…and how people are caught up in them' (Abu-Lughod 1990: 42).

War, especially when recent, is a confusing, horrifying, complex and upsetting rupture to 'come to terms with' and cannot be simply understood in terms of oppression and resistance between the individual and the state, but also between the individual and competing interpretations of the war, their personal revulsion, ability or inability to comprehend and account for brutalities which took place.

Thus conspiracy theories concerning elements of conflicts do not so much point to limits of understanding and a lack of knowledge, as they do to a wider sense of disenfranchisement, particularly when it comes to writing and narrating one's own history. As Skinner argues,

> conspiracy theory has become a mode of cognition for those outside the pluralistic consensus, as conspiracy theory theorists convert singular events into larger frameworks, sometimes deliberately misreading or misinterpreting evidence and thereby rocking the boat of consensus history. (Skinner 2001:96)

They can be said to 'take part in discursive interventions not only to *cope* with reality... but to reconstruct history and actively *shape* reality' (Bock-Luna 2007:190, added emphasis). The active shaping allows them a protagonist's role; they are thus no longer passive receivers of knowledge, even if they do assign themselves a passive role in recent events – a role they feel they are given by the 'international community' and NGOs – but writers of history.

Creating conspiracy theories or alternative explanatory mechanisms, relying on the past, questioning, but also acknowledging and denying, reinterpreting the past based on one's own victimhood: these are attempts and tools aimed at making sense of the past but also frameworks which offer resistance to the narratives that respondents feel 'write them out'.

CONCLUSION

This book set out to illustrate narratives about a violent past, produced by those who observed it, or experienced it in subtle and complicated ways. It aimed to point out tensions and divergences which exist between these particular approaches to the past and transitional justice initiatives in Serbia. It sought to illustrate some of the challenges that may crop up when attempts are made to label what might constitute a confronting with the past.

It did so by considering a small group of individuals for whom the wars and the atrocities came as a shock. In most cases they watched the atrocities unfolding and, based on what was said and not said, on what was heard, rumoured or not talked about, they drew their own conclusions, and understood the extent of the brutalities that had taken place. These were, at the time, difficult to comprehend and take on board, given the disturbing nature of the events, but even more so given that they were left without words and frameworks to understand what was happening. The sudden collapse of Yugoslavia, the onset of the wars, the loss of friends, family, and the attempts to survive amidst all the chaos exacerbated the problem, and left many struggling to find meaning in 'all that', and later; to find meaning in their own experience. It is a past in which nothing makes any sense at all. The collapse of 'ordered worlds' of meaning (Verdery 1999), has not been replaced by anything that gives coherence or credibility to the violent past. That no real meaning or answer has been found yet to questions posed by the collapse of Yugoslavia, the conflicts and brutalities which followed, is reflected in the highly contradictory, confused and incoherent narratives which unfold quickly, and in which themes and phrases are repeated constantly. They are attempts to 'come to terms' with the witnessing of what has frequently been described as 'horror' and 'terror', a 'sick' past, in which 'insane' people have caused the suffering of many. It is also an attempt to come to terms with the witnessing of the visible, physical realities of the wars; the missing, the losses, the disabled, the traumatised, the 'lost' and 'damaged' youth as well as the possibility of one's own involvement in all that.

Despite its small sample, this book has illustrated some recurring themes. First, it pointed out that that part of history is not yet 'over' (c.f. Dawson 2007) for most individuals presented here, who continue to speak of the past as if it were still occurring; an indication that these events are still subject to continued thinking, reflection and reassessment. Individuals who have the task of confronting the past are not outside of that history; their own, often very difficult, experiences of the 1990s have influenced the ways in which they reflect and speak of this period, indicating that, for them, wartime realities converged with their own lives quite frequently. This difficult experience has left a legacy of silence, but not a silence resulting from ignorance or nationalism, but rather one created by experiences of 'horror' and 'terror'. The difficulty in expressing and articulating what took place – the unspeakability of atrocities – emerged as a constant theme. The inability to speak about the past created a silence which activists and observers understand as a 'failure' and proceed to problematise the reactions of 'the Serbian public' for this. The approach of local transitional justice practitioners does not sit well with the individuals presented here, and pushes them further into silence and/or into creating counter-discourses.

In these silences, there are hints not only of horror but also of 'hidden' knowledge, things which are known but not openly spoken about. Knowledge of atrocities, and those who committed them, is pushed further and further into the margins of everyday life and consciousness, displaced by ever increasing questions of practical concerns and existence, but also by feelings of genuine repulsion and regret. In some cases this has created discourses filled with implicit acknowledgement of atrocities, but in which metaphors replace horror, in attempts to understand and give meaning to 'the unspeakable'; to acknowledge but not talk directly about it (c.f. Daniel 1996).

In other cases, knowledge of this kind of horror, of the extent of atrocities, produces denial – but one which rarely categorically denies the occurrence of events, whilst denying the responsibility of certain actors for such atrocities. Understood in the broader context of respondents' emphasis on 'horror' and 'terror', denial in this case acts to distance respondents, conceptually and physically, from the atrocities. Denial distances the 'ordinary' drafted soldiers (some of whom were friends, relatives and sons), from responsibility; from 'people like them' and 'people like me' (Serbs, 'the generals'), whilst placing responsibility for all atrocities and things which went wrong onto the 'crazy', the 'drunks', the paramilitaries and the politicians. Yet at the same time, the narrative context of such denial and distancing suggests that this is a part of an ongoing re-examination since very few of those presented here can be said to be convinced of a particular scenario or outcome of the conflicts – everything about the past is subject to confusion, and denial arises out of that. Confusion, however, does not appear to be the result of an absence of knowledge about the past; rather, it is the result *of* knowledge and speculated knowledge, which has produced feelings of horrification and repulsion and led many to question *how* such a thing could have happened.

Indeed, the distancing of responsibility from oneself through these discursive means brings into question the notion of guilt or feelings and perceptions of guilt. This was all the more pertinent in discussions of victimhood, in which the Serbs, but also 'all normal people', were identified as victims of the conflicts of the 1990s. However, the questions of guilt never became quite focused in these narratives and somehow always slipped from view, I would suggest that this might be something that can be picked up by future research.

The narratives produced here can be understood better when placed in the wider context of the current debate about the past in Serbia, which is quite exclusionary. It makes requests for certain audiences – e.g. the 'ordinary public' – to confront atrocities of the past, without taking into account other events, problems and aspects of that past the audience in question may need to deal with. It excludes their problems and their methods of engagement. The kinds of things which the individuals presented here clearly need to address, in addition to confronting atrocities committed by the Serbs against others, is the question of their own very negative experience of the 1990s. They have no outlet for this, as the public debate fails to engage them. Moreover, the only time that they are asked about the past is through surveys which do not ask whether they regret what happened, or feel sorry about it, and which do not capture the complexity of their relationship to the past. Since they are asked about their own experience very rarely, they feel that they have been made unimportant and invisible, or visible only to the extent that their primary function ought to be acknowledgement of what they perceive as collective guilt. In an attempt to come to terms with what happened, as well as their own marginalisation, the respondents here have begun to create their own narratives and to continually ask questions.

This is visible in the creation of counter-discourses on the conflicts, victims and atrocities. In the spaces created by silence, and as a response to what is often perceived as the dominant discourse on atrocities (i.e. the question of Serb guilt and responsibility which needs to be acknowledged) 'alternative discursive spaces' (Chuengsatiansup 2001:63) opened up, and in these resistance and subversion of dominant narratives took place. These, in which narrative functions as a 'weapon of the weak' (Scott 1989), allowed individuals who find their own experience or ideas about the conflicts marginalised to counter their disenfranchisement by addressing their own invisibility from the dominant idea of victimhood, and by creating alternative histories, of conspiracy where the powerful outsiders were identified as the source of a number of problems. Considered together, these strategies indicate high degrees of confusion, uncertainty, incomprehension, regret and anxiety, expressed in an inarticulate way. These narratives are not rehearsed, since they are so rarely spoken aloud. Buried somewhere within these layers are implicit and sometimes explicit acknowledgements of horror, atrocities and revulsion at what was done, and how.

What relevance, then, does this bear for transitional justice, and the idea of coming to terms with the past? It illustrates that transitional justice projects need to think much more broadly about their aims, if their focus is on a confrontation with the past at a societal level. It should include a 'from below' perspective (as already suggested by McEvoy and McGregor 2008), which considers the sites and spaces outside of easily visible paradigms. Within this, it should be made much clearer what 'coming to terms with the past' might entail. Thus far, 'coming to terms with the past' is used in a way which at once implies a shared understanding based on the normative aims of transitional justice (as outlined by Vinjamuri and Snyder 2004) and is confused as to what its actual practical applications are. Does this refer to public or publicly visible acts such as acknowledgement, memorialisation and apology? If so, then transitional justice projects often ignore the fact that the very same processes (such as acknowledgment) can and do exist at the level of private and individual discourses, as the narratives presented here have demonstrated. In other words, we should not ignore the 'ordinary', or their everyday worlds and discourses, nor think of them only as passive recipients of 'our' knowledge about the conflicts. Invisibility of certain voices from the public debate on confronting the past in Serbia does not mean that they have nothing at all to say on the issue (Kidron 2009).

Given that much of this reflection is buried, out of view, or obscured by silence, and certainly not expressed publicly, the question for transitional justice projects should be how to access such narratives? And is there any merit in *insisting* that they be public or appear visible to the public? Some acknowledgement and regret exists at a private level, but does not become known. Is there, therefore, any value in such private reckoning? Certainly, since simply knowing that some acknowledgement exists at a private level means that we can perhaps alter the ways in which we access those discourses and voices, and call for more qualitative, exploratory work in this field.

As I have noted several times throughout this book, there is nothing peculiarly 'Serbian' about these silences or denial. I am often asked at seminars and presentations whether the findings of this research can be applied in different contexts. Due to my background in cultural studies and ethnography, my instinct warns against attempts to compare cultural practices and beliefs, and yet, in conversation with friends from Northern Ireland and Cyprus, I am consonantly surprised at the number of similarities that crop up. For one, it would appear that most people, given the opportunity to talk about the deaths and murders of their former compatriots, or indeed any human being, would rather remain silent. And, given this very common impulse to *not* discuss violence of the past openly or frequently (or indeed, any violence in any number of contexts), it is surprising that transitional justice and confrontation projects persist in their pursuit of public testimony as an indication of the initiatives' success. Being *seen* to participate, and being *heard* saying the right thing, not remaining silent and invisible, is still pursued as the most appropriate approach to transitional justice. It does not take into consideration that some individuals and communities have no possibility or ability to discuss these problems openly or articulate them in a way seen as acceptable by the dominant discourse.

In broader terms, this has significance for transitional justice projects in general, and Serbia in particular. First, the findings of this book highlight that there is a disconnect between the activist, practitioner and academic interpretation of transitional justice projects and the ways in which the past interpreted and (not) spoken about by the audiences at whom those projects are aimed. The exclusion of the audiences and their agency from the project raises questions about what transitional justice projects include and exclude (Miller 2008). It also raises broader questions about how practitioners engage with communities and how they choose to speak about them and on their behalf.

Literature on transitional justice often addresses the incompatibility of international transitional justice projects and local practices (e.g. Millar 2012), however, as this study shows, more attention needs to be given to internal, local tensions between domestic practitioners and their audiences. Local practitioners of transitional justice in Serbia are not a homogenous group, but a majority of the most important initiatives has interpreted the dominant discourse of 'confronting the past' in a way which has clearly alienated their audience.

This has special resonance in light of the recent calls for the establishment of a regional truth and reconciliation commission (abbreviated to RECOM). Whilst this is an extremely important initiative and will have great merit, it must at the same time be aware of prescribing what confrontation with the past is or is not. How, if it proceeds with the public-isation (Johnson 1986:52) of war narratives and testimonies, can it tap in to the silent, disenfranchised voices? And how can it encourage those individuals to participate, given that they have difficulty in making their private narratives about the past, public?

The point is this: the pursuit of a particular narrative as an indication that a 'coming to terms with the past' has taken place or has been successful is a misguided approach because confrontations with the past are not fixed nor do they ever reach an 'end' point. Günter Grass, whose work is often labelled as *Vergangenheitsbewältigung* or 'coming to terms with the past' (see Flood 2008) noted in an interview that: 'You can't come to terms with the past ... the word [*Vergangenheitsbewältigung*] suggests you can come to terms with it, and I'm not of this opinion, I will never be ready for that' (in Flood 2008). The idea that a singular type of confrontation with the past exists, and can be expressed unequivocally and clearly in narrative, is misguided. Individuals need coping mechanisms, both as a way of shielding themselves from the horrors of the past, and because they wish to escape the possibility that they may have somehow caused it, or played a role in it. In that sense, denial, euphemism, conspiracy and silence are all unavoidable 'coping' mechanisms. These influence and shape narratives of the past, and often mask implicit regret or revulsion towards atrocities and deaths of civilians. It is difficult to separate one discursive element from the other.

Based on this, confrontation with the past should not be understood only in the context of the positive connotations which it has picked up (such as acknowledgement), but should be viewed as a potentially rather 'ugly' process. After all, how does one go from not talking to talking, from not acknowledging to acknowledging and so on? In this case, it happens through having to look at, to talk about extremely violent events, brutalities and often incomprehensible acts, such as death and murder. Looking at and talking about these is not pleasant, nor easy, or always possible. In effect, when we talk about confrontation with the past, we should be talking about plural confrontations, and developing transitional justice mechanisms which will engage with these many types of confronting and facing.

In the pursuit of transitional justice and confrontation with the past, it must not be forgotten that, in effect, we are dealing with societies, groups and individuals for whom 'worlds of meaning' (Das et al. 2004) were changed – catastrophically so – and that what we observe now are their attempts to piece together the strands of the past in order to make sense of it, and how it all went wrong. Any attempt to discuss the idea of confronting the past should take these dynamics into account. And if there is to be an overall, single, take-away message from this book, it is this: facing the past is also an exercise in reconstruction of reality and normality, and an attempt to go back to the 'before' when atrocities and horror did not exist. As such, mess and complications are to be expected, and any attempt to 'convert' these narratives into something more homogenous will be futile. Therefore, we should seek to understand such contradictory narratives as a necessary process of confronting the past, however we might understand that term.

NOTES

Chapter 1 Introduction

1. There is a significant literature on this issue, although not in the Serbian context. For an overview, see Seu (2010) and Cohen (2001).
2. Henceforth, Bosnia.
3. In English, this process is variously labelled as confronting the past, facing the past, dealing with the past and coming to terms with the past across academic and practitioner literature in Serbia. There is no consensus or consistency as to its application. In Serbian, the phrase most frequently used by practioners is *suočavanje sa prošlošću*, which translates as 'confronting the past', a phrase I adopt in this book.
4. My focus in this book is the war narratives of the selected respondents. There are, of course, many other ways of understanding, dealing with and remembering the conflicts, for instance in literature, film and art, but they are beyond the scope of this book. I do not believe it appropriate or productive to include these in the *analysis*, as such works require the tools of literary criticism or film analysis and belong to different disciplinary paradigms.

Chapter 2 Confronting violent pasts

1. Henceforth, Helsinki Committee.
2. The full title of the initiative is: Intiative towards the establishment of a Regional Commission Tasked with Establishing the Facts about All Victims of War Crimes and Other Serious Human Rights Violations Committed on

the Territory of the Former Yugoslavia in the period from 1991–2001, See RECOM Initiative, http://www.zarekom.org/

3. The surveys in question are the Strategic Marketing Research Agency, *Public Opinion in Serbia: Views on Domestic War Crimes Judicial Authorities and The Hague Tribunal* (April 2005) and Organization for Security and Cooperation in Europe (OSCE), *Public Opinion in Serbia: Views on Domestic War Crimes Judicial Authorities and The Hague Tribunal* (Belgrade, December 2006) see Subotić (2009:368).

4. This relates mainly to practitioner and scholarship approaches to 'confronting the past' in Serbia, rather than transitional justice scholarship more generally.

Chapter 3 A short summary of events: The 1990s conflicts, war crimes and NATO air strikes

1. There are several spellings of this: Priština (Serbian), Pristina ('international-ised') and Prishtina, which is closer to the Albanian *Prishtinë*. I use 'Serbian' versions for all place names throughout this book as it reflects the ethno-graphic reality of the research context. Therefore, using the international or Albanian version in this case would have not been consistent with the rest of the text.

2. At the time of writing, his trial is still under way.

Chapter 4 'That was just not normal': The 1990s as a decade of sickness, insanity and horror

1. In Serbian: *užas, užasno, strah, strašno, zastrašujuće*

2. I am grateful to Ger Duijzings for pointing this out in this context.

3. In an interesting parallel, Clark (2008:35–43) outlines a surprising number and extent of physical and psychological illnesses recorded in the Serbian popula-tion in the 1990s. Phenomena such as spiritual healing and paranormal beliefs also experienced popularity in Serbia during this time (Clark 2008:42). In a somewhat ironic twist, when Radovan Karadžić, a fugitive from the ICTY, was arrested in Belgrade in 2008, he was discovered to have been practicing 'alternative medicine' – 'bioenergy' – during the years that he was on the run.

4. The Serbian word used very frequently to describe this period is *preživljavanje*.

5. Ger Duijzings helpfully pointed this out.

6. In adopting this approach of describing respondents through their stories and lives, I have been greatly inspired by the approach taken in Ivana Bajić's PhD thesis, *Belgrade Parents and Their Migrant Children*, 2008.

7. All respondents' names are pseudonyms.
8. Josip Broz Tito, Communist leader of former Yugoslavia.
9. Diminutive of Slobodan.
10. 'No milk': it is interesting that shortages of milk were the most frequently mentioned, even by the oldest respondents who had no small children or any children at home. Milk is not used very much in cooking, and coffee in Serbia is usually drunk without it. Adults do not frequently drink it either. Milk however, is symbolic: it is life-giving, nourishing, and comforting.
11. Trg Republike is a square in the centre of Belgrade.

Chapter 5 'You can't believe it's happening': Knowledge, Silence and Terror

1. This word derives from Albanian word for Albania, Shqipëria, but in the Serbian context is often used in a derogatory manner to refer to Kosovo Albanians.
2. Towns in north and northwestern Bosnia, near the border with Croatia.
3. To make the sign of the cross. In Serbia, a practice often followed by older or more religious people in conversations where something deemed particularly evil or terrible is mentioned.
4. For an illustration of this, see Miller (2006:316).
5. Catherine Baker, in as yet unpublished research, notes that in her work on soldiers and interpreters during the Bosnian conflict similar patterns can be observed. In one particular instance, former British soldiers discuss the Ahmići massacre in Bosnia by referring to the BBC drama *Warriors*, a fictionalised account of British deployment to Bosnia. Baker notes that respondents may sometimes refer to fictional films where violence is present 'in order that that violence can be noted within the space of the interview, but without the respondents themselves having to evoke it through thoughts and language' (Baker, personal communication). This is a point currently being developed in forthcoming research.

Chapter 6 'I try not to think about it because it is far too horrific': Denial, Acknowledgement and Distancing

1. See e.g. Fond za Humanitarno Pravo 2005 for an overview.
2. For an overview see Obradović-Wochnik 2009.
3. Catherine Baker helpfully pointed out this terminology.
4. This discussion of ethnicity and ethnic identity and the ways it features in discussions of war crimes is rather brief and I realise other scholars may find much more

to say about the 'ethnic' aspect of this. However, this section is brief for a reason. In the earlier versions of this manuscript, I attempted to tackle the question of confrontations with violence and war though the framework of identities – ethnic, national, group and so on – to see whether they had any explanatory power in this case. They did not – not in any meaningful way, because the question of ethnicity, one's own or that of others, hardly ever featured in narratives which talked about the war even though they sometimes labelled these wars 'ethnic' conflicts. This is perhaps demonstrated in this book, given that I have thus far presented a number of respondents' interviews, without the question of ethnicity cropping up. There are some hints, as here, and some more substantive comments about Serbs as victims (discussed in the next chapter), but on the whole, violence and the 1990s in general were seen in terms of horror, terror and the inexplicable, rather than something which was interpreted through 'ethnic' frames.

5.   The Serbian word used was *inat*.
6.   Nebojša Pavković and Vladimir Lazarević were officers in the Serbian Army, indicted for, and later convicted of war crimes against humanity in Kosovo.
7.   Used extensively during the wars, especially in Bosnia.
8.   Municipality in Western Kosovo.

Chapter 7 'Haven't Serbs also been killed?': Victimhood, Resentment and Marginality

1.   This point can be extended further. According to unpublished research on Serbian victimhood narratives by Brendan Humphreys, University of Helsinki, such narratives require an acknowledgement or validation from a 'neutral' external party, i.e. someone who is not 'us', someone who does not already agree that 'we are the victims'.
2.   This also resonates with their ideas about the causes of the ethnic conflicts, which usually implicated external parties such as the international community rather than ethnic others.
3.   I am grateful to Catherine Baker for pointing this out.
4.   The respondent is referring to a health spa or *banja*, where those with illnesses may go for treatment or recuperation.
5.   There is also an interesting gender dynamic here. Those who most frequently discussed these issues were older female respondents. Interestingly, they also frequently discussed children and young people when relating the issues of disease and disability. This gender dimension may yield an interesting analysis, but unfortunately space and conceptual considerations prevent me from considering this in more depth.
6.   In Serbian, a derogatory name for Muslims.

Chapter 8 'Was it all a part of a secret plan?': Subversion, Resistance and 'theorising fears' through Conspiracy

1. I am grateful to Catherine Baker for pointing out the following: although all generations held some form of conspiratorial ideas, it is particularly the older generations – i.e. those who grew up during socialism – who seemed to believe that the West was implicated in the destruction of Yugoslavia. Did the international politics of the Tito regime have an influence on this type of discourse in the present day? This is a point which merits further investigation, but one which is beyond the scope of this book.

2. The Aviano air base is in Italy, not Kosovo.

3. The original Serbian word used is '*navijačko*' which is almost impossible to translate into English. The Serbian original carries with it connotations of bias, partisanship and fandom (in a sporting sense).

REFERENCES

Aaronovitch, D. (2009) *Voodoo histories: the role of conspiracy theories in shaping modern history* Jonathan Cape: London

Abu-Lughod, L. (1990) 'The Romance of resistance: tracing transformations of power through Bedouin women' *American Ethnologist* 17 (1) pp. 41–55

Adorno, T. W. (1986) 'What does coming to terms with the past mean?' in *Bitburg in moral and political perspective* ed. G. Hartmann, translation T. Bahti and G. Hartmann. Bloomington: Indiana University Press, pp. 114 – 129

Allcock, J. B. (2000) *Explaining Yugoslavia.* New York: Columbia University Press

Amanpour, C. (1999) 'Paramilitaries' in *Crimes of war: what the public should know* eds. Gutman, R. and D. Rieff, eds. London: W.W. Norton & Co, pp. 266–268

Anastasijević, D. (2008) 'What's wrong with Serbia?' Brussels: European Stability Initiative http://www.esiweb.org/index.php?lang=en&id=310&function=print Published 31 March 2008, Accessed 1 December 2011

Arriaza, L, and Roht-Arriaza, N. (2008a) 'Social reconstruction as a local process' *International Journal of Transitional Justice* 2 (2), pp. 152–172

Arriaza, L and Roht-Arriaza, N. (2008b) 'Social repair at the local level: the case of Guatemala' in *Transitional Justice from Below: Grassroots Activism and the Struggle for Change,* eds. McEvoy, K. and L. McGregor. Oxford: Hart Publishing pp. 143–166

B92 (2006) 'Milošević otišao, "proleće" na Trgu' http://www.b92.net/info/komentari.php?nav_id=191943, published 10 March 2006, accessed 19 March 2006

Baines, E. (2010) 'Spirits and social reconstruction after mass violence: rethinking transitional justice' *African Affairs* 109 (436), pp.409–430.

Baines, E. (2007) 'The haunting of Alice: local approaches to justice and reconciliation in Northern Uganda'. *International Journal of Transitional Justice* Vol 1, pp. 91–114

Bajić, I. (2008) *Belgrade parents and their migrant children* Unpublished PhD thesis, University College London

Bandura, A. (1999) 'Moral disengagement in the perpetration of inhumanities' *Personality and Social Psychology Review* 3 (3), pp. 193–209

Bandura, A., Caprara, G. V., Barbaranelli, C., Pastorelli, C. and Regalia, C. (2001) 'Sociocognitive self-regulatory mechanisms governing transgressive behaviour' *Journal of Personality and Social Psychology* 80 (1), pp. 125–135

Barker, C. (2000) *Cultural studies: theory and practice* London: Sage

Barker, C. and Galasinski, D. (2001) *Cultural studies and discourse analysis: a dialogue on language and identity* London: Sage

Bar-Tal, D (2003) 'Collective memory of physical violence: its contribution to the culture of violence' in *The role of memory in ethnic conflict,* eds. Cairns, E. and M. D. Roe, London: Palgrave Macmillan

Baudrillard, J. (2001) *The Gulf War did not take place,* Translated by P. Patton Sydney: Power Publications

Bax, M. (1997) 'Mass graves, stagnating identification, and violence: a case study in the local sources of 'the war' in Bosnia Herzegovina' *Anthropological Quarterly* 70 (1), pp. 11–19

Beatty, B. (1999) 'Conspiracy theories: secrecy and power in American culture' *Canadian Journal of Communication,* 24 (4)

Beč, J. (2005) 'Od *hate speech* do *hate silence*: banalna ravnodušnost' in Helsiki Committee for Human Rights, *Srebrenica od poricanja o priznanja* Belgrade: Helsinki Committee for Human Rights, pp. 13–18 available at http://www.helsinki.org.rs/doc/Svedocanstva22.pdf Accessed 10 February 2012

Belgrade Centre for Human Rights (2008) 'Public perception in Serbia of the ICTY and the national courts dealing with war crimes' available at http://english.bgcentar.org.rs/index.php?option=com_content&view=article&id=406:attitudes-towards-the-international-criminal-tribunal-for-the-former-yugoslavia-icty-&catid=103, Accessed 10 March 2011

Belgrade Centre for Human Rights (2009) 'Public Perception in Serbia of the ICTY and the National Courts Dealing with War Crimes' available at http://english.bgcentar.org.rs/index.php?option=com_content&view=article&id=406:attitudes-towards-the-international-criminal-tribunal-for-the-former-yugoslavia-icty-&catid=103, accessed 10 March 2011

Bellamy, A. (2003) *The formation of Croatian national identity: a centuries-old dream?* Manchester: Manchester University Press

Bennett, W. L., Lawrence, R. G., and Livingston, S. (2006) 'None dare call it torture: indexing and the limits of press independence in the Abu Ghraib scandal' *Journal of Communication,* 56, pp. 467–485

Berger, A. A. (1997). *Narratives in popular culture, media and everyday life.* Thousand Oaks, CA: Sage.

Bersoff, D. M. (1999) 'Why good people sometimes do bad things: motivated reasoning and unethical behaviour' *Personality and Social Psychology Bulletin* 25 (1), pp. 28–39

Bićanić, I. and Franičević, V. (2006) 'The Poor, excluded and transition losers in the Southeastern European transition economies' in *Poverty and social depravation in the Mediterranean: trends, policies and prospects in the New Millennium* eds. Petmesidou, M. and C. Papatheodoru. London: Zed Books, pp. 188–217

Bideleux, R., and Jeffries, I. (2007) *The Balkans: a post-communist history* London: Routledge

Bieber, F. (2002) 'Nationalist mobilisation and stories of Serb suffering: the Kosovo myth from 600th anniversary to the present' *Rethinking History* 6 (1), pp. 95–110

Bjelić, D. I. and Savić, O. eds (2005) *Balkan as metaphor: between globalisation and fragmentation* Cambridge, MA: Massachusetts Institute of Technology Press

Bock-Luna, B. (2007) *The past in exile: Serbian long-distance nationalism and identity in the wake of the Third Balkan war* Berlin: Lit Verlag

Borer, T.A. (2003) 'A taxonomy of victims and perpetrators: human rights and reconciliation in South Africa' *Human Rights Quarterly*, 25(4) pp. 1088–1116

Bougarel, X., Duijzings, G., and Helms, E. eds. (2007) *The new Bosnian mosaic: identities, memories and moral claims in a post-war society* Aldershot: Ashgate

Bourdieu, P. (1977) *Outline of a theory of practice* translated by R. Nice. Cambridge: Cambridge University Press

Brubaker, R., Fieschmidt, M., Fox, J and Grancea, L. (2006) *Nationalist politics and everyday ethnicity in a Transylvanian town* Princeton, New Jersey: Princeton University Press

Buckley, M. and Cummings, S. N. eds. (2001) *Kosovo: perceptions of war and its aftermath* London: Continuum

Bugarski, R. (1996) 'Mitologizacija političkog diskursa' in *Mit: zbornik radova* ed. Bekić, T., Novi Sad: Univerzitet u Novom Sadu, Filozofski Fakultet

Bugarski, R. (2002) *Nova lica jezika: sociolingvističke teme* Beograd: Biblioteka XX Vek

Bujošević, D and Radovanović, I (2003) *The fall of Milošević: the October 5th Revolution* Basingstoke: Palgrave Macmillan

Byford, J. (2006) *Teorija zavere: Srbija protiv 'novog svetskog poretka'* Belgrade: Belgrade Centre for Human Rights

Byford, J. and Billig, M. (2001) 'The Emergence of antisemitic conspiracy theories in Yugoslavia during the war with NATO' *Patterns of Prejudice* 35 (4), pp 50–63

Cairns, E. and Roe, M. D. (2003) *The Role of Memory in Ethnic Conflict* London: Palgrave Mcmillan

Caruth, C. (1991) 'Unclaimed experience: trauma and the possibility of history' *Yale French Studies*, 79, pp. 181–192

Caruth, C. ed. (1995) *Trauma: explorations in memory* Baltimore: Johns Hopkins University Press

Chuengsatiansup, K. (2001) 'Marginality, suffering and community: the politics of collective experience and empowerment in Thailand' in *Remaking a world: violence, social suffering and recovery* eds. Das, V., Kleinman, A., Lock, M., Ramphele, M. and P. Reynolds. Berkley and Los Angeles: University of California Press, pp. 1–30

Clark, J. N. (2008) *Serbia in the shadow of Milošević: the legacy of conflict in the Balkans* London: Tauris Academic Studies

Clark, J. N. (2009) Judging the ICTY: Has it achieved its Objectives? *Journal of Southeast Europe and Black Sea Studies* 9 (1–2), pp. 123–142

Clarke, S. (2002) 'Conspiracy theories and conspiracy theorizing' *Philosophy of the Social Sciences* 32 (2), pp. 131–150

Cohen, S. (1995) 'State crimes of previous regimes: knowledge, accountability and policing of the past' *Law and Social Enquiry* 20 (1) pp. 7–50

Cohen, S. (2001) *States of Denial: Knowing about Atrocities and Suffering* Cambridge: Polity Press

Comaroff, J. and Comaroff, J. (1999) 'Occult Economies and the Violence of Abstraction: Notes from the South African Postcolony' *American Ethnologist* 26 (2), pp. 279–303

Connerton, P. (1989) *How Societies Remember* Cambridge: Cambridge University Press

Crocker, D. (1998) 'Transitional justice and international civil society: toward a normative framework' *Constellations* 5 (4) pp. 492–517

Cuéllar, A.C., (2005) 'Unraveling silence: violence, memory and the limits of anthropology's craft' *Dialectical Anthropology*, 29 (2), pp.159–180

Čolović, I. (1996) Društvo mrtvih ratnika in *Republika* No. 145, available online at www.yurope.com/zines/republika/arhiva/96/145/145–15.html accessed 15 December 2009

Čolović, I. (2000) *Bordel ratnika: folklor, politika i mit* Beograd: Biblioteka XX Vek

Čolović, I. (2002) *Politics of identity in Serbia: essays in political anthropology* translated by C. Hawkesworth, Washington Square, New York: New York University Press

Čolović, I. (2004) *Kad kažem novine/When I say newspaper* Beograd: Biblioteka Krug

Danas (2004) 'Srpska Garda, partijska vojska' SPO *Danas* Online edition published 5 November 2004, www.danas.co.yu/20040511/dogadjajdana1.html accessed 17 September 2007

Daniel, V. E. (1991) *Is there a counterpoint to culture?* Amsterdam: The Wertheim Lecture Centre for Asian Studies available at http://www.iias.nl/asia/wertheim/lectures/WL_Daniel.pdf, accessed 10 October 2011

Daniel, V. E. (1994) 'The individual in terror' in *Embodiment and experience: the existential ground of culture and self* ed. Csordas, T.J. Cambridge: Cambridge University Press, pp. 229–247

Daniel, V. E. (1996) *Charred lullabies: chapters in an anthropography of violence.* Ewing, NJ, USA: Princeton University Press

Dannreuther, R. (2001) 'War in Kosovo: history, development and aftermath' in *Kosovo: perceptions of war and its aftermath* eds. Buckley, M. and S. N. Cummings, London: Continuum, pp. 12–29

Das, V. (1995) *Critical events: an anthropological perspective on contemporary India* Delhi: Oxford University Press

Das, V. (2003) 'Trauma and testimony: implications for political community', *Anthropological Theory*, 3 (3), pp. 293–307

Das, V. and Kleinman, A. (2001) 'Introduction' in *Remaking a world: violence, social suffering and recovery* eds. Das, V., Kleinman, A., Lock, M., Ramphele, M. and P. Reynolds. Berkley and Los Angeles: University of California Press, pp. 1–30

Das, V., Kleinman, A., Lock, M., Ramphele, M. and P. Reynolds,. eds (2001) *Remaking a World: Violence, Social Suffering and Recovery* Berkley and Los Angeles: University of California Press

Dević, A. (1998) 'Ethnonationalism, politics and the intellectuals: the case of Yugoslavia' *International Journal of Politics, Culture and Society* 11 (3), pp. 375–409

Davies, C. A. (2005) *Reflexive ethnography: a guide to researching selves and others* London: Rutledge

Dawson, G. (2007) *Making peace with the past? Memory, trauma and the Irish Troubles* Manchester: Manchester University Press

De Leonardis, F. (2008) 'War as a medicine: the medical metaphor in contemporary Italian political language', *Social Semiotics*, 18 (1), pp. 33–45

Dević, A. (1997) 'Anti-war initiatives and the un-making of civic identities in the former Yugoslav republics *Journal of Historical Sociology* 10 (2), pp. 127–156

Dević, A. (1998) 'Ethnonationalism, politics and the intellectuals: the case of Yugoslavia' *International Journal of Politics, Culture and Society* 11 (3), pp. 375–409

Dimitrijević, N. (2008) 'Serbia after the criminal past: what went wrong and what should be done' *International Journal of Transitional Justice*, 2 (1), pp. 5–22.

Djurić, I. (2010) 'The Post-war repatriation of Serb minority internally displaced persons and refugees in Croatia—between discrimination and political settlement' *Europe-Asia Studies* 62 (10) pp. 1639–1660

Donnan, H. & Simpson, K. (2007) 'Silence and violence among Northern Ireland border Protestants' *Ethnos,* 72 (1), pp. 5–28

Dragović-Soso, J. (2010) 'Conflict, memory, accountability: what does coming to terms wiht the past mean?' in *Conflict and Memory: Bridging Past and Future in (South East) Europe.* eds. Petritsch, W. and V. Džihić. Baden-Baden: Nomos, pp. 29–48

Dragović-Soso, J. (2012) 'Apologising for Srebrenica: the declaration of the Serbian parliament, the European Union and the politics of compromise' *East European Politics*, 28 (2), pp. 163–179.

Dragović-Soso, J. (Forthcoming) 'Collective responsibility, international justice and public reckoning with the recent past: reflections on a debate in Serbia' in *The Milošević Trial—An Autopsy* ed Waters, T. W. Oxford:Oxford University Press

Dragović-Soso, J. and Gordy, E. (2010) 'Coming to terms with the past: transitional justice and reconciliation in the post-Yugoslav lands' in *New Perspectives on Yugoslavia: Key Issues and Controversies,* eds. Djokic, D. and J. Ker-Lindsay. London: Routledge, pp. 193–212

Drakulić, S. (2004) *Oni ne bi ni mrava zgazili* Belgrade: Samizdat B92

Du Gay, P., Hall, S., Janes, L., Mackay, H. and Negus, K. (2001) *Doing cultural studies: the story of the Sony Walkman* London: Sage and Open University

Duijzings, G. (2000) *Religion and the politics of identity in Kosovo* London: Hurst & Co

Duijzings, G. (2005) *Religija i identitet na Kosovu* Beograd: Biblioteka XX Vek

Duijzings, G. (2007) 'Commemorating Srebrenica: histories of violence and the politics of memory in Eastern Bosnia' in *The new Bosnian mosaic: identities, memories and moral claims in a post-war society* eds Bougarel, X., Duijzings, G., and E. Helms. Aldershot: Ashgate, pp. 141–166

Dyer, R. (1998) *Stars* London: British Film Institute

Evans-Pritchard, E. (1987) *Witchcraft, oracles and magic among the Azande* Oxford: Oxford University Press

Eyerman, R. (2002) *Cultural trauma: slavery and the formation of African-American identity* Port Chester, NY, USA: Cambridge University Press

Feldman, A. (1991) *Formations of violence: the narrative of the body and political terror in Northern Ireland* London: University of Chicago Press

Feldman, A. (1994) 'On cultural anaesthesia: from Desert Storm to Rodney King' *American Ethnologist* 21 (2), pp. 404–418

Feldman, A. (1995) *Towards a political anthropology of the body: a theoretical and cultural history* Boulder CO: Westview Press

Feldman, A. (2003) 'Political terror and the technologies of memory: excuse, sacrifice, commodification, and actuarial moralities' *Radical History Review* 85, pp. 58–73

Fenster, M. (2008) *Conspiracy theories: secrecy and power in American culture* Minneapolis: University of Minnesota Press

Ferguson, N., Burgess, M., and Hollywood, I. (2010) 'Who are the victims? victimhood experiences in postagreement Northern Ireland' *Political Psychology* 31 (6), pp. 857–886

Ferme, M. C. (2001) *The Underneath of things: violence, history and the everyday in Sierra Leone* Berkley, CA: University of California Press

Fiske, J. (1989) *Understanding popular culture* London: Unwin Hyman

Flood, A. (2008) 'Not Coming to Terms with the Past' *The Guardian* http://www.guardian.co.uk/books/2008/oct/20/gunter-grass-die-box Published 20 October 2008, accessed 11 December 2011

Fond za Humanitarno Pravo (2005) *Izveštaj o tranzicionoj pravdi u Srbiji, Crnoj Gori i Na Kosovu 1999–2005* Belgrade: Fond za Humanitarno Pravo

Foucault, M. (1982) 'The Subject and power' in *Michel Foucault: Beyond Structuralism and Hermeneutics* eds. Dreyfus, H. L. and P. Rabinow. Chicago: University of Chicago Press

Fox, J.E. and Miller-Idriss, C. (2008) 'Everyday Nationhood' *Ethnicities* 8 (4) pp. 536–563

Fridman, O. (2011) 'It was like fighting a war with our own people': anti-war activism in Serbia during the 1990s' *Nationalities Papers* 39 (4), pp. 507–522.

Gandsman, A (2012) 'Testimonies of trauma, human rights, and the reproduction of conventional knowledge', paper presented at the Beyond Testimony and Trauma: Oral History in the Aftermath of Mass Violence conference, University of Montréal, 24 March 2012

Gibson, J. L. (2006) 'Can truth reconcile divided nations?' in *Conflict Prevention and peacebuilding in post-war societies: sustaining the peace* eds. Meernik, J. D. and T. D. Mason, Abingdon: Routledge, pp. 176–195

Giddens, A. (1991) *Modernity and self-identity: self and society in the late modern age.* Cambridge: Polity

Girard, R. (1977) *Violence and the sacred* translated by P. Gregory, London: The Johns Hopkins University Press

Glenny, M. (2011) 'Ratko Mladić's arrest is a huge step for Serbia's moral rehabilitation' *The Guardian* Comment is Free http://www.guardian.co.uk/commentisfree/2011/may/27/ratko-Mladić-serbia-boris-tadic Published 27 May 2011, accessed 27 May 2011

Gluckman, M. (1966) *Custom and conflict in Africa* Oxford: Basil Blackwell

Goertzel, T. (1994) 'Belief in conspiracy theories' *Political Psychology* 15 (4), pp. 731–742

Goldsworthy, V. (2005) 'Invention and in(ter)vention: the rhethoric of Balkanization' in *Balkan as Metaphor: Between Globalisation and Fragmentation* eds. Bjelić, D. I. and O. Savić. Cambridge, MA: Massachusetts Institute of Technology Press, pp. 25–38

Gordy, E. (1999) *The culture of power in Serbia: nationalism and the destruction of alternatives* University Park, PA: Pennsylvania State University Press

Gordy, E. (2003) 'Accounting for a violent past, by other than legal means' *Southeast European and Black Sea Studies* 3 (1), pp. 1–24

Gordy, E. D. (2005) 'Postwar guilt and responsibility in Serbia: the effort to confront it and the effort to avoid it' in *Serbia since 1989: politics and society under Milošević and after* eds. Ramet, S. and V. Pavlaković. Washington: University of Washington Press

Gow, J. (2003) *The Serbian project and its adversaries: a strategy of war crimes* London: Hurst

Gow, J. (2007) 'Dark histories, brighter futures? The Balkans and the Black Sea Region – European Union frontiers, war crimes and confronting the past' *Journal of Southeast European and Black Sea Studies* 7 (3), pp. 345–356

Gödl, D. (2007) 'Challenging the past: Serbian and Croatian agressor-victim narratives' *International Journal of Sociology* 37 (1) pp. 43–57

Grann, D. (2011) 'Murder foretold: unravelling the ultimate political conspiracy' *The New Yorker,* 4 April 2011

Gray, A. (2003) *Research practice for cultural studies* London: Sage

Gray, A. and McGuigan, J. eds. (1993) *Studying culture: an introductory reader* London: Edward Arnold

Greenberg, J. (2011) 'On the road to normal: negotiating agency and state sovereignty in postsocialist Serbia' *American Anthropologist* 113 (1), pp. 88–100

Grohl, D. (1987) 'The temptation of conspiracy theory or why do bad things happen to good people?' in *Changing Conceptions of Conspiracy* eds. Graumann, C. F. and S. Moscovici. New York: Springer Verlag

Haider, H. (2008) '(Re)Imagining coexistence: striving for sustainable return, reintegration and reconciliation in Bosnia and Herzegovina' *International Journal of Transitional Justice* 3 (1), pp. 91–113

Halbwachs, M. (1980) *On collective memory* New York: Harper and Row

Hammersley, M. and Atkinson, P. (2004) *Ethnography: principles in practice* London: Routledge

Hayner, P. (2011) *Unspeakable truths: transitional justice and the challenge of truth comissions* Abingdon, Oxon: Routledge

Hellinger, D. (2003) 'Paranoia, conspiracy and hegemony in American politics' in *Transparency and conspiracy: ethnographies of suspicion in the new world order* eds. West, H. G. and T. Sanders, Durham, NC: Duke University Press, pp. 204–232

Helsinki Comittee for Human Rights (n.d. a) 'Head of Serbia's Helsinki Commitee says serbia still "relativises" its crimes and has failed to tell young people the truth of what happened in the nineties' http://www.helsinki.org.rs/tjpast.html, accessed 2 April 2011

Helsinki Comittee for Human Rights (n.d. b) About us http://www.helsinki.org.rs/about.html, Accessed 1 March 2011

Helsinki Comittee for Human Rights (2005) 'New in the Testimonies Edition: Srebrenica: from denial to confession' http://www.helsinki.org.rs/tjsrebrenica_t02.html, Accessed 2 March 2011

Hughes, M.L. (2000) ' "Through no fault of our own": West Germans remember their war losses' *German History* 18 (2), pp. 193–213

Humanitarian Law Centre (n.d. a) Public Information and Outreach http://www.hlc-rdc.org/stranice/Public-Information-and-Outreach.en.html, Accessed 1 March 2011

Humantiarian Law Centre (n.d. b) Coalition for RECOM http://www.hlc-rdc.org/Outreach/Koalicija-za-REKOM/index.1.en.html Accessed 1 March 2011

Humphrey, M. (2002) *The Politics of atrocity and reconciliation: from terror to trauma* London: Routledge

Humphrey, M. (2003) 'From victim to victimhood: truth commissions and trials as rituals of political transition and individual healing' *The Australian Journal of Anthropology* 14 (2), pp. 171–187

Humphrey, M. & Valverde, E. (2008) 'Human rights politics and injustice: transitional justice in Argentina and South Africa' *International Journal of Transitional Justice*, 2(1), pp.83–105.

Humphreys, B. (2011) 'Victimhood, Justice, Revenge', Presentation at the 'Shared Past – Conflicting Histories: Historical Knowledge, Memory and Politics in the Baltic Sea Region' Conference, Turku, Finland, September, 2011

ICMP (n.d.) International Commission for Missing Persons worldwide: Southeast Europe http://www.ic-mp.org/icmp-worldwide/?page_id=534, last accessed 10 December 2011

ICTY (n.d., a.) 'The Former Yugoslavia conflicts' http://www.icty.org/sid/322 last accessed, 11 December 2011

ICTY (n.d., b) 'Achievements' http://www.icty.org/sid/324 accessed 4 January 2011

ICTY, (n.d., c) 'The Prosecutor of the Tribunal against Vojislav Seselj: Indictment' available at http://www.icty.org/x/cases/seselj/ind/en/ses-ii030115e.pdf last accessed, 2 February 2011

ICTY (2002) 'Statement on behalf of Biljana Plavšić' http://www.icty.org/sid/8072 accessed 7 May 2012

ICTY (2004) 'Milan Babić pleads guilty to one count of crimes against humanity' http://www.icty.org/sid/8482 accessed, 7 May 2012

ICTY (2006) 'The Prosecutor v. Naser Orić summary of judgement' http://www.icty.org/x/cases/oric/tjug/en/060630_Oric_summary_en.pdf, accessed 29 March 2012

ICTY (2008) 'Radovan Karadžić in tribunal's custody', http://www.icty.org/sid/9869, accessed 1 March 2012

ICTY (2009) 'Five senior Serb officials convicted of Kosovo crimes, one acquitted', http://www.icty.org/sid/10070 accessed 1 March 2012

ICTY (2011) 'Judgement summary for Gotovina et al.' http://www.icty.org/x/cases/gotovina/tjug/en/110415_summary.pdf accessed, 1 May 2012

Idrizi, V. (2007) 'The Kosovo perspective: the importance of ownership' in *The European Union and transitional justice: from retrubutive to restorative justice in the Western Balkans,* ed. Kostovicova, D. Belgrade: Humanitarian Law Centre pp. 116–117

Jalušić, V. (2007) 'Organised innocence and exclusion: "Nation-States" in the aftermath of war and collective crime' *Social Research* 74 (4) pp. 1173–1200

Jameson, F. (1995) *The Geopolitical aesthetic: cinema and space in the world system* London: British Film Institute

Jansen, S. (2000) 'Victims, underdogs and rebels: discursive practices of Serbian protest' *Critique of Anthropology* 20 (4), pp. 393–420

Jansen, S. (2002) 'Violence of memories: local narratives of the past after ethnic cleansing in Croatia' *Rethinking History* 6 (1), pp. 77–94

Jansen, S. (2003) ' "Why do they hate us?" everyday Serbian nationalist knowledge of Muslim hatred' *Journal of Mediterranean Studies* 13 (2), pp. 215–237

Jansen, S. (2005) *Antinacionalizam: etnografija otpora u Beogradu i Zagrebu* Belgrade: Biblioteka XX Vek

Johnson, R. (1986) 'What is cultural studies anyway?' *Social Text*, 16, pp. 38–80

Johnson, R. (1997) 'Reinventing cultural studies: remembering for the best version', in *From sociology to cultural studies: new perspectives* ed, Long, E. Malden MA: Blackwell

Johnson, R, McLennan, Schwartz, B. and D. Sutton. Eds (1982) *Making Histories: Studies in History Writing* and Politics Minneapolis: University of Minnesota Press

Johnson, R., Chambers, D., Raghuram, P., and Tincknell, E. (2004) *The practice of cultural studies* London: Sage

Judah, T. (2000) *The Serbs: history, myth and the destruction of Yugoslavia* New Haven: Yale Nota Bene

Judah, T. (2002) *Kosovo: war and revenge* New Haven: Yale Nota Bene

Kaminski, M., Nalepa, M. and O'Neill, B. (2006) 'Normative and strategic aspects of transitional justice' *Journal of Conflict Resolution* 50 (3) pp. 295–302

Kandić, N. (2010) 'Dealing with the past – step by step' in *Conflict and memory: bridging past and future in (South East) Europe* eds Petritsch, W. and V. Džihić. eds. Baden-Baden: Nomos, pp. 229–234

Keeley, B. (1999) 'Of conspiracy theories' *The Journal of Philosophy* 96, pp. 109–126

Kelsall, T. (2003) 'Rituals of verification: indigenous and imported accountability in Northern Tanzania' *Africa* 73 (2), pp. 174–201

Kent, L. (2011). 'Local memory practices in East Timor: disrupting transitional justice narratives' *International Journal of Transitional Justice*, 5(3), 434–455

Kerby, A. P. (1991) *Narrative and the self*, Minneapolis: Indiana University Press

Ker-Lindsay, J. (2011) *Kosovo: the path to contested statehood in the Balkans* London: IB Tauris

Kidron, C. A. (2009) 'Toward an ethnography of silence' *Current Anthropology* 50, (1), pp. 5–27.

Kostovicova, D. (2006) 'Civil society and post-communist democratization: facing a double challenge in post-Milošević Serbia' *Journal of Civil Society* 2 (1), 21–37

Kostovicova, D. ed. (2007) *The European Union and transitional justice: from retrubutive to restorative justice in the Western Balkans* Belgrade: Humanitarian Law Centre

Kritz, N. J. ed. (1995) *Transitional justice: how emerging democracies reckon with former regimes* Vols. I–III Washington, DC: United States Institute of Peace Press

Krohn-Hansen, C. (1997) 'The Anthropology and ethnography of political violence' *Journal of Peace Research* 34 (2), pp. 233–240

Krstić, I. (2002) 'Rethinking Serbia: a psychoanalytic reading of modern Serbian history and identity through popular culture' *Other Voices* 2 (2), http://www. othervoices.org/2.2/krstic/ accessed 13 February 2007

Kulyk, V. (2006) 'Constructing common sense: language and ethnicity in Ukrainian public discourse' *Ethnic and Racial Studies* 29 (2), pp. 281–314

Kusno, A. (2003) 'Remembering/forgetting the May Riots: architecture, violence, and the making of Chinese cultures in Post-1998 Jakarta' *Public Culture* 15 (1) pp. 149–177

La Fontaine, J. S. (1998) *Speak of the devil: tales of satanic abuse in contemporary England* Cambridge: Cambridge University Press

Lakoff, G. (1991) 'Metaphor and war: the metaphor system used to justify war in the Gulf' *Journal of Urban and Cultural Studies* 2 (1), pp. 59–72.

Lambourne, W. (2008) 'Transitional justice and peacebuilding after mass violence' *International Journal of Transitional Justice* 3 (1), pp. 28–48

Lamont, C. (2010) 'Defiance or strategic compliance? the post-tudjman Croatian Democratic Union and the International Criminal Tribunal for the Former Yugoslavia' *Europe-Asia Studies* 62 (10) pp. 1683–1705

Levi, P. (1986) 'The Memory of offense' in *Bitburg in Moral and Political Perspective*, ed. Hartmann, G. Translation T. Bahti and G. Hartmann. Bloomington, Indiana University Press, pp.130–137

Logar, S. and Bogosavljević, S. (2001) 'Vidjenje istine u Srbiji' *Reč* No. 62/8, 7–34

Longinović, T. Z. (2011) *Vampire nation: violence as cultural imaginary* Durham, NC: Duke University Press

Lorey, D. E. and Beezley, W. H. (2002) *Genocide, collective violence and popular memory: the politics of remembrance in the Twentieth Century* Wilmington: Scholarly Resources

Lundy, P. and McGovern, M. (2008) 'The Role of community in participatory transitional justice' in in *Transitional justice from below: grassroots activism and the struggle for change* eds. McEvoy, K. and L. McGregor. Oxford: Hart Publishing, pp. 99–120

Lupton, D. (2006) *Medicine as culture* London: Sage, 2nd Edition

Lüdtke, A. (1993) 'Coming to terms with the past': illusions of remembering, ways of forgetting Nazism in West Germany *Journal of Modern History,* 65, pp. 542–572

Magaš, B. (1993) *The Destruction of Yugoslavia: Tracing the break-up 1980–92* New York: Verso

Magaš, B. and Žanić, I eds. (2001) *The wars in Croatia and Bosnia-Herzegovina 1991–1995* London: Frank Cass

Malcolm, N. (2001) *Bosnia: A short history* London: Pan Books

Malkki, L. (1995) *Purity and exile: violence, memory and national cosmology among Hutu refugees in Tanzania* Chicago: University of Chicago Press

Malkki, L. (2002) 'From *Purity and exile: violence, memory and national cosmology among Hutu refugees in Tanzania*' as reproduced in *Violence in War and Peace: an Anthology* eds. Scheper-Hughes, N. and P. Bourgois. Oxford: Blackwell Publishing pp. 129–135

Mani, R. (2002) *Beyond retribution: seeking justice in the shadows of war* Malden, MA: Polity

Matić, V. (2001) 'Odbacivanje istine' *Reč* 62/8 pp. 75–82

McAdams, A. J. (2011) 'Transitional justice: the issue that won't go away' *International Journal of Transitional Justice* 5 (2) pp. 304–312

McCarthy, C., Rodriguez, A. P., David, S., Meecham, S., Godina, H., Supriya, K. E., and Wilson-Brown, C. (1997) 'Danger in the safety zone: notes on race, resentment and the discourse of crime, violence and suburban security' *Cultural Studies* 11 (1), pp. 274–295

McEvoy, K. (2008) 'Letting go of legalism: developing a "thicker" version of transitional justice' in *Transitional justice from below: grassroots activism and the struggle for change* eds. McEvoy, K. and McGregor, L. Oxford: Hart Publishing, pp. 15–46

McEvoy, K. and McGregor, L. eds (2008) *Transitional justice from below: grassroots activism and the struggle for change* Oxford: Hart Publishing

McGrattan, C (2009) ' "Order Out of Chaos": the politics of transitional justice' *Politics* 29 (3), pp. 164–172

Miličević, A. S. (2006) 'Joining the war: masculinity, nationalism and war participation in the Balkans war of secession, 1991–1995' *Nationalities Papers* 34 (3), pp. 265–287

Millar, G. (2012) 'Between Western theory and local practice: cultural impediments to truth-telling in Sierra Leone' *Conflict Resolution Quarterly*, 29 (2), pp. 177–199

Millar, G. (2010) 'Assessing local experiences of truth-telling in Sierra Leone: getting to "why" through a qualitative case study analysis' *International Journal of Transitional Justice* 4 (3), pp. 477–496

Miller, P. B. (2006) 'Contested memories: the Bosnian genocide in Serb and Muslim minds' *Journal of Genocide Research* 8 (3), 311–324

Miller, Z. (2008) 'Effects of invisibility: in search of the "economic" in transitional justice' *International Journal of Transitional Justice*, 2 (3), pp. 266–291

Misztal, B. (2003) *Theories of social remembering* Maidenhead: Open University Press

Mitchell, A. (2011) 'Quality/control: international peace interventions and "the everyday"' *Review of International Studies*, 37 (4), pp. 1623–1645.

Monroe, K. R. (2008) 'Cracking the code of genocide: the moral psychology of rescuers, bystanders, and Nazis during the Holocaust' *Political Psychology* 29 (5), pp. 699–736

Moore, R. (2002) 'Reconstructing reality: conspiracy theories about Jonestown' *Journal of Popular Culture* 36 (2), pp 200–220

Morris, D. B. (1993) *The Culture of pain* Los Angeles University of California Press

Mueller, J. (2000) 'The Banality of "ethnic war"' *International Security* 25 (1), pp. 42–70

Mundy, J. (2011) "Deconstructing civil wars: beyond the new wars debate" *Security Dialogue* 42 (3): 219–236.

Nagy, R. (2008) 'Transitional justice as a global project: critical reflections' *Third World Quarterly* 29 (2), pp. 275–289

Nettelfield, L. J. (2010) 'From the battlefield to the barracks: the ICTY and the armed forces of Bosnia and Herzegovina' *International Journal of Transitional Justice* 4 (1) pp. 87–109

Nikolić-Ristanović, V. (2002a) *Social change, gender and violence: post-communist and war-affected societies* Dordrecht: Veslagsgesellschaft

Nikolić-Ristanović, V. (2002b) 'Spečificnosti društveno-istorijskog konteksta i viktimizacije u Srbiji i njihov značaj za concipiranje modela istine i pomrenja' *Temida* December 2004, No. 4, Viktimološko Društvo Srbije: www.org.yu/temida.htm, Accessed 10 February 2007

Nikolić-Ristanović, V. and Hanak, N. (2006) Truth, reconciliation, and the Serbian Victimology Society *Peace Review*, 18 (3), pp. 379–387

Nordstrom, C. (1995). 'War on the front lines', in *Fieldwork under Fire: contemporary studies in violence and survival*, C. Nordstorm and A. Robben, eds. Berkeley: University of California Press

Nosov, A. ed. (2006) *Serbia and Srebrenica 1995–2005* Belgrade: Youth Initiative for Human Rights. Accessed from http://www.yi.org.yu/english/Publications/Documents/knjiga%20Srbija-Srebrenica.pdf Accessed 4 January 2007

Obradović-Wochnik, J. (2009) 'Knowledge and acknowledgement in Serbia's response to Srebrenica' *Journal of Contemporary European Studies* 17 (1) pp. 61–74

Olick, J. K. and Robbins, J. (1998) 'Social memory studies: from "collective memory" to the historical sociology of mnemonic practices' *Annual Review of Sociology*, 24, pp. 105–140

Olick, J. K., Vinitzky-Serioussi and Levy, D. (2011) *The Collective Memory Reader* Oxford University Press

Orentlicher, D. F. (2007) ' "Settling Accounts" revisited: reconciling global norms with local agency' *International Journal of Transitional Justice* 1(1), pp. 10–22

Orentlicher, D. F. (2008) *Shrinking the space for denial: the impact of the ICTY in Serbia* Open Society Justice Initiative available at http://www.soros.org/initiatives/justice/articles_publications/publications/serbia_20080520 last accessed 8 December 2011

Ostojić, M. (2011) *International judicial intervention and regime change in Serbia 2000–2010*, Unpublished PhD Thesis, London: Queen Mary, University of London

Ostojić. M. (2013) 'Facing the past while disregarding the present? Human rights NGOS and truth-telling in Post-Milošević Serbia' in *Civil Society and Transition in the Western Balkans* eds. Bojcic-Dželilovic, V., Ker-Lindsay, J., and D. Kostovicova. Basinstoke: Palgrave McMillan

Parish, J. (2001) 'The Age of anxiety' in *The Age of anxiety: conspiracy theory and the human sciences, eds.* Parish, J. and M. Parker. Oxford: Blackwell Publishers and the Sociological Review, pp. 1–16

Parsons, T. (1975) 'The Sick Role and the role of the physician reconsidered' *The Milbank Memorial Fund Quarterly. Health and Society* 53 (3), pp. 257–278

Pavlaković (2005) 'Serbia transformed? political dynamics in the Milošević era and after' in *Serbia since 1989: politics and society under Milošević and after* eds. Ramet, S. P. and V. Pavlaković, Washington: University of Washington Press, pp. 13–54

Pavlaković, V. (2010) 'Croatia, the International Criminal Tribunal for the former Yugoslavia, and General Gotovina as a political symbol' *Europe-Asia Studies* 62 (10), pp. 1707–1740

Perera, S. (2001) 'Spirit possessions and avenging ghosts: stories of supernatural activity as narratives of terror and mechanisms of coping and remembering' in *Remaking a World: Violence, Social Suffering and Recovery* eds. Das, V., Kleinman, A., Lock, M., Ramphele, M. and P. Reynolds. Berkley and Los Angeles: University of California Press, pp. 157–200

Peskin, V. (2008) *International justice in Rwanda and the Balkans: virtual trials and the struggle for state cooperation* Cambridge: Cambridge University Press

Pešić, V. (2009) 'Facing the past – the prerequisite for creating a modern Serbian state' in D. Vujadinović and V. Goati, *Serbia at the Political Crossroads Between Authoritarianism and Democracy* Vol. III, pp.1–304 Belgrade: Friedrich Ebert Stiftung, pp. 179–196 available at http://www.fes.rs/pubs/2009/pdf/10.Serbia%20at%20the%20Political%20Crossroads.pdf Accessed 1 May 2011

Petersen, R. D. (2002) *Understanding ethnic violence: fear, hatred and resentment in twentieth-century Eastern Europe* Cambridge: Cambridge University Press

Petritsch, W. and Džihić, V. (2010) 'Confronting conflicting memories in [South East] Europe: an introduction in *Conflict and memory: bridging past and future in (South East) Europe* eds. Petritsch, W. and V. Džihič. Baden-Baden: Nomos pp. 15–46

Petritsch, W. and Džihić, V. eds. (2010) *Conflict and memory: bridging past and future in (South East) Europe* Baden-Baden: Nomos

Petrović, N. (2005) *Psihološke osnove pomirenja izmedju Srba, Hrvata i Bošnjaka* Belgrade: Institut za Psihologiju, Univerzitet u Beogradu and Dokumentacioni Centar 'Ratovi 1991–1999'

Popov, N. ed. (2000a) *The road to war in Serbia: trauma and catharsis* Budapest: CEU Press

Popov, N. (2000b) 'Media shock and comprehending it' in Skopljanac-Brunner, N., Gredelj, S., Hodžić, A. and Krištofić, B., eds. *Media and War* Zagreb: Centre for transition and civil society research

Prodanović, M. (2004) *Stariji i lepši Beograd* Beograd: Stubovi kulture

Ramet, S. P. (2001) 'The kingdom of god or the kingdom of ends: Kosovo in Serbian perception' in *Kosovo: perceptions of war and its aftermath* eds. Buckley, M. and S. N. Cummings. London: Continuum pp. 30–46

Ramet, S. P. (2004a) 'Explaining the Yugoslav meltdown, 1 "for a charm of pow'rful trouble, like a hell-broth boil and bubble": theories about the roots of the Yugoslav troubles' *Nationalities Papers* 32 (4), pp. 732–763

Ramet, S. P. (2004b) 'Explaining the Yugoslav meltdown, 2: A theory about the causes of the Yugoslav meltdown: the Serbian national awakening as a "revitalization movement"' *Nationalities Papers* 32 (4), pp. 765–779

Ramet, S. P. (2007) 'The Denial syndrome and its consequences: Serbian political culture since 2000' *Communist and Post-Communist Studies* 40, pp. 41–58

Ramet, S. and Pavlaković, V., eds. (2005) *Serbia since 1989: Politics and society under Milošević and after* Washington: University of Washington Press

RECOM, n.d. 'The Coalition for RECOM' http://www.zarekom.org/The-Coalition-for-RECOM.en.html, last accessed 3 July 2011

Renard, J.B. (2007) 'Denying rumours' *Diogenes* No. 213, pp. 43–58

Riaño-Alcalá, P. & Baines, E. (2011) 'The Archive in the witness: documentation in settings of chronic insecurity' *International Journal of Transitional Justice*, 5 (3), pp.412–433.

Rill, H. and Šmidling, T. eds. (2010) *Slike tih vremena* Belgrade and Sarajevo: Centar za Nenasilnu Akciju, available at http://www.nenasilje.org/publikacije/pdf/Slike%20tih%20vremena.pdf accessed 1 March 2011

Roht-Arriaza, N. (2006), 'The new landscape of transitional justice', in *Transitional Justice in the Twenty-First Century: Beyond Truth vs Justice*. Eds. Roht-Arriaza, N and J. Mariezcurrena. New York: Cambridge University Press, pp. 1–16

Rusek, B., and Ingrao, C. (2004) 'The "mortar massacres": a controversy revisited' *Nationalities Papers* 32 (4), pp. 827–852

Scarry, E. (1985a) 'Injury and the structure of war' *Representations* 10, pp. 1–51

Scarry, E. (1985b) *The Body in pain: the making and unmaking of the world* New York and Oxford: Oxford University Press

Scheper-Hughes, N. (2004a) 'Bodies, death and silence' in *Violence in war and peace: an anthology* eds. Scheper-Hughes, N. and P. Bourgois. Oxford: Blackwell Publishing pp. 175–185

Scheper-Hughes, N. (2004b) 'Undoing: social suffering and the politics of remorse in new South Africa' in ' in *Violence in war and peace: an anthology* eds. Scheper-Hughes, N. and P. Bourgois. Oxford: Blackwell Publishing pp. 459–467

Scheper-Hughes, N. and P. Bourgois (2004a) 'Introduction: making sense of Violence' in *violence in war and peace: an Anthology* eds. Scheper-Hughes, N. and P. Bourgois. Oxford: Blackwell Publishing pp. 1–32

Scheper-Hughes, N. and P. Bourgois eds. (2004b) *Violence in war and peace: an anthology* Oxford: Blackwell Publishing

Schwandner-Sievers, S. and A. Di Lellio (2006) 'The Legendary Commander: the construction of an Albanian master-narrative in post-war Kosovo' *Nations and Nationalism* 12 (3), pp. 513–529

Schwandner-Sievers, S. (2007) 'Emotions and transitional justice: on the restorative potetnails of symbolic communication in Kosovo' in *The European Union and Transitional Justice: From Retrubutive to Restorative Justice in the Western Balkans* ed. Kostovicova, D., Belgrade: Humanitarian Law Centre pp. 99–105

Schwartz, B. (1991) Social change and collective memory: the democratization of George Washington *American Sociological Review* 56, pp. 221–236

Schöpflin, G. (1997) 'The Functions of myth and taxonomy of myths' in *Myths and Nationhood* eds. Hosking, G. and G. Schöpflin. London: Hurst & Co

Scott, J. C. (1987) *Weapons of the weak: everyday forms of peasant resistance* New Haven, CT: Yale University Press

Scott, J. C. (1989) 'Everyday forms of resistance' *The Copenhagen Journal of Asian Studies* 4, pp. 33–62

Sen, A. (2006) *Identity and violence: the illusion of destiny* London: W. W. Norton and Company

Seu, I. B. (2010) ' "Doing denial": audience reaction to human rights appeals' *Discourse & Society* 21 (4), pp. 438–457

Shaw, R. (2007) 'Memory frictions: localizing the Truth and Reconciliation Commission in Sierra Leone' *International Journal of Transitional Justice* 1 (2), pp. 183–207

Shaw, R. and Waldorf, L. (2010) *Localizing transitional justice: interventions and priorities after mass violence* Palo Alto, CA: Stanford University Press

Silber, L. and Little, A. (1996) *Yugoslavia: death of a nation* Harmondsworth: Penguin

Simić, O. and Daly, K. (2011) ' "One Pair of Shoes, One Life": steps towards accountability for genocide in Srebrenica' *International Journal of Transitional Justice* 5 (3), pp. 477–491

Simon, L., Greenberg, J. and Brehm, J. (1995) 'Trivialization: the forgotten mode of dissonance reduction' *Journal of Personality and Social Psychology* 68 (2), pp. 247–260

Simpson, K., (2008). 'Untold stories: unionist remembrance of political violence and suffering in Northern Ireland' *British Politics*, 3 (4), pp. 465–489.

Sivac-Bryant, S. (2008) 'Kozarac school: a window on transitional justice for returnees' *International Journal of Transitional Justice* 2 (1), pp. 106–115

Skeggs, B. ed. (1995) *Feminist cultural theory: process and production* Manchester: Manchester Univeristy Press

Skinner, J. (2001) 'Taking conspiracy seriously: fantastic narratives and Mr Grey the Pan-Afrikanist on Montserrat' in *The Age of anxiety: conspiracy theory and the human sciences* eds. Parish, J. and M. Parker. Oxford: Blackwell Publishers and the Sociological Review, pp. 93–111

Skopljanac-Brunner, N., Gredelj, S., Hodžić, A., and Krištofić, B., eds. (2000) *Media and War* Zagreb: Centre for transition and civil society research

Smith, A. L. (2004) 'Heteroglossia, "common sense", and social memory' *American Ethnologist* 1 (2), pp. 251–269

Smith, W. (2001) 'Conspiracy, corporate culture and criticism' in *The Age of anxiety: conspiracy theory and the human sciences* eds. Parish, J. and M. Parker. Oxford: Blackwell Publishers and the Sociological Review, pp. 153–165

Sontag, S. (1978) *Illness as metaphor* London: Allen Lane

Sontag, S. (2003) *Regarding the pain of others* London: Hamish Hamilton

Sontag, S. (2004) 'Regarding the torture of others' *The New York Times*, published 24 May 2004, available at http://www.nytimes.com/2004/05/23/magazine/

regarding-the-torture-of-others.html?pagewanted=all&src=pm, accessed 9 December 2011

Sorabji, C. (1995) 'A very modern war: terror and territory in Bosnia-Herzegovina' in *War: a cruel necessity?* Eds. Hinde, R. A. and H.E. Watson. London: Tauris Academic Studies

Sorabji, C. (2006) 'Managing memories in post-war Sarajevo: individuals, bad memories and new wars' *Journal of the Royal Anthropological Institute* 12, pp 1–18

Spark, A. (2001) 'Conjuring order: the New World Order and conspiracy theories of globalisation' in *The Age of anxiety: conspiracy theory and the human sciences* eds. Parish, J. and M. Parker. Oxford: Blackwell Publishers and the Sociological Review, pp. 46–62

Spoerri, M. (2011) 'Justice imposed: how policies of conditionality effect transitional justice in the former Yugoslavia' *Europe-Asia Studies* 63 (10) pp. 1827–1851

Sriram, C. L. (2007) 'Justice as peace? liberal peacebuilding and strategies of transitional justice' *Global Society* 21 (4) pp. 579–591

Stanić, R. (2006) 'Uvod u drugi život Slobodana Miloševića' *Evropa* No. 101, pp. 10–14

Strand, H. (2011) "Deconstructing civil war: a rejoinder" *Security Dialogue* 42 (3), pp. 297–302

Strauss, C. (1990) 'Who gets ahead? cognitive responses to heteroglossia in American political culture' *American Ethnologist* 17 (2) pp. 312–328

Subotić, J. (2009) *Highjacked Justice: dealing with the past in the Balkans* Ithaca: Cornell University Press

Subotić, J. (2010) 'Explaining difficult states: the problem of Europeanization in Serbia' *East European Politics and Societies* 24 (4), pp. 595–616

Subotić, J. (2011) 'Expanding the scope of post-conflict justice: individual, state and societal responsibility for mass atrocity' *Journal of Peace Research* 48 (2), pp. 157–169

Szasz, T. (2001). *Pharmacracy: medicine and politics in America* Westport, Conn.: Praeger

Sztompka, P. (2000) 'Cultural trauma: the other face of social change' *European Journal of Social Theory*, 3 (4), pp. 449–464

Tate, W. (2007) *Counting the dead: the culture and politics of human rights activism in Colombia* Berkley: University of California Press, Kindle Edition

Taussig, M. (1984) 'Culture of terror – space of death: Roger Casement's Putumayo Report and the explanation of torture' *Comparative studies in society and history* 26 (3), pp. 467–497

Taussig, M. (1987) *Shamanism and the Wild Man: a study in terror and healing* Chicago: Chicago University Press

Taussig, M. (1989) 'Terror as usual' *Social Text* (Fall-Winter), pp. 3–20

Taussig, M. (2004) 'Talking terror' in *Violence in war and peace: an anthology* eds. Scheper-Hughes, N. and P. Bourgois. Oxford: Blackwell Publishing pp. 171–174

Teitel, R. G. (2003) 'Theoretical and international framework: transitional justice in new era', *Fordham International Law Journal* 26 (4) pp. 893–906

Thompson, M. (1994) *Forging war: the media in Serbia, Croatia and Bosnia-Herzegovina* London: Article 19

Trbić, B. (2000) 'Taboo Serbia: an interview with Janko Baljak' Senses of Cinema, http://www.sensesofcinema.com/2000/11/baljak/ last accessed 11 December 2011

Tromp, H. (1995) 'On the nature of war and the nature of militarism' in *War: a cruel necessity?* Eds. Hinde, R. A. and H.E. Watson,. London: Tauris Academic Studies, pp. 118–131

Tsang, J. (2002) 'Moral rationalization and the integration of situational factors and psychological process in immoral behaviour' *Review of General Psychology* 6 (1), pp. 25–50

Turner, G. (1996) *British cultural studies: an introduction* London: Routledge

van Dijk, T. (1990) 'Social cognition and discourse' in *Handbook of Language and Social Psychology,* eds Giles, H. and W. P. Robinson John Wiley & Sons pp 163–183

van Dijk, T. (1992) 'Discourse and the denial of racism' *Discourse and Society* 3 (1), pp. 87–118

Vasović, M. (2000) 'Epidemic warnings in Serbia' Institute for War and Peace Reporting published 7 January 2000 http://iwpr.net/report-news/epidemic-warnings-serbia accessed 11 December 2011

Večernje Novosti (2006a) 'Zdenko Tomanović: rekao mi je da ga truju' *Večernje Novost* http://www.novosti.co.yu/code/navigate.php?Id=3&status =jedna&vest=86489&datum=2006–03–12 published 11 March 2006, accessed 12 March 2006

Večernje Novosti (2006b) 'Socijalisti ubedjeni da je za smrt njihovog lidera odgovoran tribunal' http://www.novosti.co.yu/code/navigate.php?Id=3&status=jedna&vest=86489&datum=2006–03–12 published 11 March 2006, accessed 12 March 2006

Večernje Novosti (2006c) 'Smilja Avramović: Mrtvačnica za Srbe' http://www.novosti.co.yu/code/navigate.php?Id=3&status=jedna&vest=86489&datum=2006–03–12 published 11 March 2006, accessed 12 March 2006

Verdery, K. (1999) *Political lives of dead bodies: reburial and post-socialist change* New York: Columbia University Press

Vinjamuri, L. and Snyder, J. (2004) 'Advocacy and scholarship in the study of international war crimes tribunals and transitional justice' *Annu. Rev. Polit. Sci.* 7, 345–62

Volčič, Z. (2006) 'Blaming the media: Serbian narratives of national(ist) identity' *Continuum: Journal of Media and Cultural Studies* 20 (3), pp. 313–330

Vujičić, M. (2005) 'Pijavice duha isisavaju dobrotu' *Feral Tribune*, 8 December 2005 www.feral.mediaturtle.com/look/weekly1 accessed 12 December 2007

Vulliamy, E. (1999) 'Concentration camps' in Gutman, R. and Rieff, D. eds. *Crimes of war: what the public should know* London: W.W. Norton & Company pp. 102–106

Vulliamy, E. (2005) 'Srebrenica: ten years on' *Open Society* http://www.opendemocracy. net/conflict-yugoslavia/srebrenica_2651.jsp last accessed 10 October 2008

Vulliamy, E. (2011) 'Ratko Mladić's arrest is a hollow victory in a country that refuses to apologise' *The Guardian* Comment is Free http://www.guardian.co.uk/commentisfree/2011/may/28/ratko-mladic-bosnia-ed-vulliamy Published 28 May 2011, Last accessed 10 December 2011

Weller, M. (2009) *Negotiating the final status of Kosovo* Chaillot Paper No. 114, European Union Institute for Security Studies: Paris

Welzer, H., Moller, S. and Tschuggnall, K. (2002) *'Opa war kein Nazi': Nationalsozialismus und Holocaust im Familiengedächtnis* Frankfurt a.M: Fischer Taschenbuch Vlg

West, H.G. (2003) 'Voices twice silenced: betrayal and mourning at colonialism's end in Mozambique' *Anthropological Theory* 3 (3), pp. 343–365

West, H. G. and Sanders, T. (2003) *Transparency and conspiracy: ethnographies of suspicion in the New World Order* Durham: Duke University Press, pp. 204–232

Williams, R. (1961) *The long revolution* Harmondsworth: Penguin

Wittlinger, R. (2006) 'Taboo or tradition? The "Germans as victims" theme in West Germany until the early 1990s' in *Germans as victims* ed. B. Niven. Basingstoke: Palgrave Macmillan

Women in Black (n.d.) 'Confronting the past' http://www.zeneucrnom.org/index.php?option=com_content&task=view&id=18&Itemid=17 Accessed 2 March 2011

Yerkes, M. (2004) 'Facing the violent past: discussions with Serbia's youth' *Nationalities Papers,* 32 (4), pp. 921–938

Youth Initiative for Human Rights (n.d.) 'Programmes' http://rs.yihr.org/en/programmes/1/TRANSITIONAL-JUSTICE accessed 1 February 2011

Zalaquett, J. (1997) "Why deal with the past?" in *Dealing with the past: truth and Reconciliation in South Africa* eds. Boraine, A. Levy, J. and R. Scheffer. Cape Town: Institute for Democracy in South Africa. pp. 8–15

Zambelli, N. (2010) 'A Journey Westward: a poststructuralist analysis of Croatia's identity and the problem of cooperation with the International Criminal Tribunal for the former Yugoslavia' *Europe-Asia Studies* 62 (10), pp. 1661–1682

Zimmermann, C. and Rodin, G. (2004) 'The denial of death thesis: sociological critique and implications for palliative care' *Palliative Medicine* 18 (2), pp. 121–128

Zverzhanovski, I. (2007) 'Watching war crimes: the Srebrenica video and the Serbian attitudes to the 1995 Srebrenica massacre' *Journal of Southeast European and Black Sea Studies* 7 (3), pp. 417–430

Živković, M. (2001) 'Jelly, slush, and red mists: poetics of amorphous substances in Serbian jeremiads of the 1990s' *Anthropology and Humanism* 25 (2), pp. 168–18

INDEX